A 1188

Passing Shots

Passing Shots

FRANK KEATING

Illustrated by John Jensen

 Robson Books

The author and publishers would like to thank the proprietors of *Punch* magazine, in which earlier versions of the text appeared.

First published in Great Britain in 1988 by Robson Books Ltd, Bolsover House, 5-6 Clipstone Street, London W1P 7EB.

British Library Cataloguing in Publication Data

Keating, Frank, *1937*–
    Passing shots.
    1. Sports – Humour
    I. Title
    796'.0207

ISBN 0-86051-532-X

Printed in Great Britain by
St Edmundsbury Press, Ltd,
Bury St Edmunds, Suffolk.

Typeset by AKM Associates (UK) Ltd.
Southall, Greater London.

Contents

Introduction

'Here he comes,' sighed Ian Botham, amiably pointing at me one Test match morn, 'the one bloke who's more fan than journalist.' Everyone laughed. I took it as a compliment. *And* we shared a few large drinks at close of play.

No boasting, though, for this is not a sports book that claims to reveal the colour of the Test-match barmaid's undies. Nor the price of an athlete's dope. It was not written with any remote hopes of changing the FA's offside law, toning down Wimbledon's pompous greed, popping out the collar-studs of the starched mandarins at Lord's, or even giving poor Frank Bruno a realistic chance of ever resisting lifelong membership of the Flat Earth Society.

It is a snug bedside book – by a fan for a fan – and I hope it might be a decently snappy indipper in the Malcolm Marshall class: quick, pithy and only sometimes overpitched; a collection of bits and bobs, fads and fancies, dashed off week by week as we reach the last decade of the planet's first and, therefore, most colossal century of organised sport. Indeed it will probably be the one and onliest, for I can reveal that spectator sport in the 21st century will be staged only in vast, barren TV studio barns, applauded by nothing but taped, hollow cheers and the cynical shuffle of soft and seedy money.

So read here about sport as a few last, lucky generations did love and laud it. Weekly doodles from *Punch* – on a generous day off from Mike Averis, sports editor of my beloved *Guardian* – encouraged always by those two actor-managers from Tudor Street, Alan Coren and David Taylor; with Lucy Morrissey expertly dotting the t's, and John Jensen's drawings embellishing the i's. Sport and sports writing is not remotely important in the general scheme of the world – how can it be when a defeat in a football match is mourned as a 'tragedy', a mundane passing shot is hailed as 'great', and a fellow on an off-day is told he 'stinks'? But it remains – just – *Fun*. And it helps if you are a *Fan*. There are still a lot of us about.

F. K. Hereford, 1988

Boot Boys

What Pevsner Forgot

I went up to join in the happy little hooley to celebrate the entry into the Football League of its blushing debutant, Scarborough, whose winning of the quaintly named GM Vauxhall Conference transported them automatically into the next season's Fourth Division of the Football League. This elevation on the undisputed merit of goals in the back of the net – as opposed to the occasional you-scratch-my-back palsy-walsy whim of the League's 92 chairmen – is unique in the organized game's 99-year-old history. They are a forward-looking lot in footer.

The new ground is a welcome addition – a homespun, spanspick place plonked in the wind-blown cleft between Oliver's Mount and Irton Moor. As is the custom, everything is painted in the club colours – in this instance that means strawberry-jam red – and, true to tradition, even though the grandstand is only eight years old, the PA announcements bounce around the rafters as raucous and incomprehensible as Britrail's, so *Here are the team changes* . . . sounds the same as *The train now standing at Platform Three* . . .

I drove back from the strawberry-field through York and Leeds, and then hopped off the motorway to criss-and-cross the Calder and canal, then twiddle round the Ribble. It was a glorious day, shafts of bright sunlight dancing through the scudding clouds, the moors spring-green and daisy-fresh. I turned left at Preston and headed home down the long, lulling M6, untwined Spaghetti Junction and so to the great west road.

It was an evocative journey for a sports nut, especially one who had come from the very newest Football League ground. In the couple of hours or so from passing right under the side-wall of Leeds United's sombre, cementy-grey, modern-Meccanoed stadium at Elland Road on the M621, I zig-zagged through a large slice of almost totally unconsidered, century-old social and

12

architectural history. Down in the dells and dales, or high on the plump hills, in various shapes and sizes, stood sentinel the football grounds of England – now, every one of them, you fancy, under some kind of threat as our habits and hobbies head, straining for change, fast into the twenty-first century. Those we have loved. Quite possibly, by 2087, not one will be in use.

At once you skirt Bradford. In that one town, you might even say, is the beginning and end of the whole short history – for certainly the cataclysmic fire in the 78-year-old grandstand on May 11 1985, wiped out, too, in five horrendous minutes, any architectural romantic's absolute devotion to tradition and nostalgia. Nothing could possibly be the same after Bradford – which the rapid, handsome and contrite rebuilding of Valley Parade itself, only serves to prove.

Bradford, however, has other relics in the same glass case. Park Avenue, now an overgrown wilderness, was not only a League soccer ground but one of the most celebrated enclosures in all the world of cricket. You could not possibly twig that now. And not long before Christmas 1986, I stood drenched, alone and forlorn, to watch the Australian rugby league team swamp Bradford Northern – along with scarcely a couple of thousand other drowned and dotty enthusiasts at Odsal Stadium (which thirty-three years ago housed 102,575 for a rugby league Cup Final replay). Odsal had been fashioned into its vast now vacant bowl from a ring of council rubbish-tips seventy years ago. Once it was going to be the Wembley of the North. It remains *Exhibit A* in the museum of once great British playtime paddocks.

Wind round Brighouse (misunderstanding of the year – clipped, southern *Daily Mail* rugby union man interviewing softly-mumbling, almost monosyllabic new rugby league player, Terry Holmes: 'Where are you living?' 'Up the road, Brighouse.' 'Big, eh? How many bedrooms?') and on through Halifax, rugby league Cup-winners, but whose soccer ground, The Shay, is so shabby now they say the only seat they polish up each Saturday is the one reserved for the Official Receiver. That, too, was once a refuse-tip, and though not long ago Tottenham Hotspur played there in front of 37,000 (and so did Red Star, Belgrade), they count the faithful congregation in the hundreds now. Not for much longer, either.

On to Burnley and, for soccer men, yet sadder still. Turf Moor, as evocative a name (and meaning just that) as you can imagine. A glistening gem of a little ground which would (indeed *did* only a dozen years ago) grace the First Division. Alas, the team lost all its vigour and it wilts and wails, now, down among the dead men. To the left, the signposts finger a detour to Accrington: this pilgrim passes by: famous founders, Accrington Stanley, expired, £60,000 in debt, after the Rochdale match of 24 Feb 1962: Peel Park once jingle-jangled with 20,000 football men: it's just a scrubland field now, not even sheep to keep the thistles down.

Other signs suggest Rochdale, Bury and Oldham, just down the lane. The latter, at least, are in vibrant health this year – little big club, still alive and kicking. Round the inner ring-road at Blackburn: somewhere in there is Ewood Park, famous name with a centenary coming up. They filmed that soulful sepia Hovis ad outside its turnstiles for television. That says it all. Just a handful of miles down the A666 is Bolton's Burnden Park, lorded over by Lawton and Lofthouse, and where Lowry set his matchstick tableau of the times, *Going to t'Match*. Times long gone now.

Left turn at Preston, which they used to call 'proud' when Finney feinted and weaved. At least they're out of the Fourth now, plastic pitch and all. Then slice down the highway valley between Manchester and the Mersey, and its whole bible of football folklore, and on to the historical stations past Crewe – Stoke and Wolves and Walsall. On the day of my journey, it looked as certain that Birmingham (who took to this game with such a pioneering will and vim a century ago) would have all three of its legendary clubs – Villa, Brum and West Brom – scrabbling undignified and anonymous around the Second Division come the autumn.

These grounds of appeal could soon be remotely attractive only to the misty-eyed student of history. Luckily, and at long last, a professor in such an esoteric subject has emerged. In the nick of time, a young, devoted enthusiast with owlish, nil-nil, thick-lensed spectacles and a notebook has logged the era's end – and the new beginnings. Simon Inglis has travelled 9,000 miles and taken in 150 grounds as his contribution to posterity. He has even paid his respects to the long dead, like this panegyric to Park Avenue, so beloved by both football and cricket: 'The grandstand has a slate roof. The slates were stacked up and returned to Wales, whence they first came in 1907, for recycling.

A farmer bought some roof sheeting for his barn . . . Still visible are the perimeter walls, a very bumpy and neglected pitch, and three sides of crumbling, overgrown terraces. The floodlight bases also survive, as do a few old turnstiles, overwhelmed by trees, bushes and scrap . . . there is a ghostly atmosphere, almost as if the departed stands still cast a cold shadow over the pitch and warn one not to tread on too many memories.'

Inglis has revised and updated his triumphant book of 1983 on the pyloned cathedrals of England and Wales to take in Scotland. The result, *The Football Grounds of Great Britain* (Collins Willow), is a pluperfect job. No football fan, social history boffin, nor student of architecture can remotely afford to be without it. I dare say the latter collective of pink-shifted, crayoning creeps sniff disdainfully at that for, as Inglis and football men have discovered, architectural books are full only of the dullest churches and faceless office blocks; none of them considers football grounds.

Even Nikolaus Pevsner, author of the many-volumed *Buildings of England*, the most comprehensive survey of British architecture ever accomplished, mentions only *two* grounds in passing – Wembley and Hillsborough. Ludicrous snobbery. Pevsner describes a perambulation of Everton, its parks, churches and public buildings, but totally ignores the solid mass of Goodison. Similarly in Highbury, there is no indication that Pevsner was even aware of Arsenal's existence, despite the 1930s grandeur of the façade.

The architecture of every aspect of life – even sport – is far too precious to leave to the architects.

Final Judgment

At their mothers' knee, the English used to be told they were ye werry best at ye lot. But what, these days, do they still do better than anyone else? Make motor cars? Or marmalade? Make hay? Or laws? Or brogue shoes? Or children's TV programmes? All, apparently, now relegated to Div II. Universal consensus is that we remain only the world's absolute, hunky-dory, genu-ine, A1 aces – at keeping goal.

That fact has just about been a certainty this century – and never more so than in the last two decades, when England's yellow-jerseyed net-minders have been Gordon Banks and Peter Shilton. In autumn 1985, in (of all places) France, a schoolboys' magazine voted Shilton one of 'Europe's Ten Topmen', after he overtook Banks's 73-cap record. He was only four places after Mitterrand.

Shilton – who, oddly, was Banks's immediate successor at both Leicester City and Stoke, as well as England – has taken the one-eyed former king's geometry, agility and calm, and added a rousing, bullying, musclebound presence. His commanding aggressions will bowl over, without ceremony, fellow defenders as readily and dismissively as opposition forwards. Shilton's cry of 'Mine!' is about the most certain thing in soccer, these days.

Since the beginning of the Sixties there have been some formidable claimants as *supremo* of the sticks. There was Lev Yashin, the dynamic Muscovite all in black; Dino Zoff, Italian in the farmhand's hat; the two trapezing South Americans, Gilmar of Brazil, and Mazurkiewitz of Uruguay; then, of course, the instinctive Irishman, Jennings, and – for a time – the spring-heeled compatriots, Clemence and Bonetti. In fact, but for Clemence, Shilton would have played more than a hundred games for England.

Shilton could well have been England's sole defender of the five-yard box for fully fifteen years. When Sir Alf Ramsey began to dismantle that last side of true quality after the 1970 World Cup, he at once handed the gloves to Shilton. His first game was against East Germany at the beginning of the 1970–71 season, and he played in front of such legendary 'where-are-they-nows?' as Bobby Moore, Terry Cooper and Alan Mullery. The goals were scored by Allan Clarke, Martin Peters and Franny Lee. In other words, it was a long time ago.

It may have been the memory of Mexico, when poor Bonetti had played an awesomely unfortunate game as deputy for Banks – he had not had a match for months – that made the new national manager, Don Revie, decide on playing Shilton and Clemence in alternate internationals. Neither men liked it – indeed, in 1976, Shilton refused to go on an England tour, saying he had better things to do with his summer than sit on the subs' bench. He said at the time, 'Ray and I are friends, but

16

there is always some barrier between us. No two men can be said to have exactly the same talent. One must always be better – and I just want the opportunity to show that it's me.'

When Ron Greenwood took over, he persuaded Shilton back – then continued to alternate the two goalkeepers in an even more indecisive turn and turnabout. But they knew the World Cup in Spain was coming up, when he would have to make one of them the first choice. He decided on Shilton – and he has been there ever since, for Bobby Robson, the current manager, may have had doubts about every other position in his pack of ten, but never about the man in the pullover. Robson is an emotional man – and all the better for that – and at talk of professional soccer's grand old days of two or three decades ago, his face gets more rubbery and his eyes moisten. He doesn't come over as such in his after-match touchline interviews, these days, perhaps, but in his spirit burn candles of romance. Of Shilton he says: 'Since the middle 1950s, I've seen them all. And played against most of them. Swift and Trautmann, Gilmar and Yashin, Jennings and Zoff. And, of course, Gordon (Banks) was rivetingly brilliant. But, quite honestly, we have never seen a better one than Shilton. He has everything. He not only protects his obvious quarters – that rough area from the penalty-spot – he is totally in charge of what goes on in the 18-yard "box", plus *another* 20 yards as well! He demands. He motivates. He expects every colleague around him to be seeking the same as him – which is, quite simply, *perfection*.'

The other Robson crucial to England's World Cup challenge this year is the captain, Bryan. He also is in awe of his goalkeeper's 'perfectionism'. It was almost unsettling, he said, to come back into the dressing-room after a rattling good victory in which no goals had been conceded – and amidst all the cheery jollity and banter of triumph, 'There would be "Shilts", massive on the bench, with his head in his hands, and concentrating on assessing his performance, re-running his performance through his mind, dwelling on some tiny, minis- cule miscalculation that no one but he would have even noticed.' Then suddenly, with a slap of his hand on a muddy thigh, he would snap out of his private post-mortem, be one of the lads again, and begin to prepare for his shower.

Safe hands for the top corner, or the bottom. A good five-yard 'body spread' to narrow an angle. Even a spitfiring tack, arms outstretched, for the goal-line photographers, is no us if a goalie lacks *judgment*. Thirty years ago, one of the best football writers of all, Donny Davies, enthused about goalkeepers in one of his very last pieces for the *Manchester Guardian* before he was killed, along with half United's team, in the slush on a Munich runway: 'The basic qualities required for good goalkeeping very little, if at all, from age to age. They are keen vision, prompt reflexes, adequate physical endowments covering height, reach, muscular agility, courage, daring and judgment . . . ah, yes, judgment, that master quality which brings all others into play at the right time. In this quality of judgment are included so many important things, such as divination of an attacking forward's intentions, a correct sense of positioning, and a knowledge of when to sally forth from goal and then to stay put.'

It is the possession of this quality in such a marked degree that – with all his other, aforesaid and singular attributes – makes Shilton heir to the legendary line. He is probably the finest the old game has ever seen.

Double Standards

There was a spring in the step of the cricket-lovers as they walked to Lord's on the morning of August 27, 1948. It was Don Bradman's 40th birthday and he was due to bat at Lord's for the last time. He would surely celebrate with a century. (He did.) After breakfast that morning, friends had called at a tiny flat in Grove End House – scarcely a Trott-tonk from the famous old ground – to urge the widowed occupant, Ethel Stoddart, to come and see the little Oz wizard bat on his farewell appearance. They could not persuade her. 'I have not watched a cricket match since the spring of 1915,' said the grey, perky old lady. But this Bradman was the greatest ever, her friends insisted. She refused even to consider putting on her hat. And she eyed the old Victorian tobacco jar on her dressing-table. 'Perhaps he is,' she said, 'but he wasn't a rugby international too, was he?'

The loyal Ethel was the widow of A. E. Stoddart – 'my dear, victorious Stod' – who blew his own brains out with an ornate duellist's pistol in his Maida Vale bedroom, in April 1915. He remains the only man to have captained England at both rugby union and cricket.

I was telling that bitter-sweet tale in a Dublin bar recently when a few of us over for The Match got to wondering why there were so few double-internationals at rugger and cricket. You'd have thought, with the carefree amateur *ethos* governing both games through the century, that there would have been many more than there have been at soccer, a far more professionally demanding and specialist game. We could count only ten who have played for England at both rugger and cricket, but as many as 14 cricketing footballers – if you include the wartime internationals, Hendren and Compton, to the list of Lyttleton, Gunn, Gay, Foster, Fry, Sharp, Makepeace, Hardinge, Ducat, Arnold, Watson, and, last of the noble line, chirpy Arthur Milton, the Bristol postman.

At rugger, after the anguished Stoddart (demon bat and Blackheath winger) we could come up with only nine – most of those had qualifications so dubious as to be unconsidered today and labelled 'unregistered overseas players'.

Such ruminations arose – and in a long night spent reviving Guinness shares, don't forget, so don't all you usual clever-clogs bother to write if I've missed your grandad's best friend – because there may just be the teeniest outside chance that England's fly-half last Saturday, Rob Andrew, could go on to win his England colours at cricket. For he is said to be highly thought of by the gnarled old sages of Yorkshire CCC. Certainly he played some good knocks for Cambridge.

It is over thirty years since a cricketer last played rugby for England. In 1956, M.J.K. Smith, later to be a sterling Test captain, was picked at fly-half against Wales at Twickenham, made two goodish breaks, but had a drop-kick attempt charged down which led to the winning Welsh try and was never chosen again. Since when, good England rugger bods (all full-backs incidentally) like Tony Jorden, Alistair Hignell and Dusty Hare have each played county cricket well, but not remotely made a Test selector's journey really necessary.

Rugby is pushing it a bit in claiming even nine British double internationals – our lists did not bother to include 'colonials', such as the New Zealanders who have played rugby for the All Blacks and cricket for the All Whites; though, being in Dublin, we did get in a round to pay respects to Dr Kevin O'Flanagan, who played both rugger *and* soccer for the Republic on either side of the last war. In those days, the English rugby team had no shame at all in calling up unqualified foreigners – even if they did play a decent game. In 1949, for instance, they 'Zola'd' a South African Rhodes scholar, Clive van Ryneveld, up to Twickenham to bolster the squad, and nobody raised an eyebrow, let alone anything like the outcry stirred by the barefoot matchbox mite thirty-five years later. Van Ryneveld played four games for England in 1949 – went home to become an MP and to prepare to captain the South African cricket team *against* England a couple of years later.

The same year that van Ryneveld was playing rugger as an Englishman, a New Zealander, Martin Donnelly, was putting the English cricketing bowlers to the sword (a sumptuous 206 in the Lord's Test, for instance). Twickenham could well have blushed – for two winters previously they had given Donnelly his *England* cap, versus Ireland, in the centre!

In its cavalier fashion, the England rugby selectors had contrived another selection ten years earlier that should have inspired a querying double-take at least. Full-back for Obolensky's match against the New Zealanders at Twickenham in 1936 was one H.G. Owen-Smith – the same fellow who, seven years earlier, had made 129 for South Africa *versus* England at Leeds, inspiring *The Times* correspondent to rave over 'this undoubted new Trumper in the making'.

Welshmen, though some wouldn't thank me for saying so, are allowable holders of a sporting *double* nationhood. Their finest all-rounder in this sense must be Maurice Turnbull, who played with such vim for England at cricket, and rugby, hockey and squash for Wales. He was killed in action with the Welsh Guards in 1944. He might have made a more trenchant England cricket captain than, say, the amateur likes of F.G. Mann or Freddie Brown. So, too, Wilf Wooller, Welsh rugby gallivant with a boxful of tasselled caps who surely deserved at least one blue one for England at cricket.

Like M.J.K. Smith, Reggie Spooner played many innings for England at cricket, but won only one cap at rugby – against Wales at Swansea in 1903. In Reggie's case, he was later delighted to be dropped for the next match against Ireland in Dublin – for three of the England team caught typhoid fever.

Two recovered, but the left-wing, R. Forrest, of Blackheath (though he played in the next match against Scotland a month later in March), had died of the disease by the end of April.

C.B. Fry remains sport's most legendary renaissance man. He played cricket and soccer and most other things for England, of course – and could well have been capped at rugby too, for he turned down a Blue at Oxford (then almost a sure passport to the England team) because he wasn't feeling too well on The Day. It was his two contemporaries who began the carefree colonial approach to England rugger colours: R.O. Schwarz, purveyor of googlies for South Africa, played three games at fly-half for England at the turn of the century; and Sammy Woods went even better a few years earlier – playing three Test matches each at cricket for both England (1895) and Australia (1888), while simultaneously winning 13 rugby caps for England as a rampaging wing-forward.

Woods was a soul-mate of W.G. Grace, who (not many people know this) captained England six times at bowls. Woods probably made a point of not telling the Doctor that rugby had a tradition of clubhouse drinking, making sure he was saved for the cricket and immortality. For if Grace had spent his winter evenings as he did his summer's, he would surely not have middled a thing.

For instance, a few months after Woods had changed his rugby allegiance from Australia to England in the winter of 1895, he sat next to W.G. at the dinner that celebrated the latter's hundredth century – for Glos v Somerset, 288 at 50 an hour and chanceless. Reported Woods next morning: 'The Doctor drank something of everything before and during dinner. And afterwards he sent for the whisky bottle. You just cannot make the Old Man drunk. His nut's too large. Around midnight, some of us thought to start for home, but the Old Man said to me. "Shock'ead, get two others, and we'll play two rubbers of whist." So we did.'

Woods's rugby captain for England was poor Andrew Ernest Stoddard. He tried to combine the social pleasures of rugby and cricket. And look what happened to him. Young Rob Andrew might be well advised to stick to his rugby clubhouse – and give the bar of the cricket pavilion a miss. Like Mrs Stoddart said, Bradman never played rugger, did he?

West is Best, Mun

It has been many moons, I fancy, since the Welsh have so tremulously been crossing their fingers and hoping for the best as their battered Cortinas and scarlet Escorts single-file this Saturday morning across the Severn Bridge and up the M4 to Twickenham. England, for once, are waiting to ambush them something rotten. The rugger-fogeys' pre-match plonk in the car-park should have turned into a most satisfactory red whine by tea-time.

English hearts are in trim after the dramatic boldness of their result against France (to be sure, they lost; but to *deserve* to win a game was a giant step for macho mankind in England). Wales have had to wait three weeks longer than the others to begin their Championship season. It has given them more time to bicker, more gloomy days to work up a pessimistic thirst in the taprooms of those dingy pubs of theirs which serve that watery-thin bitter called 'Felinfoel' (pronounced 'Feeling Foul' by a borderer like me when I have to endure it).

Simply, till Saturday, the Welsh are not sure whether they have any sort of decent team. The leeks are very limp for the time of year, look you. Wales is going through one of its palpitating periods of rugby introspection. It is fun to behold: every other fellow you talk to thinks a different player should be pulling on the red shirt this weekend. The selectors, of course, are main sponsors for this simpering state of mind. Then the English snipers, like me. It unnerves the Celts when the Anglos take their very occasional turn to get cocky and strutting about their own rugby. Why, the English (who came back with nothing) even laughed when the bedraggled Welsh team came back from the inaugural World Cup in the summer of '87 having fluked the 'bronze' medal (surely the most unlikely sporting medal since Don Cockell took the silver to Rocky I's gold, in the San Francisco boxing-ring in 1955).

But the quintet of Welsh selectors – self-styled 'The Big Five' since their inception in 1924 – have been taking most of the blame. Not for the first time, they have started a spiritual civil war. For down in South Wales, east is east and west is west, and never the twain shall meet . . .

West is preening best these days. Anywhere east of Cardiff, you come across pale, forlorn rugby men who narrow their eyes and purse their lips and mutter with venom about 'the West Wales Rugby Freemasonry'. Any player from an Eastern club who fancies his chances for Wales had better think again, is the received wisdom. Failing that, he should learn Welsh, join the Swansea Rotary Club or sign on for Llanelli Seconds.

The other day I took a drive, from East to West. 'The Big Five? They haven't been along to see anyone at our club since we charged half-a-crown at the gate. Haven't seen nor heard of one of them since decimalization. And no one would know them if they did show their faces,' said one Gwent club official. He told me to look up the composition of the teams in the disastrous Welsh trial match in the New Year – and, sure enough, though Pontypool, Abertillery and Pontypridd were the top three clubs in the season's Merit Table Championship, not one forward from any of those sides warranted a place in the trial.

Of course, in recent years Ponypool's spectacular successes have forced them to muscle in on the Big Five's deliberations – and in the last ten seasons, men from 'Pooler' have won 107 caps. But, to prove their point, Gwent's remaining six first-class clubs have provided only a measly, humiliating 2.8 per cent of the Welsh international players. Forty-three per cent of the Welsh senior clubs are in Gwent – yet, including Pontypool's huge contribution, they have been asked to give only 15.3 per cent of their players to the cause of Wales since 1979.

On my recce from East to West, I began with a good and comradely evening at Pontypool, where the famous clubhouse is above a pub, and the beer's better. The team put on another of their relentless displays, and an astonishing 5,000 turned up to see them do it. Pontypool Park is owned by the local council, so, legally, anyone can get in for nothing as long as he says he's just taking his dog for a walk. More dogs watch rugby at Ponty than anywhere else. The pooches are nearly all black-and-white. Folk thereabouts think that makes for a cheaper dog licence.

Talking point is invariably the Big Five. One utterance of 'the scandal of the selectors' is worth at least a pint. 'Well, you saw for yourself tonight, boy. Our Davie Bishop is the best scrum-half in the world. But will he get a game for Wales? Not on your life! Best in the world isn't good enough for them West Walians, is it?'

Then up and down the criss-cross road through Crumlin, signs to the right and left to Newport, Abertillery, Ebbw Vale and Cross Keys and Newbridge (the youthful Neil Kinnock's two 'alternate weekends' teams), and so down the valley-cut to Bridgend and the West – and the shrine at Stradey, where Llanelli play. Here the passions rise for Jonathan Davies, the perky, insouciant, daringly cocky new product from the Welsh fly-half factory. He joined the *sospan* side in the summer from nearby Neath – which is still 'East' to a Llanelli man on the 'tanner' bank, where one or two pallid grey-beards scuffed their feet and sucked their teeth and confided, 'He still doesn't realize our scarlet No. 10 jersey's been worn by geniuses far less fancy-Dan than him; serve him right if the selectors gave him a sharp shock by dropping him. Mind you, just for one match, 'cos he's a marvellous player.' They are spoiled for their surfeit of stars in the West, they will tell you. Gwent? They don't understand the finer points. If Jonathan Davies is the flamboyant successor to the last real Prince of Wales, Llewelyn, who died in 1292, then that David Bishop over there is no more than a trouble-making Wat Tyler.

Then, against the west-end corner, huddled against the corrugated in his anorak, with his arms around his son's shoulders, appraising Davies and his tricks and treats, I spotted the onliest Phil Bennett, another scarlet jinker who once created the winds as opposed to sniffing them. The Western line goes on. But then I remembered the dozen winters ago to the very week, when a previous Big Five put the boot in – on the other foot – and there was such a weeping and gnashing in the West when, out of the blue for the England match at Twickenham, they dropped Bennett, and didn't even make him a substitute.

They announced the team and half a nation mourned. John Bevan was in, with Dai Richards his sub. Then, in no time, both of them had reported bad injuries: Bennett was back in. Maxie Boyce, that jowly, jovial jester from Glynneath, penned his immortal hymn of how he was watching the Harlech one newstime, and the name *P. Bennett* had not come up in the No. 10 spot in the new Welsh team. So he rang the man from Rediffusion to report a fault. The vanman came up and tinkered with the back, there was the name *P. Bennett* restored again.

Not only restored but, within the twelvemonth, Phil was captain of Wales, and for the match against England he had written out his first dressing-room exhortation to his troops in red on a scrunched-up slip of paper. I saw it once. The British Museum – or, rather, the Imperial War – should confiscate it for display. It read: 'Boys, look what these English swine have done to Wales. They've taken our coal, our water, our steel; they buy our houses and only live in them a fortnight each year. What have they given us in return? Absolutely nothing! We've been exploited, raped, controlled and punished by the English. C'mon, Gareth boy, look what they've even done to your fishing rights! Buying up all the banks for directors and their fat English wallets. Those are your riverbanks, Gar', yours and mine and all us boys', not the English – not these men we're going out to play this very afternoon!'

1977 score: Wales 14, England 9.

East may be east, and west west . . . but this Saturday, for an hour and twenty minutes at least, Wales will be united against the common, fogeyed foe. Bickering will only resume when Wales are beaten.

The Black and White Frostbite Show

English rugby union's bright-white new year dawn has, for the umpteenth successive time, turned into a dingy dusk well before the end of Feb '88. 'P2, L2' reads the latest succinct lamentation; and on Saturday it looks likely to get a further notch worse, for the white-kneed Scots do so enjoy treading on wimps in white in their own raucous glen at Murrayfield.

But what's this? Scots *wha hae* (if that means 'beware') for the England selectors in their desperation have turned to the dynamic, long-legged colt they funked choosing in the first place. In doing so at this stage, however, they have loaded an awesome heap of pressure on the slim shoulders of Christopher

Oti, the first black man to win an England cap at rugby union in all of eighty years.

The 22-year-old Cambridge undergraduate can run like the wind, and if his English compatriots can get the ball to him he could be very lethal indeed. That latter determination, alas, is likely to prove more difficult than you might imagine. England's other winger, the RAF pilot Rory Underwood, is just as nippy off the touchline tarmac – but in twenty-odd games for England, even Rory's mum can remember him receiving only two passes from his colleagues that didn't have the dreaded Red Cross seal of imminent disability stamped on them. In a couple of dozen internationals, that's meant the sacrifice of standing frostbitten and forlorn as a corner-flag for 1,000 minutes – just to receive one pass. They don't even let the wingers chuck the ball into the line-out any more. If England on Saturday wantonly continue to starve Underwood and Oti of their rights, then the selection panel should be arraigned before Twickenham County Court for bringing a fairly decent game into disrepute.

Christopher is the son of a Nigerian businessman, and after a grounding in rugger at an English prep school stayed to relish the game at Somerset's rest-work-and-playschool, Millfield. He read for a General Arts degree at Durham; then to Cambridge, where he enrolled in the 'Sportsman's PhD' course, which is currently Land Management. He has electrified the last two university matches at Twickenham with his voluptuous sprinting. But that was against boys: it will be a man's game on March 5, and we shall see what we shall see. I have a hunch it will be worth staying in for.

A friend of mine, the father of one of Oti's Cambridge rugby colleagues, reported that the rest of the team described the fellow they call (yawn, yawn) 'Black Flash' as, variously, 'an affable gentleman'; 'polite, brave and physical'; and 'a brilliant matchwinner'. As I say, he goes on to the field on Saturday dauntingly overweighed with expectations. Jolly good luck to him.

Mind you, England might well have been playing *two* black wingers, and so break their eighty-year-old multi-racial duck in even more style. A year ago, Rosslyn Park were playing another dashing 21-year-old on the wing. Indeed, Martin Offiah's dramatic running was a feature of last spring's Barbarians' tour to Wales as well as the season's final Twickenham curtain, the Middlesex Sevens. If England were daring in 1988, we thought, they had to pick him. But the Wigan rugby league club were too quickly on the ball and signed up the student of Business Studies at Liverpool Polytechnic before the Twickers' types even had time to get in a twit about it. Offiah has been a revelation, breaking a whole clutch of try scoring-records on his way to his first England cap of, doubtless, many. They don't mess around in the Rugby League.

They have also christened Offiah with one of the best sporting nicknames I've come across for some time. Throughout the North, he answers simply to the name 'Chariots'. Better, I reckon, even than that bestowed on the Polish World Cup footballer of 1978, Rikki Duda, who joined the American soccer team, Chicago Sting. So buzzingly well did he play in his debut game that, by half-time, his colleagues were referring to him only as 'Zippity'.

The only other black man to play for England at rugby union was James Peters, who won five caps between 1906–08. Twickenham's official England history still logs him as 'Darkie' Peters. Well, they would, wouldn't they? He was born in Salford in 1880, moved with his parents to work in Bristol Docks, where he was educated at Knowle School. He played at both inside and outside-half, and the only photograph I've got of him suggests the looks and quicksilver reactions of a Sugar Ray Leonard, the superlative American middle-and-welterweight boxer.

When Peters graduated from Bristol's junior Dings rugby club to the city's senior side, there was even a letter in the *Bristol Post* complaining of the choice of (quaintly and insufferably) 'this pallid blackmoor'. Nor did that paper's sports reporter think much of the young man's first appearance in the blue-and-white hoops. On the Monday morning, he wrote: 'Peters's ambition appeared to be to break away as he might do playing junior football and the result was that time after time he was collared with the ball. His excessive lack of judgment had a detrimental effect on his partner, Billy Needs, and the result was that all Bristolians present had the mortification of seeing the worst half-back play that has been seen since the club became "first-class".'

Peters persevered to become a favourite through the old city, but after two years he got a job at Devonport dockyard and, a fully-fledged fly-half now, was soon the talk of the county. Vying for the position for England were D.R. Gent, the Old Cheltonian soon to be rugby correspondent of *The Times*, and Adrian Stoop, Rugby, Oxford, Harlequins' immortal and all that. But they chose Devon's Peters. The official history records that his first performance (v. Scotland in 1906) was 'most pleasing'. He played four more times, keeping out Gent and Stoop, and scoring tries against France (1906) and Scotland (1907).

He lost three fingers in a dockyard accident but continued playing, to the apparent delight of all sporting Devonians, till he was 32, when Twickenham charged him and others of conspiring to introduce rugby league into the county and banned him from any further contact with the sublimely snobbish rugby union. Things haven't changed much. So Peters gently chided them for their childishness – and finished his career playing rugby league for Barrow.

The Black Flash – and Chariots, too – have a most agreeable-sounding mentor to follow.

The Wild West

It is a typical West London soccer scenario. Ups and downs, ins and outs. While Queen's Park Rangers are back at Wembley this weekend for the Milk (*née* League) Cup Final, Fulham are dropping like stones for one of their all too regular neighbourly visits to join contented little Brentford in the Third Division. Meanwhile, up the Fulham Road, Chelsea managed to shoot themselves in both legs over Easter when they let in a comical ten goals in two successive matches to scupper their already pretty optimistic notions of getting in on the League Championship itself. Life is never dull in this neck of the woods.

Looking back, I suppose I was a fair weather supporter. I wasn't one of those Fulham fans who wouldn't be seen dead cooped up among the hoops of QPR. Or vice versa. And if Chelsea had a decent fixture, I would be there, scuffing around the cinders in front of the turnstiles and waiting to catch a glimpse of a star or two when the visitors' team bus arrived. It must have been nearly twenty years ago that I went to Stamford

Bridge with John Cleese. They were, as the reporters used to say, 'entertaining' Liverpool. One of Bill Shankly's first relentless sides. We had to pay a tout to get a ticket, and we barracked Roger Hunt, an earnest runner off the ball whom Alf Ramsey had preferred to Jimmy Greaves in the 1966 World Cup. Even then, the young Basil Fawlty had some marvellous lines in exasperated sarcasm. Every time Chelsea's goalie, Peter 'The Cat' Bonetti, caught the ball and punted it back to the half-way line, John would stretch himself to his full height and shout, 'Cat, you must kick it higher, man, *higher!*' It had us all in stitches – and afterwards we went round the corner to the flat of my then girlfriend, the actress Jo Kendall, and she made us crumpets round the fire and we listened to the rest of the results on *Sports Report. Tarum-Tarum-Tarum-Tarum-Tar-iddely Um-Tarum* . . . Happy days.

Mind you, I was always Fulham at heart. When I first came up to bedsitland, I drifted down by the riverside one Saturday and got well and truly hooked when Tosh Chamberlain slipped as he was taking a corner, missed the ball and centred the corner-flag instead. For an awful moment we all thought Maurice Cook was going to nod it in.

I remember, to the minute, when my allegiance to Fulham began to waver. At half-past seven on the evening of Tuesday August 23, 1966. That was the night Sir Stanley Rous switched on the new floodlights at QPR's Loftus Road – and not only that, for in the summer Fulham had unaccountably sold our Fulham Reserves idol, Rodney Marsh, to the Shepherd's Bush club for an insultingly paltry £15,000. We all trooped up the Fulham Palace Road and across Hammersmith to see how Rodney would fare under the avuncular guidance of dear old Alec Stock. Encouraged to play as zanily as he wanted to, he was a glorious revelation. He scored four goals before half-time on that bright-light night against (I think) Colchester, and we were converted; not so much QPR-ites, but Rodney worshippers.

I will think warmly of that youth of mine (and Rodney's) when I stroll up Wembley's Empire Way this Sunday to watch the Rangers. For within a year, those twenty seasons ago, Marsh had not only taken QPR out of the Third Division but had got them to the League Cup Final itself. Along with Swindon Town (inspired by another talented solo circus artist, Don Rogers), that QPR side must have been the lowliest ragbag of misfits ever

29

to have graced a Wembley Final. That morning in March, we all congregated for bacon sandwiches at the Bush cafe. Then a congregation of some 4,500 with banners and bugles, crocodiled a few miles up the Harrow Road to the dilapidated old concrete shrine. The lilting, haunting, chant of *Rod-nee! Rod-nee!* had the traffic stopping on the North Circular when taxi-drivers got out of their cabs to clap the parade and offer us a thumbs-up. (The musicians John Tilbury and Gavin Bryars were Rangers fans, and that season they incorporated the few bars of the chant in a piece they arranged for a concert in the Purcell Hall – and the reviewer wrote in the *Musical Times*, 'Did Marsh really score in Cardew's treatise or was it an hallucination?')

Such looney tunes had no affect whatsoever on West Bromwich Albion, however. Not to begin with, anyway. The First Division sharks set about the *minnows* (another good olde tyme football reporters' word) with a lip-smacking appetite. We were high above the corner-flag at the Tunnel End, the better, alas, to see Clive Clark, the perfidious Albion's quicksilver wingman, score two easy, early goals with a smug swagger. We held glum faces in our hands, for an utter humiliation seemed on the cards. For three-quarters of an hour, Rodney didn't even have a touch. He tried one flamboyant, over-head bicycle-kick, missed the ball completely – and 99,000 people laughed their heads off. We squirmed with embarrassment.

At half-time, old Alec Stock was frantic fast off the bench in his spotted silk muffler and British Warm army officer's overcoat. In the dressing-room, he pinned Marsh and his fellow front forward, Les Allen, against the wall and shouted at them: 'If we're going to lose six-nil, then let's lose six-nil with a bit of pride. If you two are not going to pull your fingers out, then you have my full permission to stay in here and not even bother to go out for the second half.'

They went out. And all of a sudden, Allen was fizzing. He fussed and chivvied around Rodney, inspiring the boy to get his act into gear. And so it came to pass, and Marsh started running at West Brom with that full-tilted, falling-waiter, tripping shuffle. He never needed to look at the ball when he dribbled. Like a boxer, he just kept his beady stare on the opposition's eyeline.

Marsh fed Morgan, who scored a beauty to make it 1–2. Then, twenty yards out, Rodney chassied left, then right – and

30

rolled a tantalizing, soft-shoed slipper of a daisy-cutter for the far corner. It was inch-perfect. The First Division goalie was deceived totally. The rigging hissed. It remains one of the best scores I have ever seen. Now it was 2-all – and with a few minutes left, Rodney bewitched the defence again and laid the ball into the path of his dervish of a hook-nosed Cockney right-winger, Mark Lazarus, who walloped in the winner to make it 3-2. Lazarus indeed! And that evening we lit bonfires on Shepherd's Bush Green. *Rod-nee! Rod-nee!* wafted up to the stars. And the coppers joined in.

Now Rangers are back at Wembley again. Comparatively, they are a pretty well-established bigtime club now. They have even pioneered the age of the plastic pitch – as well as the old joke: 'Do you prefer grass to Astro-Turf?' 'I dunno, I've never smoked Astro-Turf!' On Sunday, they play Mr Robert Maxwell's Oxford United, a club which has had as unlikely a recent rise into the big time as Rodney's Rangers did two decades ago. Marsh is a successful entrepreneur in Florida now. I trust he will be tuning his good ear to the crackly World Service commentary from Wembley on Sunday.

A keen, passing aspect of the afternoon will be to watch how Mr Maxwell himself takes the defeat when Oxford lose – as they surely must, if only for West London's old time's sake. We know his is very good at winning, when his great arms can jerk into almost uncontrollable out-stretched and Messianic actions. One of the Christmas competitions set by *The Guardian* was to compose a letter from Mr Maxwell written to the United manager on the day in April that Oxford are relegated from the First Division (which remains a possibility). The same could yet be penned this Sunday tea-time. The three winners were:

To whom it may concern: You're fired. Fraternally, pp., R.M.

You are redeployed forthwith as coach to Vaduz-Maxwell (Div 2, Leichtenstein). Travel warrant enc., Maxwell.

Gravy train stops here. You have hit buffers. See my daughter in Petty Cash. M.

Talking Turkey

Bobby Robson's Englnd soccer team will clatter, chalk-faced and nervous, up the tunnel at Wembley to play Turkey this Wednesday night looking only for, as the jargon has it, 'a result, Brian'. Anything fancy in the way of decoration – like, say, a skein of mazy dribbles or half a dozen goals that slap and hiss at the rigging – would be too much to ask. But there's asking. What's Turkish for *Wodderloderubbish!*

England crucially need to beat the mightily modest Turks by whatever means, to ward off the possibility of ignominy when they travel to Yugoslavia on Armistice Day to play the final qualifying match for next summer's European Nations' Cup, which will be held in West Germany. It would be a right turn-up if England's hooligans holidayed in Bavaria next year while England's footballers and Mr Robson were kicking only their heels on the Costa Brava. It could happen yet.

England's yellowy autumn pessimism stems from an awful drubbing they took in the September friendly match against the West Germans in Düsseldorf. The ageing, and suddenly fallible, Shilton let only three in, but more by luck than judgment apparently – indeed, by all accounts, England could have been six down by half-time so gormless was the defensive dithering in the face of Germany's smart and speedy routines. The full-backs that day, Anderson and Sansom, were said by observers not to have woken from their nightmare for the full ninety mins, and the midfield was so resoundingly alarmed that, as the ever splendid David Lacey put it in *The Guardian* next day, 'The forlorn Reid shuffled around like a man in his pyjamas who had been woken up in the early hours to find the house full of firemen; (while) Hoddle's contribution was that of a man drawn reluctantly from a sunbed to mend a leak.'

Mind you, the captain, Bryan Robson, was injured and missed the match. You don't say? Poor brittle-boned Bry. Has he actually missed more matches for England than he's played? I'd bet on it. Other sports have *official* non-playing captains.

Whenever Robson jnr is mentioned, I think of that injury-prone and very hittable American pugilist, Chuck Wepner, who, they said, used to turn up for his fights in an ambulance. And, if he did hear the sound of the first bell, once he'd seen stars, his immediate post-fight excuse was, 'Sorry, I musta slipped on the blood in my corner!'

Surely England cannot blow it on Wednesday? If they do, poor put-upon Robson snr – at the best of times, in his after-match touchline interview, all watery-eyed and rubbery-faced like a Les Dawson playing Grandma Giles – could at least coin a new variation for the 1990s: '*Sick as a turkey, Brian.*' The old one is approaching its seventieth birthday as part of the sub-culture's language, apparently, according to *Match Weekly* magazine: 'Spurs gave birth to the famous footballing cliché "sick as a parrot" when, returning from a trip to Argentina in 1908, the team was given the ship's parrot as a mascot by the captain. The bird lived happily in Tottenham High Road for ten years before dying in 1919, on the very day that Arsenal deprived Spurs of their First Division place. Hence . . .' Ahh, the value of research.

To avoid further entry into soccer's book of quotations, Mr Robson might this week consider *widening* Wembley before the match. Give the wingers a bit more space to pull the Turks apart. Quite legal, apparently, as Glasgow Rangers so cheekily illustrated a couple of weeks ago when they compressed the width of their Ibrox pitch to bottle up the reportedly elusive wingmen from Dynamo Kiev. The rules state, simply, that the width of a football field 'must be not less than 100 yards by 50 yards, or 90 metres by 45 metres'. Which leaves a lot of room for manoeuvre.

If Mr Robson pinches a yard or two from the greyhound track at Wembley this week then England should have no problem. For wingers are coming back, twenty-one years after Sir Alf Ramsey banished them and won the Cup with nine muscular midfield men, plus Banks and Charlton. Now the likes of John Barnes and Chris Waddle are reviving the ancient arts.

They'd better be picked this week. Seven and Eleven. Cheap at the price. The matinée idols are back in biz. The dance-floor dandies with the touchline chassé. Poetry is back in motion. Such as in Alan Ross's classic hymn to Sir Stanley Matthews:

. . . he weaves in towards,
Not away from, fresh tacklers,
Who, turning about to gain time, are by him
Harried, pursued not pursuers.
Now gathers speed, nursing the ball as he cruises,
Eyes judging distance, noting the gaps, the spaces
Vital for colleagues to move to . . .

Barnes has been particularly thrilling. I've seen him play only twice this year. In the spring, for Watford, he was a chirpy enough yellow canary, but he was caged and seemed to be whistling the tunes half-heartedly, more careless than carefree. They don't rate that sort of thing at Anfield. The soloist at Liverpool has to satisfy the full orchestra. Then they'll play him in. And how! Barnes was quite breathtaking in red.

Barnes does it both ways. He can be a diddly dribbler, or direct and uncomplicated with a whizzbang of a shot. B was also for Best, surely the best of them all. Funnily enough, down the years, M was the letter for these corner-flagging, mazy mesmerists – Billy Meredith and Alan Morton; Mullen of Wolves and Mitchell of the Magpies; Mitten of Manchester and Medley of Spurs; not forgetting good ol' Arthur Milton of Glos and the Gunners. Nor, of course, the onliest twinkletoes, Sir Stan himself.

London's appetizing new literary imprint, *Sportspages*, which has recently been founded by Simon & Schuster, kicks off with timely reissue of John Moynihan's glorious celebration of pre-'66 Saturdays and Sundays, *Soccer Syndrome*. One time, when the venerable Matthews appeared in one of his last command performances in the capital, Moynihan cadged a spot on the very byline at White Hart Lane: 'I could have touched him as he wiggled up the line. Hands held out slightly, the shuffle, the spurt, and then there was the heaving and straining and pushing and shouting as the Spurs defence jostled to put the ball away . . . Stanley always going through on the outside, coming again, and Withers in trouble again, not knowing whether to go forward, not knowing whether to take the bloke and make a fool of himself again, or hang back . . . and then Stanley was near goal again and we could hear the delicate slap, slap of his boots which you never hear from the terraces because of the noise.'

Now, true greats are true greats, I agree, and in sport anyway you must never dare to compare them with moderns. But, honestly, the sort of collective anticipation and exultation described by Moynihan back in the mists of thirty-odd winter ago is the sort of thing that could riddle the cockles of Barnes's Anfield this season. If he keeps it up – and Wembley, too. Certainly if Mr Robson widens the pitch.

England to qualify. On a prayer and a wing.

Hart in the Right Place

In a sleeves-uprolling, off-yer-bottoms gee-up, fit to join such legendary exhortations as Hal's before Harfleur, Winston's after Dunkirk, or Tebbit's behind the bicycle-shed, Mr Terry Venables arrived at White Hart Lane and proclaimed, in royal and purple plural, '*We have no time to fanny around no more.*' Quite so, and in the last couple of weeks we have seen how such inspiring oratory has blown cold or hot on the Hotspurs.

His new set of lads had, said the former Sr El Tel of Barcelona, gotta get organized at the back, find a flaming lot more fluency down the flanks, and more midfielders in midfield, not to mention a heck of a dollop of potency, punch and panache upfront in the area, like. In short, no more fannying around.

At least the late Señor talks like north London football managers should. He no longer, we are told, needs an interpreter. Rabbit, rabbit, rabbit . . . And it must be said that together with, and in direct contrast to, Mr Robert Maxwell's pat and plonking, brontosauran speeches down the road at Watford, the British football season has been cheerfully enlivened just as it was traipsing in for half-time with sagging shoulders – everyone already well cheesed-off with flailing limply along, in the wake of Liverpool FC's ruddy relentlessness in England, and Rangers' shin-kicking, cold-blue shirtiness in Scotland.

Terry, of course, is exactly the right name for the very model of a modern midfield general, a supremo of the squad. The next generation dug-out dictators will, I guarantee, all be Garys,

Waynes or Darrens, but without question Terry is very much the monicker of the moment for upwardly-mobile management men. Second best name is Barry (as opposed to Barrie, which has bookish connotations). These are true facts. Anyone can discover them by diligent research in back copies of Rothman's football *Yearbook*, which lists even the Christian names of apprentice substitutes. Fifteen years ago, Terrys (69) outnumbered Barrys (38) with the rest nowhere. Now Garys (77) have streaked ahead, Terrys are down to 21, with Waynes and Darrens showing them a clean pair of heels.

So it is no coincidence that the other young sporting entrepreneur of 1987 who made a million out of Jo Bugner's gormless boxing challenge at the same White Hart Lane, answers to the name of Barry. Both Terry and Barry Hearn were both born in Dagenham in the mid-1940s, in housing estates overshadowed by the seemingly unending roof of the vast Ford motor-car factory. Both are, as the jargon has it, streetwise. Both detest fannying.

Venables remains the only English soccer player to have won international caps at every possible level – schoolboy, junior, under-19, under-23, and full, grown-up 1st XI – just two caps in 1965 before being discarded by another Dagenham lad, Alf Ramsey. Word was about by then, that young Venables' football brain was already far sharper and faster than his chubby little wing-half's legs. In Alf's breathless, early England sides, there were definitely no Brownie points to be won by serenely standing on the ball in the centre-circle and weighing up the intelligent options. You had to give and take, get rid of it, and hare about like mad. Pinball stuff – or, rather, Alanball.

It was around that time that Terry kept beating me at ping-pong. I, too, have competed on the international stage. It was a week-long, marathon series in the sun. It usually got to 18-all, but there is no way a romantic spin-server can ever beat a dedicated professional forehand driver with a massive competitive instinct. It always ended up 21–18 to Venables T. Also, he always bagged the best bat, the only one with any decent rubber dimples. Let me explain.

It was the summer of 1965 and we were in Nice in the south of France. I was, of all unlikely things, making a film on the life of the newly late Somerset Maugham. Terry was captain of Tommy Docherty's vibrant young Chelsea side, which was having a close season training to sunbathe and playing a few friendly matches against local Riviera teams. We were all staying at the same, very ritzy hotel, and whose private beach, just across the Promenade des Anglais, was this ping-pong table. I could usually see off Osgood and Cooke, Hinton and Hollins. But Terry V. always had this dab forehand and, as we called it in those days, will to win.

In the evenings, Mr Docherty would make a token gesture of insisting the rest of the lads tucked themselves early into bed – and then he'd settle down with his captain at a bar table and talk tactics with the salt, pepper and vinegar pots. It was gloriously heated, comradely and memorable stuff, and there was no doubt even then, in his early twenties, that Venables was on course to be an outstanding coach. To me, the enthusiastic, insecure Scot and the quick-witted, canny Cockney looked an unbeatable team. Their Chelsea team of tyros had already won promotion, just taken the First Division by storm, and dramatically won through to the FA Cup semi-finals. Sitting in on those late-night disputations would have made anyone place a large bet on their Chelsea being *the* team of the next ten years.

Then Venables would amiably cry off and hoik himself to bed, Docherty would stay for a couple more nightcaps – and, as soon as the young man had gone, astonishingly launch into the most vitriolic and abusive attacks on him, calling to account his captain's lack of fidelity, team spirit, leadership, discipline and general soccer nous. Young Venables was, insisted the eccentric headmaster, a dangerous trouble-maker.

Next day, as if nothing had happened, manager and captain were again seen publicly in warm, fraternal embrace – before the very same late-night scenario would take place. It was no way to run a railway, I thought, and when I got home I was cancelling every bet and forecasting with certainty that the team of the Seventies would not, in fact, last more than a few more months in the mid-Sixties. No one believed me, but I was right: almost at once, Venables was transferred to Tottenham for £80,000 and, not long afterwards, Docherty ('I've had more clubs than Jack Nicklaus') also moved on with his cap and bells to begin his melancholy meander through the Divisions.

I often thought of those few relishing, and relishable, not to say remarkable nights in France, as Docherty went from club to more lowly club (he is now, at the time of writing anyway, with non-League Altrincham), and Venables moved smoothly upwards till he came to the legendary Hotspurs by way of Barcelona. It was only the other day that I twigged and it all explained itself when another of those seaside table-tennis opponents of two decades ago, John Hollins – now, himself the manager of Chelsea – recalled the nub of the relationship between his first captain and manager, in the course of one of those strikingly good Saturday morning profiles in *The Independent*. Recalled Hollins: 'We were mostly very young, including Terry, and for a while everything stemmed from the Doc. But because of Terry's personality, his sharpness and sheer enthusiasm for the game, he was soon matching Docherty thought for thought, word for word, crack for crack. The Doc sensed he was being threatened, understandably I suppose, because Terry was so sharp and clever, particularly when it came to talking about the game.'

That season, between our French ping-pong and Venables being transferred, Chelsea travelled back to the south to play a second-leg UEFA Cup-tie in Italy. They held a first-leg advantage of 4-0, so the Doc, ever flamboyant, reckoned they should look to double it by playing their normal attacking game. And so he sent them out. But once on the pitch, Venables, still only 22 remember, redeployed his men and rejigged the whole strategy. As Hollins recollects: 'Terry simply changed everything. We marked man-to-man and pushed Marvin Hinton back to sweeper. It worked brilliantly. Docherty may not have noticed, but if he did nothing was said – but, for Terry's career at Chelsea, it was only a matter of time.'

Twenty-one years on, back at Tottenham, it is intriguing to watch Mr Venables coping with his latest challenge. He does like to get organized. Like he said to the lads, when Tommy the Doc sent them out to that Italian kick-off all those years ago, *'Fellas, we have no time to fanny around no more.'*

Top Gunners

The first occasion (of quite a few: all deserved) that I found myself in *Private Eye*'s Pseuds Corner was on the Wednesday of Cup Final week, in May 1971. Arsenal's 'double' year. I had written, 'I honestly don't think I could make a close friend of a man who supported Arsenal,' which I agree was pretty wet. But you *still* know what I meant.

The poor old Gunners remained the butt of the weary jokes. Lucky Arsenal had long become Boring Arsenal. Not any more, it seems. All of a sudden, a brand-new team of unknown and unlikely sprogs are looking to make a serious challenge for the League title in the New Year – and with football of a refreshing, youthful fizz. And what's more, in their centenary season. Exactly one hundred years ago this week, on the afternoon of December 11, 1886, a group of comrades, from the Dial Square workshop at the Royal Arsenal munitions factory, crossed the Thames by ferry to the Isle of Dogs, where they played and beat the Eastern Wanderers on some scrubland ringed with sewers. A fortnight later, on Christmas Day, they all met for a lunchtime ale at the Royal Oak, next to Woolwich Arsenal railway station, and officially chipped in their first subs and elected officers. By a narrow vote, they decided not on Dial Square FC, but on the far grander Royal Arsenal.

That particular Arsenal 'double' side of 1971 were the last London club to win the Championship – an indictment of the capital's standards over the last two decades. Much loved, of course, by their immediate family in north London, that last successful Arsenal side were derided by the rest of the country for always putting efficiency ahead of excitement. Multitudes would offer a collective yawn when they trotted out for an away fixture. They were managed, not by a rasping, gasping TV pundit – as were other clubs at that time – but by Bertie Mee, a quiet, well-mannered physiotherapist who had the style and the pale lovat suits of a country solicitor. They nudged and nurdled a succession of one-nil victories to take – or so the rest of the land

39

imagined – the prizes almost by default. There was a lot of jealousy involved – soft Southerners never having to work for anything and never having it so good.

Looking back, though, it wasn't a bad team at all. Bob Wilson in goal, making up for his crummy geometry (especially down at the near post) with grit and gumption; McLintock, McNab, Rice and Simpson forming the wall in front of the clattering, often evil, ton-of-bricks tackles of Storey; the two Georges, Charlie and Armstrong, doing the nifty stuff, to let the two rough-hewn runners, Radford and Kennedy, off the lead as often as possible.

The brains of the side, the quiet Mr Big, was George Graham, a slim, generous, experienced prober and prodder, who was usually in the right place at the right time without noticeably breaking sweat. He was the calming influence, and they called him 'the Stroller'. And it was to Graham that Arsenal turned fifteen summers later when the manager, Don Howe, resigned in an understandable huff having heard that the club had approached '*El Tel*' of Barcelona, Sr Venables, to see if he was inclined to re-stoke some home fires. Bad luck on Howe, but is the way of these things. Graham inherited Howe's cadre of youngsters – and they suddenly began to play with flair and a sureness of touch, in spite of the cautious, gentlemanly Graham telling us on the day he took the job: 'I look, first, for efficiency. I have a limited future if I look for attractiveness first – and we finish in the middle of the table. That is not where Arsenal belong. Like our team of 1971, we might not be pretty to watch, but I'm determined, like them, that we will have all the qualities that foreign teams admire about the British – fitness, resilience, application, conviction, and the will to win.'

Stroll on, Stroller, we thought (as we yawned, and reached for the fish-paste sandwiches), George Graham's Gunners are going to be full of the same old groanworthy guff and huff of the legend. But not a bit of it. The boys struck up the band – and suddenly Highbury is happy and the team of tyros actually seem to be enjoying themselves of a Saturday afternoon.

Funny, this bias against Arsenal. Yes, it must be envy. The first sports book I ever remember buying, for 1s 6d on Gloucester's old GWR station, was a pamphlety thing called *Up the Gunners!* which celebrated the club's League Championship after the war. There was an article in it by Denis Compton (whom I much admired), naturally, about his brother Leslie, the big jet-haired stopper centre-half and Middlesex wicket-keeper, and lots of pictures of Tom Whittaker, another manager-physio, fingering Ronnie Rooke's knobbly knees on the dressing-room couch. George Swindin, Wally Barnes, Forbes and McPherson, Lewis, Logie, Roper and Mercer . . . Perhaps it was the boastful tone of the book: 'No one who enters the hallowed Highbury halls of marble can fail to be affected by the aura of this great club' sort of stuff. Even to an eight-year-old Western bumpkin, this seemed nauseating presumption.

On Cup Final day, 1950, my father and I went to see Swindon Town play (in those days there was a full League programme on Final day at Wembley), and afterwards we heard on the car wireless how Reg Lewis's goal had won the thing for Arsenal against Liverpool. In spite of it being Denis's last game on the wing, I still found an anti-Arsenal feeling welling up.

Quaintly, the same thing happened a quarter of a century later when I was working for Thames TV. Another delightful man was a security officer at our Euston Road studios – and whenever I used to greet that uniformed and smiling, still petite, wizard of dribble, Jimmy Logie, I could never stop myself thinking, 'Lovely man, what a pity he played for Arsenal.' In the early-middle 1970s, I saw Liam Brady come on as a substitute at Highbury for his first-ever senior game. At once you could sniff his aura of being out of the ordinary, even though he looked as lost, lightweight and worried as Stan Laurel at the top of a one-reeler. Why did such a wispy clever-clogs have to come to Arsenal, I thought: why couldn't he have taken the usual route from Dublin to Man United, who would really appreciate his talents?

All to do with the snooty tone of that little pamphlet. In it, the old amateur international, Bernard Joy, had written: '"A bit crude when eating," had stated the report of an Arsenal scout. He was referring to a well-known international whom Arsenal were interested in buying, and is shows how deeply the club vet a man, and how personal background can sometimes damn a player even when he has the necessary football qualifications.' Get you, Gunners, I thought, aged eight.

Although Arsenal celebrate their centenary this week, you might say that they really should have had a bigger fling last year, for 1985 was the golden jubilee of the arrival of the marble

41

halls of Herbert Chapman, truly the founder of the modern club and its swish and swanky reputation. The advertisement which he answered, in an *Athletic News* of 1925, read: 'Only people who will not spend big money on transfer fees need apply.' He took no notice of that, in the event. His first success was to get London Transport to change the name of their Underground railway station from 'Gillespie Road' to, simply, Arsenal. He put a huge clock in the stadium, and kept it there 'as a benfit to spectators', even though the FA wrote furious letters saying it would impinge on the referee's authority. He held a floodlights' demonstration at the ground as early as 1932, pioneered the 10-yard penalty area (again with heated objections from the FA), introduced rubber studs on players' boots, urged the invention of a white ball, and was first seriously to suggest research into composition 'all-weather pitches. He also produced a series of revoltionary teams, all based on strength, purpose and presumption. Through the 1930s, they won five League titles and two FA Cups.

Chapman also changed the team's all-red strip into the more classy and Corinthian white-sleeved shirt. They first ran out in the now-famous uniform at Highbury for a match against Liverpool on March 4, 1933. But red had been the colour ever since that Christmas Day meeting at the Royal Oak in 1886. Two of the pioneers that day in the pub were newly down from the Midlands to work at Woolwich, Messrs Bates and Beardsley. Back home they had played for Nottingham Forest. The agenda at the opening meeting reached the item: *Kit?* Beardsley said he had an idea.

The club's centenary history, *Arsenal 1886-1986* (Hamlyn), is by far the best of its kind I have come across, rewardingly researched and handsomely illustrated. In it, the authors, Martin Tyler and Phil Soar, relate how Beardsley that afternoon simply 'wrote to Nottingham Forest asking if they could help . . . (and they) generously sent down a complete set of red shirts . . . and a ball, useful, for the new club didn't have one of those either.'

Many happy returns are in order, and, I suppose, in this week anyway, many apologies and a firm purpose of amendment about any future groans. But, in future, if you find them coming on a bit too strong, know now that you can blame Nottingham Forest for starting it all. Trust Brian Clough to get some sort of oar in, however tenuously.

Derby Day

In the Anfield district of Merseyside, just off Walton Breck Road, there is a dusty little thoroughfare called Houlding Street. Historians of the sub-culture should be popping past on pilgrimage this special week which ends with Liverpool AFC meeting Everton at Wembley. In over a century it is, astonishingly, the very first time these neighbouring giants and enemies have ever walked out together to contest an FA Cup final. Reds versus Blues on the lush green velvet.

John Houlding was founding father of the famous feud. He was a moustachioed Victorian brewer who liked to get his own way – and did to the extent of being a sometime Tory MP, JP, and Lord Mayor of Liverpool. He owned all the land round Anfield Road, and what money his workers made in a long week they spent far faster of a Saturday night on the ales and stout from Houlding's Sandon Hotel. His supporters called him 'Honest John'; to others, with grudging fear, he was 'King John'.

One hundred and two years ago, a Sunday school team of ragamuffins from St Domingo's Church bagged a pitch in Stanley Park when it was first opened to the public at weekends. Houlding (perhaps he was running for Parliament that year) sponsored them, buying kit, letting them change in the pub, enclosing the ground, and charging them only a nominal £100 per annum for rent. He named them 'Everton' and the little pitch was known as 'Anfield'. They played very good football and four years later, in 1888, they were one of the first twelve members of the newly-founded Football League – which gave them legal entitlement to charge admission money. When they started doing so Houlding, ever the entrepreneur, upped the rent to £250 and demanded exclusive rights to sell all ales, stout and refreshments. St Domingo's sports committee refused, and offered only £180 for rent.

Houlding evicted them on the spot and said he would form his own, more complaisant team. 'Everton Domingo's' moved north across Stanley Park to some scrubland which was described as having 'degenerated from a nursery to a howling desert'. By 1892 it had been transformed into 'Goodison Stadium' and was opened by Lord Kinnaird, FA supremo. Meanwhile, down the hill, the furious Houlding had demanded that his new team be allowed to keep the name 'Everton'. Both the League and FA refused so, grandly, he baptised them 'Liverpool'. At this, the *rugby* club of that name threatened court action – so Houlding simply stuck *AFC* on the end.

The first local 'derby' was played at Goodison in 1894. Everton won easily by 3–0 – indeed, for the next sixty years, almost continuously Everton remained the senior club. Its stadium was grander, and so was its football. It was not until 1971 that Liverpool's messianic manager, Bill Shankly, could boast with that aspirate-hissing fervour of his – 'There's only two great teams on Merseyside these days: Liverpool and Liverpool Reserves!'

Shankly, a rasping one-off from Lanarkshire mining stock, fashioned a dramatic series of winning sides through the Sixties and early Seventies. Some would say he almost literally gave his life to Liverpool. Just before his retirement in 1974, Joe Mercer had jokingly remarked 'Shanks is getting past it. These days he's letting the left-half take his own throw-ins.' He had a brief, forlorn, retirement – feeling spurned by the club he had helped rebuild and, astoundingly, going to watch Everton on a Saturday more often than he went to Anfield. After his funeral, I remember Johnny Giles saying, 'Shanks died of a broken heart after seeing Liverpool go on to even greater success without him. Giving his whole life to a football club was a gruesome mistake.'

Since when, Liverpool have had three managers, each promoted from inside the club. From the little 'Boot Room' under the stands at Anfield came first another formidable ex-miner, the Geordie Bob Paisley, and then Shankly's original 'bucket-and-sponge' man, Joe Fagan. A year ago, in 1985, the team's prodigiously gifted Scottish centre-forward, Kenny Dalglish, picked up the torch, saying he would simply 'carry on the tradition'. As player-manager, Dalglish has endeavoured to restore the club's reputation after the horrors in Brussels by the only way he knows – through relentless performances on the field.

He has succeeded in that. Why, at the time of writing, both Liverpool and Everton could be not only challenging for the FA

Cup at Wembley on Saturday, but also for the historic 'double'. With a fortnight to go, they are each haring, neck and neck, for the League Championship. (Though piners for olde-tyme romantic football are still banking on a late dash by West Ham United.)

Everton's recent story is a touching one. After squirming for two decades in the shadow of their neighbours across Stanley Park, they roused themselves three winters ago under the managership of their taciturn, sad-faced, and stocky little wing-half, Howard Kendall – helped very much more than somewhat by his unsung coach and former midfield colleague, Colin Harvey. Other than by Liverpool, in the last two seasons Everton have been unstoppable. One of them hits the buffers this Saturday teatime.

Odds are, I'm afraid, that it will not be a pretty match. Both sides are more full of pragmatists than poets. Both have fashioned predictability to a fine art, *viz* the long-ago Shanklyism, 'We're not "mechanical", we're "methodical". Who wants to be "unpredictable" if you can perfect being "predictable"? Joe Louis was predictable. He'd hit a man, who'd fall to the floor. Count to ten. Out! Goodnight! Louis was predictable all right. I'm glad Liverpool are predictable too.'

And at football, it must be said, Kendall's Everton have learned alot from Shankly – as well as from his successor, Paisley, whose short, sharp sermons said much of the same – such as, in 1979, 'Oh yes, we've had bad times here at Anfield: one year we came second.' Or, 'If a team beats us once, they spend the rest of the season doing a lap of honour: I remember Burnley's manager, Adamson, once crowing how they'd beaten us one night and that his fellows were in a different league. At the end of the season, they were.'

Saturday soccer down there is likely to be technical, taut, tight-lipped and ashen-faced – though the whole *occasion*, to be sure, will be awash with Merseyside passions of either red or blue. The rivalry can break up families, as in the folk singer Bridie's lament, *Romeo an' Juliet:*

Juliet's Dad was Everton mad,
While Romeo's Pa was a Shankly lad.

The rest of England, uncommitted, will pretend to watch the civil war unfold while being nonchalantly careless as to its outcome. Well before half-time, I warrant, we will all be sucked in by the swirl of the clamorous drama. The only Merseysider known to have been indifferent to such stuff was the 1975 nutcase hero of Roger McGough's darling *Football Poem:*

I'm a schizofanatic, sad burrits true
One half of me's red, and the other half's blue.
I can't make up me mind which team to support
Whether to lean to starboard or port.
I'd be bisexual if I had time for sex
Cos it's Goodison one week and Anfield the next.

Before him, the only man who might, in his heart, have sung that song was old 'Honest John' Houlding, the brewing alderman of a century ago.

On the Ball

Brian Glanville lives down the street from me. Most days you spy him at least once whizzing past on his drop-handled bike, a satchelful of books and boots on one shoulder, a net of footballs on the other. More than likely he's off to the park to put in some work on his penalty taking. In Glanville's teams, captains – even if they are nearer sixty than fifty – always take the pens and I fancy Glanville has never, since Charterhouse Under 12s, deigned to play for a team that hasn't let him be captain. They can lump it or he'll leave them.

When his spokes haringly hum down Holland Park's hill, you're probably better averting your eyes, doing up a shoe-lace, or crossing the street – for more often than not the Reg Harris sprint will screech to a stop, as overture to an overwhelming performance which takes in the goodliness and beauty of his good and beautiful children and the infamy and awfulness of critics, publishers, producers and other ponces and poodle-fakers he has come across that morning. The whole glorious

46

outrage will be laced with Italian aphorisms, venemously spiky Jewish jokes, and the snidest of English public-school scorn.

A word in edgeways is out of the question for this is only preliminary spiel to give him a run at his always resounding, despairing crescendo – namely *The State of the Game*. Plays, musicals, short stories, novels and acclaim can come and go to this rum emperor and guardian of Soccer's conscience, for he has been bewitched and bothered by his entrancing bitch of a game all his life. He remains besotted by it, nagging and gnawing over its poor old bones in the *The Sunday Times* each week, and in a multitude of magazines the world over (all translations, it goes without saying, by the author himself).

For over thirty years, this beaky, prolific pamphleteer of the Pressbox has been raising for good his supplicating voice: usually at one and the same time, he has been the Steele & Addison, the Barnum & Bailey, the Job, Jeremiah & Jolson ('You ain't seen nothing yet, folks!') of English association football. Not to mention the *catenaccio* branch of The Family down Juventus way. He prefers attack to defence, and punches in combinations. And as with many rippingly savage left-hookers, he can be a romantic softie outside the ring. Instance, offhand, two throw-away lines in successive issues of *The Sunday Times* in September 1986. Of Bobby Robson's performance in the World Cup, he said of the England manager: 'It is less germane to ask whether you would buy a second-hand press conference from this man than whether the judgment (or lack of it) he showed in the summer justifies his re-appointment for another five years.' And when that other Establishment figure, the FA secretary, Ted Croker, suggested newly-promoted Wimbledon were 'small-time', Glanville replied that we might as well all pack up: 'The day English football cannot find room at the top for Wimbledon, whatever Croker may think . . . we can say goodbye to the game as we know it; and still like it.'

The Establishment has always been the butt of Glanville's scorn. Another of his beefs concerns cricket claiming all the best tunes. A quarter of a century ago, Glanville edited a sumptuous soccer anthology, *The Football Companion*, for Eyre & Spottiswoode (a famous duo who always reminded me of an inseparable pair of olde-tyme, square-toed, Brylcreem-parted full-backs: ah, where, too, are they now? Gone to Andover to publish bibles, it seems). In his Introduction to that eye-opening volume in 1962, Glanville began: 'We have been told, *ad nauseam*, that football is a game without a literature. What has astonished me, over the year spent in making this collection, is just how rich the material is.'

Now, in a brand-new rejig and rethink for Hodder & Stoughton (who sound somehow like a much more enduring, streamlined pair of overlapping counter-attackers in the modern idiom), Glanville starts his *Joy of Football* with even more trenchant contradiction of the conventional wisdom that football has produced no writing worthy of being preserved, with the opening sidewipe – 'much that passes for literature in the lauded realm of cricket now often seems whimsical or over-written.' Fair point. The thing about cricket writing, however, is that it has a vast literature to feed off. It has an historical momentum. In-jokes, anecdotes and statistics need not be explained. The leading players, too, are steeped in the lore, legend and literature of the game. Not so in soccer. Though Glanville, typically, disagrees: 'An ingrained snobbery towards football in Britain, where the upper classes first originated the game, then abandoned it for so many years, has led to a curious, conditioned disdain for writing about the sport, quite unknown in Europe or Latin America, where everybody follows it. In the last twenty years or so, a number of excellent writers have emerged in Britain, liberated by the consequences of our bloodless "social revolution", the rise from the working classes of actors, writers and academics, who love football and comprise a new audience. Journalists such as Hugh McIlvanney, David Lacey, and Hunter Davies . . . Eamon Dunphy and John Moynihan.'

As well as Hunter, whose pieces here naturally include snatches from his memorably enlightening labour of love on his happy Hotspurs of the early 1970s, *Punch* is in evidence, with selections from other soccer buffs who have written regularly in that magazine – Hattersley on his beloved Wednesday, Arlott on Reading, Parkinson on Barnsley, and a couple of other bits to make up the weight.

Older, but just as familiar, fish are landed by Glanville – de Montherlant, no less, and Camus, Nabakov, Giraudoux, Arnold Bennett and, of course, Priestley's very definition of the Saturday soccer congregation: 'To say that these men paid their shillings to watch twenty-two hirelings kick a ball is merely to say that a violin is wood and catgut, that *Hamlet* is so much paper and ink.'

There is the statutory litany of the saints. Alan Ross in the tangerine: 'If Matthews dominates a match, calling up the thunder on the wings for all to admire, Mortensen is the lightning that strikes immediately after'; Geoffrey Green on Di Stefano's peacock-struttin' *completeness* – or on George Best, 'the son of instinct rather than logic'; Arthur Hopcraft on 'the delicious exhilaration' of the flowing lines of Bobby Charlton's football; and Paul Gardner on the 'never-ending clarity, freshness and *perfection*' of Pelé.

In another part of *The Sunday Times* the other week, there was a nice phrase about the human division in spectator sport between, as Mark Lawson put it, 'the doers and ooh-ers'. Glanville understands the difference well: 'To examine spectator sports too closely may simply be to destroy them. The appearance may itself be the essence. What we see and know on the field is, like a theatrical performance, perhaps the reality. What goes on offstage, or off the field, is almost secondary; marginilia.'

Quite. What *hic* of mackintoshed hacks have presumed to cluster backstage at the whistle after a full 90 mins at Covent Garden: 'Tell me, Dame Kirl, girl, what about that high note that ended your second aria?' 'Well, Brian, I just went for it, like, and next thing I knew it hit the back of the Upper Circle.'

Thus, in this new treasury of 80-odd pieces, Glanville especially prizes *jeux d'esprit* such as those he includes from John Moynihan, who contributes the feet-on-the-ground, head-in-the-clouds romance of Saturday's man on the terraces, looking forward to his Sunday morning in the park. Oohing, then doing.

Glanville here cues in Moynihan, gloriously, to lift the game from its high-altared cathedrals and pontifical, specialist splendours, and plonk it back where it intrinsically belongs – with his mud-splattered, worm's-eye views from a council pitch. Moynihan fleshes out, with love, such local-rag one-liners as *Apex Reserves 6, Rawl-plugs 5*. And, oh, the cockeyed optimism of the real football man when he sets off, bleary but expectant, for his Sunday morning fix. On the way, it cruelly begins to bucket down: "It can't be on," I said. "It's pissing." "Keep your fingers crossed," he said, "I've waited a week for this. It can't be off." "There isn't a chance," I said, always a defeatist. How many times had it happened this winter at Hackney Marshes,

Parliament Hill Fields, and Hampstead Heath Extension? As our left-back had often said about the Chelsea Royal Hospital pitch, "It only has to have a quick slash and that's it, *the bastard.*" The rain seemed to ease a bit as we reached the ground, but there he was . . . I recognized the groundsman, a small, beaky-chinned man wearing a faded pin-striped suit, sodden and clipped at the ankles with bicycle-clips. His brown eyes protruded, his mouth was in it permanent openness, and as we ambled up it spoke in shrill cockney: "*It's HOFF!*" . . . We looked down, mumbling that we might be able to play if the rain stopped. Hoping, praying, crossing fingers. "I'm telling you it's hoff. And when I say it's hoff, it's hoff. *HOFF!*".'

The lofty Glanville, too, understands such provincial poig-nancies . . . whoops, there he goes now, whizzing outside my window on his drop-handled roadster. So it's safe to whip out and catch the post. His hunched back, as ever, is bedecked with books and boots and balls. He's off, no doubt, to put in further work on more viciously inswinging corners from the left wing. Bless his shinguard-encasing, ever colourful, little cotton socks.

And Brian Begat Nigel

Brian Clough's son, Nigel, could not only get the very first of his father's long line of bespoke football teams through to the FA Cup final at the end of this Saturday's semis, but also give himself a chance, as they say, to nudge the selector, and make his Dad the first England international to sire a ditto son. Certainly Clough Jnr's contributions have been decisive in helping Nottingham Forest this far and another strollingly elegant show this weekend and in the grand finale on north London's famous green velvet in the second week in May could force Mr Bobby Robson's hand when he comes to choosing his squad for this summer's European Championship in West Germany.

Well, unless I'm bonkers and blind to a celebrated couple of names staring me in the face, I cannot think of one pair of father-and-son England soccer internationals. Cricket, of course, has oodles of them – there have been the Cowdreys, Parkses,

Huttons, Hardstaffs, Manns, Tates and Townsends. And they could play easily two whole teams made up of filial duos from the other Test-playing nations. But in soccer, not a single 'One day all this will be yours, my son.'

Fathers and sons have *played* together in the same league side: James and William Butler for Grimsby Town in 1916; and Alec and David Herd, who were inside-right and inside-left respectively for Stockport County v Hartlepool in May 1951. On the same day in April 1936, Harry Wait was between the sticks in the poloneck for Walsall's 1st XI, while his son, Harold, was turning out as custodian for Walsall 2nds. That was the year Tom Johnson was centre-half in Sheffield United's Cup final team (beaten by Arsenal). Tom's Dad, Harold, had won Cup winner's medals for United in 1899 and 1902 – and his elder brother, Harry, had won one too in 1925, also for the Blades.

Clough *père*'s two games for England were in 1960, against Wales and Sweden. Not bad company either, for he was No.9 to Jimmy Greaves's 8 and Bobby Charlton's 10. Joe Baker took his place, and then Bobby Smith, but many old timers reckon Clough deserved more opportunities in the white shirt before he damaged a knee so badly, in 1962 at Bury, that he had to retire; he was 26. In 271 games for Middlesbrough Clough scored an astonishing 251 goals; nobody in history was faster to 200 goals (219 games), and only Dixie Dean (283 in 300) keeps Clough out of the all-time record books.

Young Nigel, 21, is a fair enough chip off the old block as a goal-scorer, but it is as a maker rather than a taker of chances that he is building his reputation. He is not very fast, but he is extremely quick on the uptake and thus a warm pleasure to watch. After his two sumptuous strokes bombed Arsenal out of the Cup in the last round, Brian Glanville of *The Sunday Times* called him 'a joy' and Colin Malam in the *Sunday Telegraph* hailed his 'inspired' match-winning performance as 'a touch of genius obviously inherited from Dad'. In *The Guardian*, ace analyst David Lacey wrote: 'Young Clough is a one-paced player who thinks and reads situations quicker than most. He has the rare gift of knowing what he is going to do with a ball as he recieves it and possesses the sureness of touch to deliver the accurate early pass so essential in opening up space amid crowded defences. He plays the stunned, first-time return ball to perfection, and turns on a dropping ball as well as most of the great creative players of the past.'

Lacey also observed, however, that his nimbleness, or lack of it, could be a drawback. And, sure enough, when a pass played to him is miscued, say, and demands a couple of quick steps and perhaps a despairing stretch, Clough sometimes stands aloof, hands on hips, in the surely-you-don't-expect-me-to-run-for-that pose, reminiscent of Johnny Haynes, the old Craven Cottage impresario.

Kid Clough, they say, is as bright as a blazer button. He needs to be for it must be quite a burden being the son of a father famed for the same line of work. 'Oh, yes, not bad, but he'll never be as good as his Dad' sort of stuff. When the teenaged Peter Alliss was of the mind to make his way as a tournament golfer in the 1950s, his father, the great Percy, gave him £50 and packed him off to the Spalding Tournament a St Andrew's, saying that if he spent it and didn't win any prize money he could walk all the way home to Bournemouth. In the clubhouse, a member remarked to young Peter, 'You putt just like your Pa,' then deflated the boy with, 'No, on second thoughts, you're even worse!'

The delightfully bluff Richard Hutton, another to tread in the old man's footsteps, had hero-worshipped Yorkshire's long-dayed knight throughout his boyhood; indeed, at the age of ten, had disgraced himself at Headingley by sobbing uncontrollably when Lindwall had clean bowled Sir Len second ball – 'a factmade worse,' recalls Richard, 'because as far as my young eye could judge, there had been an easy single off the first ball!'

At boxing, an adorable little bruiser, Brian, was twelve when his Dad, Jack London, bald, bandy and eminently beatable, was kayoed in six to lose his British heavyweight title to Bruce Woodcock. When Jack poked his two lovely black eyes into the Blackpool homestead next morning, young Brian vowed to avenge the family name one day. He did, thirteen years later: he flattened Joe Erskine at the White City on a night on which, as the official British boxing *Yearbook* described, 'London was transformed into a fighting fury, smashing Erskine twice to the canvas, where he was counted out on one knee, refusing to get up for any more.' Brian, of course, went on to fight both Floyd Patterson and Muhammad Ali for the world title, but the good fellow was less than a 'fighting fury' on those occasions, indeed when he jacked in the latter job he simply got off the floor, shrugged, and described himself as 'no more than a prawn in this game'.

Offhand I can't think of any sports-daughters who have followed Mum or Dad into the big-time. But I wonder what happened to this little girl? I quote from an article by F.B. Douglas-Hamilton in the 1933 edition of *The Boy's Own Annual*: 'He was grimy. His scrum cap was torn; and his jersey was split. His best friend would not have recognised him. Then his scrum cap was torn from his head and I heard a shrill, childish voice cry, "Look! Look! There's Daddy!" A thousand or more eyes at Twickenham turned and saw a little girl of about three sitting by her young mother. And the player, who was the holy terror of his opponent, looked up. His mouth parted with a loving smile. He waved his hand for one fleeting moment, and then he dived at a man who had the ball. "Wavell Wakefield!' ejaculated a man at my side. "Isn't he wonderful!".'

Some might even say the same about Cloughie. Certainly, if young Nige brings him home the bacon this weekend.

Leg Glances

But Did You Enjoy the Play?

The pong remains in spite of the officials' liberal aerosol of new mown-grass-plus-a-waft-of-linseed-oil. I cannot recall a more peg-on-the-nose welcome for a new cricket season. After such a boring and boorish series of, well, series through the winter, you just want to turn over and go to sleep again. Long before the first crocus I wasn't even bothering to stick a morning mitt out of bed to tweak the radio on for news of the latest fiasco, either spiritual or temporal.

Nor could my friends. The playwright, David Hare, diagnosed jaundice perfectly in *The Spectator* the other day: 'Because the team does not look as if they are enjoying the game, nor can I . . . The radio goes on at six-thirty. And yet I find, for the first time, England have finished a series in which I could not summon up any interest at all. It was all a bit like *The Invasion of the Bodysnatchers*. Without Botham, Lamb, Gower or Gooch, the team are all pods. Their replacements – more like the *Midwich Cuckoos*, this – are strange, void men with fair hair who all want to bat at Number Five, where they always fail.'

Hare should write one of his thumping radical plays about the dispiriting sameness of Mrs Thatcher's latest England XI. Perhaps the Guild of Brit Playwrights could script a combined job – for there are a heck of a lot of them about. Better still, this Saturday at Lord's, instead of MCC v Champion County (Nottinghamshire: do you realize Mr Chris 'No Go' Broad could well have the honour of taking first strike to get a new joyous season under way?), why not MCC v Gentleman Playwrights of England?

You'd have no problem raising a side. It would be a question of who to leave out. It is astonishing how many playwrights are mad about the game. How about this for a team, just off the top of my head: Hare, Pinter, Stoppard, Gibbs, Harris, Tinniswood,

Gray, Harwood, Ayckbourn (capt), Welland, Potter.

Hare, the statutory leftie opener with strokes all round the wicket like Bob Barber; Pinter, a sticker, a gumchewer, silent and sombre but, as he himself wrote of Len Hutton once, 'never dull, his play was sculptured, his forward defensive stroke a complete statement.' At No. 3, Stoppard, a bit of a razzle-dazzle Ranji, a 'Trumper leaps out to drive'; Tom would also be wicketkeeper because he likes keeping perplexed slips in fits.

Real batting order ballast would be provided by the two sound old pros. Peter Gibbs (*Arthur's Hallowed Ground, Rumblings*, etc, etc) was once P.J.K. Gibbs, Oxford and over 7,000 runs for Derbyshire between 1966 and 1972; and he would be the only player on the field allowed, in most chivalrous fashion of course, to communicate verbally with an umpire, because of the knowing BBC play that he wrote a year or two back about white-coat tribulations, *Benefit of the Doubt*. At No 5, we have Richard Harris, another prolific notcher, whose *Outside Edge* had the cricket-widow, Miriam, sighing about her Boycottian hubby: 'I don't know if I prefer Rog to have a good innings or a bad one. If it's a good one, he relives it in bed, shot by shot, and if it's a bad one he actually replays the shots until he gets it right. He can make a really good innings last all winter.'

No problem notching up runs with those two, so now we could let loose, in the Botham spot at No. 6, our busking, extemporary swiper, Peter Tinniswood, he of the faded, jauntily-peaked Winston Place cap and a Brigadier's cocked-wrist-and-left-elbow up. Trouble with the dashing, flashing Tinniswood is that he can be frightfully rude about his upright captain, Mr Ayckbourn. In his public print, *The Brigadier's Brief Lives*, the Vimto-swigging all-rounder complained how Ayckbourn had 'single-handedly ruined more Scarborough cricket festivals than any creature . . . for in the evenings you are dragged off to see one of his so-called plays, which apparently the wretch directs himself . . . Good God, the positions in which he places his actors on the stage are quite ludicrous. There's never anyone on the boundary, and the slips are always hopelessly congested.'

Good captain Ayckbourn laughs off such jibes. As he told *The Times*: 'My schoolboy ambition was to play for England. I am a member of Yorkshire and watch them a lot. We have our own theatre team . . . I know Robert Atkins (pioneer of the Royal Shakespeare Company) used to cast his plays entirely on whether you could get a fast bowler who could also play Iago, but I tend to try not to do that.'

The bowling at Ayckbourn's command for our opening fixture at Lord's this weekend would have the lot – pace, lyricism, lulling flights, devious and diddly. Simon Gray once wrote of discovering in the nets at Cambridge his ability to impart 'a curious but effective top spin, holding the ball in a grip that must have come from imagination or pre-natal memory . . . flicking my wrist and twisting my fingers at different points of the arm's varying arc'. Ronald Harwood, as a boy in South Africa, admits to being awestruck watching Denis Compton, with his twirly 'Chinamen' and a wide grin of pleasure on his face, take 5 for 70 at Newlands forty years ago. 'Years later I saw him at Lord's during a break for rain. By chance I sheltered with him under a roof near the Warner Stand. "What about that 5 for 70 in the Third Test against South Africa?" I asked. "Yes," said Denis, "that was fun."'

With Gray and Harwood taking care of the spin, the new ball will be shared by every side's know-all and necessary Lancashire Leaguer, the burly swinger, Welland, and the demon from the Forest of Dean, Dennis Potter. Well, he's been coached by his daughter, Sarah, who really does open the bowling for the England women's XI. And, for good measure, I've never once met a man from the Forest who hadn't had a grandad (sometimes two) who once bowled W.G. in the nets at a church fête in Coleford.

Non-playing 12th man would have to be Samuel Beckett, one-time all-rounder for the Gentlemen of Ireland. Scorer is Adrian Mitchell who, in the penultimate scene in *Another Country*, began jotting down his favourite team, in batting order, 'a Marxist, a Liberal, a Homosexual, a Sadist . . .' though he never did get down to the wicket-keeper's proclivities.

Coach and physio would be the cricket nut Michael Meyer, who has translated sixteen plays by Ibsen and sixteen by Strindberg; he would be good with foreign umpires. Team Groupie, naturally, would be that immortal Tinniswood creation, Miss E.W. 'Gloria' Swanton, and Team Patron, of course, E.R. 'Regina' Dexter.

If rain stopped cricket, we could have some play readings from the Lord's balcony. Stoppard, whirling his willow, could start with his definitive cricket bat speech from *The Real Thing*:

58

'If you can get it right, the ball will travel 200 yards in four seconds and all the batsman has done is give it a knock – like knocking the top off a bottle of stout, and makes a noise like a trout taking a fly. But if you *don't* get it right, the ball travels ten feet, you drop the bat and dance around shouting, "Ouch! Ouch!" with your hands in your armpits.'

I recited that speech once to our doughty second-wicket-down Peter Gibbs, in the pub that houses the Bush Theatre. His still keen, bluey-grey county cricketer's eyes misted up, as he told me of his very last innings for Derbyshire, against Warwickshire at Edgbaston. Funnily enough, of Peter's twelve first-class centuries, six were at Edgbaston. This final one determined him on retirement and full-time playwriting: 'I was, of course, known as a bit of a stodge, a stonewaller. But here on that last sunlit day at Edgbaston, in a split second I saw the light. My illustrious namesake, Lance, was fighting down his off-spinners. Suddenly, a sublime feeling. Just one ball. I hit it off the back foot through mid-wicket, an old-fashioned attacking shot of the richest vintage imaginable. No, not a pull, just one of the most difficult shots remotely possible. And in that instant, I played it to absolute perfection. Sublime. Sensational. Yet when I got back to the pavilion the moment tormented me. Here was I, at the very end of my career, after seeking to reach that same supreme satisfaction every time I had been at wicket, but now fully aware that I might never reach it again, not even once, in many, many blue moons. And, worse, being totally aware that somebody like Barry Richards was strolling out and doing such things at will every day of every summmer.'

Ouch! Ouch! But what a way to go, and I find that just typing Gibbs's story somehow refreshes the spirits and sharpens the relish and anticipation for a new season. Perhaps everything will be all right after all; the last four months have been simply an upsetting dream; and the new April sun is freshly-laundered bright and, as our Team Manager put it, 'From ashes ancient Gower is come . . . I see them stand like greyhounds in the slips . . . *the game's afoot!*'

Capel in Hand

As the final credits roll up on a generally gormless, gumboot summer, the cricket season at least has a chance to sail serenely into its autumn sunset with a decent Cup final at Lord's this weekend. Merited and just unities have been bestowed on the NatWest final, for unquestionably the two best county sides of 1987 will answer the umpires' bell at 10.40am on Saturday. Nottinghamshire, led by the bristling, narrow-eyed Hadlee, Rice and Broad, should start as slight favourites over the more bucolic Northamptonshire of Lamb, Larkins and the gallivanting new find of the season, David Capel.

Both sides, last month, were neck-and-neck to the Championship wire, so this should be the spiciest of contests. The two counties are alphabetic and, almost, geographic neighbours, both with ancient cricketing traditions. There, the resemblance ends: Nottinghamshire's past has been littered with garlands – 18 Championships (or shares of); Northamptonshire CCC have never won a Championship in the 110 years of existence.

Notts have never not fancied themselves, so I have always had a softer spot for Northants. Perhaps because, when I was being weaned on the pastoral charms of the game in summer holidays at the Cheltenham Festival, they were always the easiest team for Gloucestershire to roll over – and in going down cheerfully enough they would wave the most colourful of favours. Like, say, a wardrobe-full of striped amateur blazers, or teak-brown old bats bound in pink Elastoplast, or George Tribe's twiddly full repertoire, or Freddie Brown's purply nose and spotted, knotted, red neckerchief.

In the three years following the war, when I first saw them play, Northants were captained successively by Mr P.E. Murray-Willis and Mr A.W. Childs-Clark. The former averaged just 11 in 35 innings, the latter 17 in 85 (with the very best bowling of his career, three for 72 for 'Shrimp' Leveson Gower's XI versus Oxford University at Reigate). Then came Brown, an amateur who could at least *play* a bit, indeed captained England as the last of the true-bluers good enough to be looked up to by even the most gnarled and class-conscious pro. Before Freddie, in 26 seasons, Northants never once held a single-figure position in the Championship; ten times they were bottom, six times bottom-but-one.

Brown at least suggested to his team that it was not outside the realms of fantasy that they might be good enough to win a match, even occasionally. He would choose his side, write it out, slap the piece of paper down in the committee-room, and exit defiantly, leaving his secretary (Lt Col St George Coldwell, no less) to help calm the apoplectic cabinet of pompous burghers. Brown's right-hand man (and successor as captain) was Dennis Brookes, silver-haired, sentry-smart opening bat, who scored just on 29,000 runs for the county, never drank anything (they said) but half a pint of brown ale, and then only after scoring one of his 67 centuries for the county. He became chairman of the Northampton Magistrates' bench – but no more engaging or motley bunch could have been put up before him of a morning than the crew he used to lead out through those 1950s summers: Tribe and Manning, the colonial mesmerists; Jakeman and Barrick and Broderick; the Davis brothers, and Keith Andrew, probably all county cricketers' choice as the best wicket-keeper of his time.

Then came Tyson, and even Andrew had to retreat a few yards back to the sightscreen. Can any man between Grace and Botham have been watched around the shires with more tingling awe than Tyson? Just for a couple of summers till the typhoon blew itself out – or, I suppose, realized there were more things to life than professional sport (he emigrated to Australia where he became a leading journalist, a schoolmaster, and Victoria's director of coaching; this summer he is back in England on a teaching stint and enjoying some lush green grass again).

I sat next to the erstwhile Typhoon at the Centenary Test banquet a few years ago. There could have been no more gentle and companionable dinner neighbour – but when I had first seen his place-name, my spine riddled with a momentary chill, and all of a sudden it was a quarter of a century before and he was pacing out the tumultuous, gathering run. It was the first time Gloucestershire had come up against him. Heroes hijacked.

It was late in the evening and Tyson was at the end of a breathtakingly fast spell, every delivery of which scared our cockles into our socks. We had never seen anything like this. Nor, I fancy, had our doughty men of 'Glorse'. Arthur Milton went, at once and wisely, to Nobby Clark; then Martin Young and George Emmett, after hanging on grimly, were blown away by Tyson. Jack Crapp, brave as ever on the burning deck, signalled for a night watchman.

In the pavilion, Silvikrin-sleek and weather-beaten old George Lambert answered the call. He was Gloucester's own fast bowler, and though usually a swiping No.8 he fancied himself with the bat. Also, this time, his pride at being the nippiest bowler in the Cotswolds was being challenged by this balding, bounding, ruthless young stringbean out there. A man's gotta do what a man's gotta do, and George picked up his bat, bragging, 'This cock can't bowl, you wait and see!'

Crapp nursed him away from Tyson for five minutes, but then George had to face the last three balls of the evening. The Typhoon hollered in at him. First ball clanged into Andrew's gloves 35 yards behind before George had even finished sketching out his forward prod. So did the second. The third did a comprehensive strimming job on the hairs of George's nose as he essayed a backward jack-somersault into the arms of the square-leg umpire. Close of play.

It was a much paler, still shaking, Lambert who returned to the dressing-room. Dear Old Sam Cook met him on the steps with a treble whisky and a light-ale chaser. 'Get those down you, George boy, after a good night's kip he's going to be twice as quick in the morning!'

Tyson, of course, was recruited by Northants from Durham University – his first ball in his first practice match for the county in 1952 was snicked to second-slip with such velocity that it almost took Fred Jakeman's knee with it to the boundary, so his reputation for being fairly swift was made immediately. The north-east has always been a breeding ground for Northants cricketers (as well as Staffordshire and, especially with the present side, Yorkshire). Irrespective of Tyson's tenuous link, however, the veriest, all-time greatest Northants' Geordie must remain Colin Milburn. I bump into him once in a while and his presence still lights up the day. Or occasionally hear him on the radio: witty, pithy, generous because he knows what's goin' on down there and does not believe that no one else can play. But, of course, he can only see it with one eye. What a tragedy.

I can remember the day I read the news. I was in France, in the warm but not quite the deep South, in Cahors on the River Lot. Happy days: café-cognac and the continental *Daily Mail*. It always arrived exactly two days late – so it must have been 25 May, 1969. OLLIE LOSES EYE IN CAR CRASH. A million miles and 18 years later the impact of that headline remains numbing. It was a loss for Northamptonshire, okay, but much more for English cricket – Colin was just becoming a rallying beacon for the youthful goodness, zest, and image of the 'new' professional cricket – ironically, the first ever John Player Sunday League match had been played only 19 days before his cruel accident.

Milburn had been the Falstaffian totem for that Northamptonshire side of the middle 1960s. They finished 3rd, 2nd and 5th in successive Championships – their best ever run. Good names, too, what with the likes of those canny insurance brokers, Crump and Lightfoot; the nicely named Breakwell; and, of course, the then young 'bank clerk who went to war', David Steele. Their next decent patch was in the middle Seventies – 2nd in the Championship and victory in the Gillette in 1976, their first ever trophy. The beguiling Bedi, the dapper Mushtaq, and the snorting Sarfraz led that parade, and this weekend's two stalwarts, Geoff Cook, the captain, and the sometimes super-charged Wayne Larkins, had also come through.

Now, in the middle Eighties, their cracking latest side saw out this midsummer smelling the possibility even of three glittering prizes. But Yorkshire beat them in the Benson & Hedges final in July, and by the middle of August, Nottinghamshire had smoothly accelerated past them in the Championship when, at the beginning of the month, they had been looking unassailable. There is some way to go there yet, of course, but for safety's sake, as well as fair's fair, Northamptonshire should be looking to settle for at least something this Saturday.

I fancy most of the uncommitted will be rooting for them. For they have cheered up this cheerless summer – just as their Northamptonshire predecessors have done all down the century.

Hundreds and Thousands

He should have done it by now. If not, he will be the curse of
Fleet Street, not the toast of it. For most mornings during the last
few weeks have had the sports editors re-checking the diary to
make sure they had sent a man to Warwickshire's cricket match.
The picture blocks have been made and the stats have long been
set in type. All that remains is for Dennis Amiss, 43-year-old,
honest-gazed, affable, pipe-smoking master batsman, to score
just one more century to put himself in the elite list of those who
have made a hundred 100s in first-class cricket. Who's to say,
too, that any selectors with gumption might have brought him
back for England, after the calamitous June, for the Test team
against India?

Amiss joins the exclusive and celebrated score of centurions –
Grace, Hayward, Hobbs, Mead, Woolley, Hendren, Sutcliffe,
Sandham, Ernest Tyldesley, Bradman, Hammond, Hutton,
Compton, Ames, Graveney, Cowdrey, John Edrich, Turner,
Zaheer Abbas, and, of course, Boycott.

As Amiss has, almost unconcernedly, batted through these
midsummer weeks to reach his landmark, so has Boycott been
painstakingly looking for his 150th century – one more than
Sutcliffe, to make him the most prolific Yorkshire centurion of
all time. Such things mean a lot to you, Geofrey, lad, and quite
right too. Can it really be 50 centuries ago that Geofrey
nervelessly took that pace down the pitch at his home ground,
Headingly, in 1977 to clip Greg Chappell through mid-on for
the boundary that posted his hundreth? It seems like yesterday.

The emperor's two-fisted salute. The wonky grin ecstatically
wonkier than ever. His supporters mobbed him and one of them
stole his cap. But they could not ruffle his hairpiece that
afternoon. (The night before the epic knock, though he had been
in bed by nine, Boycott for once had an almost sleepless night. So
had his fellow opener, Mike Brearley, a couple of rooms down
the hotel corridor. Geoffrey just lay on his pillow, contemplating
his century to come. Mike read *Zen in the Art of Archery* by Eugen

64

Herrigel, the German philosopher. Next day, Mike got a duck, and Boycott ended with 191 for Queen and country.)

Amiss had been a previous Test opening partner to Boycott. On one occasion, as they were walking together to the wicket, Dennis wished Geoffrey 'Good luck' as they moved to their respective ends. Boycott called him back. 'It ain't a matter of *luck*, lad,' he said, 'it's skill.' Both were teenage prodigies of the sort we seem to have run out of in English county cricket. Amiss made his first appearance for Warwickshire in 1960 when he was 17. Three years earlier, he had hit 60 for Oldnow Road School in a junior match at Edgbaston and had been told by the county, 'Get in touch with us on your 15th birthday.' Yorkshire had been well aware of Boycott at the same age, but let him hone his grafting qualities in the pressurized local leagues till 1962.

Boycott, prodigiously, and Amiss are the last of a breed,. Indeed, it looks a good bet that no native English batsman will ever again reach his centurion's milestone. Next to his hundred 100s will obviously be Vivian Richards, who started this season with 86, but the target is surely too remote now for Clive Lloyd and Alvin Kallicharran, both 78, Sunil Gavaskar, 74, or Gordon Greenidge, 65. Keith Fletcher, the canny, gnomic chuckler from Essex heads the current Englishman's list with just 62, followed by his protégé, Graham Gooch, with 54. Amiss should close the book on this subject.

As I write, the hope is that Amiss will not keep the shires on edge as Hobbs did in 1925, when he was chasing WG's then record of 126 centuries. For almost four weeks of high summer, the cameramen's caravan trundled after him. Forties and fifties, seventies and eighties . . . but no hundreds. On August 13, a sweltering Saturday, the Movietone men cranked their cumbersome camera on to the, even then, rickety roof of the old pavilion at Taunton. Hobbs came in around three o'clock. Raymond Robertson-Glasgow, occasional inswing and incomparable essayist, was bowling for Somerset. The Master was a mess of nerves: 'He was anxious; the strokes were calculating, even stuffy; he was twice nearly lbw, once at each end. At about 30 he gave a chance to wide mid-on, which went wrong. But at close of play he was in the early 90s. Then – a Sunday, for more waiting. But nice for the Somerset gate. On the Monday morning, J.J. Bridges and I were the bowlers. I bowled a no-ball in the first over, which Hobbs hit to the square-leg boundary. Someone

afterwards suggested that the no-ball was bowled on purpose. It wasn't! Hobbs never needed any presents at the
wicket. In Bridge's second over Hobbs scored a single to leg that gave him what he has told me was the toughest century of the lot.'

In contrast, by the by, Jim Bridges scored one of history's great 99s – on his native patch at Weston, and not-out, too, for the last man ran himself out trying to get the strike. I cannot discover whether it was Robertson-Glasgow who did the deed; if so, the writer made up for it with a grand memoir of his sometime new ball mucker, with the devilish inslant: 'Jim had temperament; in success his face lighted up as if from within, and then he was ready to bowl out the world: Grace, Trumper, Ranji. Again, the slips would floor a catch, or a short-leg would seem to stray, and darkness came down. He would frown hugely, close his mouth on a dark medley of oaths, and signal fielders hither and thither without success. But he had endurance and would bowl from memory rather than give up.'

Anyway, Hobbs's hundred at Taunton . . . when he clipped Bridges to leg for the famous single, I did hear once that the Movietone men on the roof of the Pav were changing their film so never actually recorded the shot on film, but prevailed upon Hobbs to play it again in close-up at close of play.

By coincidence, Grace's hundreth 100 also arrived against Somerset, thirty summers earlier. When Hobbs shyly raised his bat to acknowledge the applause, his captain had come out with a glass of ginger wine with which to toast him. When the Doctor did it, he hollered for a bottle of champagne, quaffed a few glasses of the stuff there and then – before continuing on to 288. The old boy had just passed his 48th birthday.

Amiss comes to his century of centuries five years the Doctor's junior, but in about 400 innings fewer. I first saw him in his debut Test at The Oval against the West Indies – golly, surely not? – 21 years ago. He made 17, lbw Wes Hall, to let J.T. Murray come in and fashion a sublime partnership of 250-odd with the nonpareil Graveney. Amiss took some time to establish himself in the England side but then, through the early Seventies, he let rip in astonishing fashion – cover driving savagely with sometimes an almost Hammondesque, spring-coiled beauty, and playing through square-leg and midwicket with a creaming disdain.

66

In 1974, he was in blistering prime every time he went to the wicket! From Christmas to Christmas, he hit a record 1,379 runs, including one riveting piece of endurance in Jamaica – 262 not out to save the match on his own. But Amiss bridged two worlds, for the game was suddenly changing for opening batsmen. Helmets had not been thought of yet. If he had mastered the youthful fires of Roberts, Holding and Co, at once the more maturely cynical head-hunting of Lillee and Thomson frayed Amiss's nerve, along with all other batsmen in Mike Denness's ill-starred team. He was dropped, shell-shocked. He 'invented' and tried to market a batting crash-hat, totally remodelled his technique and backlift – and came back to prove an heroic point with a glorious 203 out of 342 at The Oval in 1976 agaist Roberts, Holding, Daniel and Holder.

Then came Mr Kerry Packer. At his age, Amiss knew the rift in cricket would result in him being put out to grass in the gentler county pastures for the rest of his career if he accepted the Austalian entrepreneur's enticements. But devoted family men need mortgages. Just as another doughty and much admired old pro used to say – and another on this most exclusive list of centurions that Amiss joins.

In those days, counties would pay 'talent' money for performances – and every time Phil Mead, imperturbable Hampshire leftie, would despatch the ball for another century (he ended up with 153), he would tug at the peak of his old blue cap in distracted acknowledgment of the applause, and before taking guard again would turn to his friend and foe, the wicket-keeper, and mutter, '*There you are then, boy, one more bag o'coal for the winter.*'

Gatting Gun

Up in the cheap seats at the Nursery End this week there will be one or two folk with a lump in their throats when Mike Gatting leads the England cricket team out through the wicket-gate, below the hallowed Establishment preserve of the Lord's pavilion. A Field Marshal has come through the ranks. It was only sixty years ago that Lord Hawke prayed God no professional would ever captain England. Now the pupil from John Kelly Boys' School – just a bus-ride north of Shoot-Up Hill to Cricklewood – represents a triumphant breakthrough for that unsung band of devoted workers who sweat and scrimp without subsidies to keep cricket alive among the urban working-class. Mind you, as breakthroughs go, this could well be a one-off.

With a dramatic recent decline in state schools' cricket – let alone egg-and-spoon races – the once 'national' game at grassroots is in a bad way and reliant in most areas on organization by a bunch of volunteer enthusiasts attached to local clubs. Ironically, in Gatting's county of Middlesex, things look particularly dire. In the week last month that the engaging young tub was named as England's new captain, the chairman of the county's Colts' Cricket Association, David Green, wrote to *The Times* pointing out that only eight secondary schools in the whole of Middlesex were now playing regular cricket, and just two primary schools had entered this summer's inter-borough competition. He said volunteer organizers were struggling to cope with the number of boys wishing to play. Soon, only boys at private schools would know of cricket: 'The decline in state school cricket has several causes – cricket requires expensive equipment and expertly maintained facilities at a time of financial stringency; fewer and fewer schools have the staff able to devote the time to run matches and recent industrial action has resulted in schoolmasters and their pupils finding other ways of spending their free time; and political pressure against sports that are competitive and are elitist is forcing headmasters and PE staff to abandon inter-school cricket.'

The following week, *The Guardian* revealed that only one school in the huge borough of Hackney was still playing any sort of cricket – and that in neighbouring Islington, there was none at all. It quoted the president of Brondesbury CC, Ted Jackson: 'The other day I tried to organize games for youngsters in Islington. The borough officials were unspeakable. There were two pitches, we understood. I was told simply that one was no longer available – and the other had been ploughed up.

Ted Jackson's Brondesbury is where Gatting comes in. First, the young man was lucky at Wykeham Primary for his teacher, Mrs Collister, liked the game, and then at John Kelly where Mr Macmillan, the art master, and Mr Phillips, PT, encouraged cricket whenever possible. (The Kelly playground remains a cricket-mad oasis.) In 1968, when Mike was 11, he answered an advert in the local rag inviting boys to make up a colts' team at Brondesbury CC. It had been inserted by Ted Jackson. From that moment, Gatting went batting. And his father, Bill, who had been made redundant as a fitter at the aircraft factory at Hendon, became steward in the Brondesbury CC bar.

From Brondesbury, it is no more than a 20-minute stroll through Kilburn and Maida Vale to Lord's. When the baby-faced podge, in his early teens, turned up with his bat for a coaching course sponsored by Wrigley's chewing-gum, Middlesex at once fancied they had a winner.

He was capped for England too early. A few months after his 20th birthday, he went on the Brearley-Boycott tour to Pakistan and New Zealand. He made 11 in two innings in his Pakistan Test and a duck against New Zealand. For the next few years the selectors were to consider him extremely dispensible. Time after time, bad luck, the rub of the green-top, over-anxiety, and padding up to straight balls when he'd first come in, made the solemn administrators determined to consign him back to the egg-and-chips motorway circuit of the county grind for the rest of his career. Time after time, Mike would force himself back into international reckoning with batting of uninhibited, even intimidating, gusto and verve.

Gatting is the granest example you could come across of the man who understands perfectly that cricket is a fully integrated *team* game, which just happens to allow individuals to flourish in context, as opposed to those – and there are many – who consider it an *individual's* game played only loosely inside a team framework. Gatt will unquestionably tuck with more vim and relish into his (always immensely hearty) supper if the team has won, in spite of his duck, than if the team has lost, in spite of his century. It's a rare quality in a Test cricketer.

Not that such an inborn and chivalrous philosophy denies him a real competitive edge. On the last-but-one traumatic trek to the West Indies by England in 1981, I had supper with Mike and his Middlesex buddy, John Emburey, in Barbados after the first day's play of the third Test. Dilley, Jackman, Botham and Emburey himself had bowled snortingly well (Richards a duck) to have the hitherto happily haymaking homesters standing at an embarrassing 237 for eight wickets. The wise old off-spinning realist, Emburey, raised a glass to toast the ambitious possibility (Lloyd was still in) that, 'if we can get the last three wickets tomorrow morning for 280 we are in with a real chance.' Gatt sipped not, but clonked the table in fury with his glass: 'We've got to get them out for 240!' he determined, fuming at his friend's sober logic.

He will be an up-and-at-'em captain. 'Okay fellows, let's bubble!' He is busy, bustling, energetic and noisy. If a dressing-room is too quiet and contemplative, he'll pick up a ball and obsessively knock in his bat for hours. Or round up a four for cards – he plays anything, from bridge to brag, with the same decisive bidding that he brings to his work at the crease. In the England party, he is second only to Gower as a crossword-puzzle demon. He doesn't suffer fools, but will always give a sucker an even break. He is a devoted family man. Team man, too – when he was freighted back from Jamaica, in the winter, for an operation on his gruesomely busted nose, the first thing he did when he left the London operating-table was turn up to a Middlesex committee meeting.

He is hooked on upmarket science fiction novels. On that 1981 tour of the West Indies, I remember him meeting at a party in the Trinidad Hilton the BBC Radio drama producer, Jane Morgan, who is a cricket buff and was having a holiday after directing her epic series of Tolkien's *Lord of the Rings*. Mike hadn't heard the series by then, of course, but his cross-examination of Jane mesmerized us all: 'How did you get across the moment when Gandalf falls into the Mines of Moravia?' 'Who plays the Ent? How can radio get across the idea of such tallness?' 'How did you possibly cast the Spider Lady, because she never talks – just breathes?' 'What, you totally cut out Tom Bombadil! Oh, Jane, how could you?' and on and on into the night. When she returned home, Jane sent him the tapes of the whole series. He was enchanted and overworked his Walkman for the rest of the tour.

He was lucky, of course, to have served his apprenticeship in captaincy under Mike Brearley, both for Middlesex and England. Brearley encouraged any team's most junior members to contribute ideas. Indeed, at the end of the classic Headingley Test of 1981, when Australia were still possible winners with only 21 runs needed and Lillee batting truculently, Gatting ran up to Brearley from mid-on: 'Just tell Bob (Willis) to try a *straight* ball at Dennis. It doesn't matter what length, as long as it's straight, I promise you.' The message was passed on – and no sooner said than done, Lillee shovelled the ball straight to the diving Gatting at mid-on!

Through Brearley's celebrated stewardship at Middlesex, as a matter of policy, a number of men were made vice-captain to see who might take over the reins – Smith, Radley, Edmonds, Emburey and Gatting. In the end, the shrewd and cricket-canny Emburey might well have got the job had he not embarked on his venture to South Africa. Gatting grabbed the chance with relish.

Pre-Brearley, Middlesex had two decades and more of itsy-bitsy leadership, often handed on from one old sweat to the other and sometimes the obviously unworkable joint-captaincy of the Comptons and Edriches, the Parfitts, Murrays and Tittlemice. Even before the war, they went in for joint command – for instance, Peebles and Robins (the latter a truly dynamic and eccentric general) one year, and Haig and Enthoven for another. Enthoven must have been quite a card. In the current issue of *The Cricketer*, Alan Gibson tells how, one spring, the Surrey captain, E.R.T. Holmes, began the season with three consecutive ducks – at which he received a telegram: *Best wishes for your thousand in May – Enthoven.*

On the field, Enthoven was popular but tactically vague and laid back. Once, for Gloucestershire at Lord's, Wally Hammond flogged the Middlesex bowlers all over St John's Wood. Glos had been batting for almost one-and-a-half days when Robins approached Enthoven to enquire: 'I suppose you're saving the new ball till after tea?'

'Oh, damn and blast it, Walter,' he sighed, 'I'd forgotten all about it!'

That will not be Gatting's style. I fancy it is going to be a rewarding pleasure as we watch the young man leading from the front. Come to think of it, Cricklewood school and all, I daresay even Lord Hawke would have mightily approved of Gatting.

Any More Fairs?

The covers will soon be wheeled on by those little men in mackintoshes for the last time in this most squelchingest of summers. Though they now have raucous Cup finals to ring down, officially, the curtain on the season, in truth English county cricket still just fades sadly away in mid-month, hardly noticed, as guy ropes are slackened and nets dismantled – and all rolled up with the marquees, and stored with the mowers till springtime.

It is fervently to be wished that the North Sea winds will relent this first week in September, for nowhere should the bunting be more cheerfully twittering nor the flower-baskets more colourfully plump than at county cricket's most celebrated farewell rendezvous. Scarborough is celebrating its Centenary Festival. It began in 1876, missed five years for each World War, and still likes to call itself Cricket's Carnival. For carnival it remains. Onlie begetter was an Etonian hitter called C.I. 'Buns' Thornson. Other patrons and organizers down the century have been Lord Londesborough, 'Shrimp' Leveson-Gower and T.N. Pearce. This year, the one-and-only D.B. Close again brings his side to take on the New Zealand tourists; then the Asda Stores company play host to a series between Essex, Hampshire, Lancashire and Yorkshire; and finally the home county round off their summer with a three-day match against Northamptonshire.

I must have been just about 11-plus when I first made my way up over the cliff walk and down to the green, green, seagull-squawking field, lined on one whole side by that forbidding five-storey mountainous Victorian terrace. It seemed quakingly awesome to me that, up to then, two men had actually cleared these chimneypots with a hit from the middle. Thornton himself did it exactly a hundred years ago this week, clean over the slate roof-tops and into distant Trafalgar Square. The bowler was one of the 'inventors' of overarm spin, A.G. Steel, and the astonishing Thornton (one of the few first-class cricketers, incidentally, to be born in Herefordshire) can only have used a whippy, cane-handled, lightweight bat, a good pound-and-a-half lighter than the cudgels used by Botham and Richards today.

Cecil Pepper, the Australian serviceman, also popped one into Trafalgar Square, off Eric Hollies, as if to announce the resumption of the Carnival in 1945. Pepper later became a first-class umpire – and, as A.A. Thompson said, 'looking, in his short white coat, so like a distinguished dental consultant in Wimpole Street thay you could not possibly have suspected him of such violence to a cricket ball.'

See, I'd read all the history. Some said Maurice Leyland, dear and deadpan Yorkshire leftie, had also cleared those maid's-room sky-lights and landed in the Square, but with typical modesty and disregard for fuss, he always poo-poohed the idea: 'Nay, lad, it just hit top roof-ridge and trickled o'er.' In 1953, Richie Benaud peppered the walls and windows with a fusillade of 11 sixes, off Tattersall and Wardle, but never quite made Trafalgar Square.

Festive batting apart, the Scarborough pitch also gave generous help to bowlers looking to readjust and polish their final summer averages and analyses – and this week, soggy summer or not, that bracing morning nip off North Marine Drive will assist, a keen breeziness that was always lovely for outswing if you were on at the Trafalgar end. Ask Fred Trueman, who used to be in his element at his beloved Scarborough.

Mind you, Fred didn't always go with the wind. One time, when the bluff Godfrey Evans was captaining the Players against the Gents in the mid-Fifties, he suggested that Fred might open up from the Pavilion end because that spring-heeled tyro tornado, Frank Tyson, was the other opening bowler in the side. The wind was particularly zappy that morning, recalled John Arlott in his classic memoir of Fred. The old war-horse turned on the wicket-keeper.

'If you think I'm going to bowl into a wind like this bugger this morning, and after all the season's work I've done, then you can bloody think again, because I shan't.'

'But c'mon, Freddie, I think Frank should bowl with the wind because he's faster . . .'

'He's only bloody faster than me if he's bowling with this

73

sodding gale . . .'

Osbert Sitwell's grandad sponsored Thornton to found the festival for the high old town. But Sitwell himself hated the game and it was purgatory for him to be dragged along as a boy. Once, when Thornton himself was batting, the budding aesthete even fell asleep midst his deckchaired family: 'I hurtled off the chair with a crash like a falling meteor. I shall never forget the sense of shame when I woke up bruised and on the ground and realized by the wooden repartee of bat and ball, and by the expressions of shock and displeasure on the face of my elder relatives, and attendants, the execrable taste of the manner in which I failed them.'

The cricketers themselves wouldn't have cared. Most of them would have been blearily hungover. Scarborough has always been the place for end-of-term revelry. And not only among the boys of languid summers long ago. Just before he died this last spring, that delightful, dancing, revel-rousing old cove, Bill Edrich, confirmed to me, one Scarborough after a particularly hooray-hooley in the Grand Hotel, that he woke up, still in his dinner-jacket, at dawn, curled up at the end of the bed of his one-time captain of England. Could it have been Mrs Norman Yardley who thought Bill was their dog who often slept with them? Bill wouldn't say, but his chortle told you 'aye'. Bill, by the way, went batting next morning – and tonked up a cheerful 78.

The bonhomie (and the booze) was always in excess at Scarborough. In 1888, at his ninth festival, Thornton bagged a brace in the same day on a sticky against the Australians. The batsman's dreared 'pair'. In the evening, as usual, the teams repaired to His Lordship's Londesborough Lodge to dine and wine. The full works for the amateurs and, on the bottom table, flagons of ale for the pros. Thornton wrote in his diary: 'A big parcel was brought for me. I at once smelt a rat, particularly as I saw old W.G.'s eagle eye fixed on me. However, I didn't want to spoil the fun and I opened it. The parcel contained the biggest pair of specs you ever saw, about a yard wide. I was to have three more by post next day. Well, this wasn't all. We went to the circus after dinner, where Lord Londesborough used to take seats for all the pros and their families, as well as for us. When the clown appeared ("Whimsical Walker" by name) he was dressed up in my own Eton blue cap, no pads or gloves like me, and when he began fumbling around in his pocket the Ringmaster said, "What are you looking for Walker?" "Oh," he said, "I got a brace of duck's eggs on the ground today, and I can't get them out!" '

Great mirth. Then back to the Lodge where the cards and the whiskies were set out. Here Thornton took his revenge, getting the butler to deliver a message to the Doctor, purporting to come from Mr Farrands, the umpire who had given W.G. out, leg before, that afternoon. It said he declined to stand as umpire next day unless W.G. apologized for what he had said about his umpiring. Grace was mortified for a while and called for even more whisky. As Thornton wrote, 'The Old Man took it all in to such extent that we had to let him know the truth during the course of the evening.' *Evening*? By then it was probably dawn.

Was it at Scarborough a couple of decades ago, that Essex went to the Music Hall prior to another good night at the Grand, and the crooner sang *I May Never Walk This Way Again*, and T.N. Pearce stood up in the stalls and shouted back, 'Can we have that in writing?' Or was that at the Leeds Palace of Varieties, and was it 'Tonker' Taylor? Certainly it was at Scarborough that F.S. Jackson, England's triumphant captain, won the toss against Darling's Aussies for the sixth consecutive time. The rotten luck and the heavy night had Darling refusing to accept the turn of the coin and, having completely stripped down to the buff there and then, demanded that Jacko wrestle him for choice of innings. Jackson imperiously intimated that if fighting it was to be, then the English champion would have to be the burly George Hirst. Darling would not take him on, fielded, and after a glass of champagne to exude and settle the marvellous cocktail of spirits the night before, Jackson strolled in to clock up a splendid 123.

Raymond Robertson-Glasgow, as you could imagine, loved being selected for Scarborough. He enjoyed those wind-assisted swingers and the green-topped nip. Once, he reckoned he was diddled out of a wicket when a clean-bowled bat argued successfully that he wasn't ready – he'd been discussing the problem of sea-mists with the square-leg umpire. And, another time – those who saw it swear so – that friendly gale whisked off a grand old lady's hat, hatpin *and wig*, and frisbeed the three of them to the feet of the deepish third-man. At the end of the over, from the marquee emerged a butler with a silver tray on which, with solemn care, he received and carried away three enjoining pieces of head-dress.

In the circumstances, the fieldsman, a pro, had acted with a deadpan decorum and at close-of-play the *grande dame* summoned him to be graciously thanked. 'Ah, Mr Fielder,' she said when he was brought to her, 'I think we have met before?', to which came the answer, 'Well, madam, *some* of us have.'

Kiwi Polish

If whingeing ol' Fred Trueman would start paying attention and stop wondering what's going on down there – 'Ah really am non-plussed, Brian, ah really am; why, my sheep-dog William can bowl better than you fellows out there this afternoon' – he would have been aware that the last decade or so has been blessed like no other with superduper Test match bowlers. Fred's successors in stamina, seam and swing have more often than not been growlingly chastised by the old cove for lack of length, line, guile or gumption. Fact is, the likes of Lillee, Botham and Willis were actually down there taking far more Test wickets than Yorkshire's pipe-puffing maestro himself had managed. Trueman took 307 – to Lillee's 355, one more so far than Botham (who also hit 13 Test centuries to Fred's none). Willis jingle-jangled in for 325.

Any month now Richard John Hadlee, 35-years-old, from Christchurch, New Zealand, could have beaten the lot of them. A sort of athletic Arthur English with his pencil-thin moustache and skinny frame that tapers from knobbly-square shoulders, Hadlee is a schemer with a frowning, foxy face who doesn't seem to be over-enjoying his job. But, oh by golly, he revels in it – and his appearance at The Oval this week could well have him putting a very shiny tin lid on one of the most sensational 12-month bowling bursts in Test match history.

When he returned home in the autumn of 1985 after his English summer with Nottinghamshire, Hadlee gave himself at most, a couple more Test match years. He accepted there was no remote chance of ever getting near Willis's wicket haul, let alone

Botham's. The England all-rounder, for one thing, was younger by more than five years. 'Ian will finish with over 400 Test wickets, for sure,' acknowledged Hadlee. 'I'll have done pretty good to pass the 300 mark before I pack in.' He had then taken 266 – nevertheless, astonishing for a Kiwi, whose previous best total in history was 116 by the popular, crabby-actioned, long-running Dick Collinge.

Last winter, New Zealand played a six match, home and away, series against the Austalians. Hadlee amazed even himself with 49 wickets, taking five wickets in an innings six times, and ten in the match twice – and a best performance of nine for 52, an analysis bettered only by Laker (twice) and George Lohmann, back in 1895. Suddenly, Hadlee had 315 Test wickets – and at Lord's last month, in the first of the current trio of Tests against England, he greeted the Bothamless England with a sometimes unplayable relish to collect another sackful – the day after which Mike Brearley wrote in his perceptive column in the *Sunday Times*: 'His meanness and aspiration never flag. His superbly fluid athleticism enables him to bowl with almost equal pace (of his youth), greater control, and more movement off a shorter run. He simply showed us the whole range of the fast bowler's art – outswing, inswing, change of pace, hostility, accuracy. As one England player put it, it was like batting against the World XI at one end, and Ilford 2nd XI at the other.'

Then more of the same at Nottingham. Now at The Oval this week, as Richard rangily moves in off that economical run, sweatbands just so, wrist cocked towards the gasometers and the Houses of Parliament, I'll reflect as always on life's relentless march. I feel my age when Hadlee bats or bowls – for his father, Walter, was captain in the first Test match I ever saw. New Zealand played England at Old Trafford in the middle of a heatwave in 1949. I was 11 and for two days we sat under the City end sightscreen. Two other men who were to become far more famous than me also turned up for their first Test that day – Brian Close, that debut day, was aged 18 years 149 days, still England's youngest; and John Reid, aged 20. The former grew up to be, well, just the one-and-only Closey, and the latter to be far and away the best ever New Zealand cricketer. Till Richard Hadlee, that is.

Following that match, Reid played a then world record 58 consecutive Tests, 34 as captain. And at one time he held records simultaneously for making most Test runs, taking most wickets, holding most catches, scoring most centuries – and doing the same in all Kiwi first-class cricket. Men like Sutcliffe and Donnelly, Dempster, Turner, Congdon and Co have all had their names writ large in the modest records of New Zealand cricket, but none bigger than that of Reid. Till Hadlee, that is. Since 1929, when they began official Test matches, New Zealand won only seven Tests in the 43 years till Richard Hadlee was first chosen. Since his first appearance against Pakistan a dozen years ago – two for 112 and a slog for 46 – they have won 17.

Walter *père*, I remember, wore spectacles, fielded at mid-on, batted in a swot-like fashion, smoked a pipe when he signed autographs, and looked more like our Maths master than a Test match captain. To us kids that day at Old Trafford, he had nothing like the appeal of his opposite number, England's Falstaffian yeoman with the purple cheeks and red-spotted neckerchief, Freddie Brown. Back home, Walter already had two sons, Barry and Dayle. Two years after that sun-baked English summer of 1949, Richard was born. Cricket was the passion in the family and, on retiring, Walter was to become, successively, local eminence, Island chairman, and then President of the country's governing body of the game. He became a much respected, shrewd and unstuffy figure at all the far-ranging meetings at Lord's.

Barry, a bat, and Dayle, new ball, were Walter's pride, and were both exuberant chips off the old conservative block. Thus, kid brother Richard had no pressure on him to be any good at the game – though in back-garden pick-ups, he was showing a carefree talent for it as he bowled for hours at Barry, ten years older, who was soon to play for Canterbury. In all, there were five brothers cricketing in that back garden. After Christchurch Boys' HS, the whole family, in turn, took over the batting, bowling, grass-rolling and tea-making for the HS Old Boys' teams. Not so the sprog. On leaving school, Richard joined the rival club side, Lancaster Park, because his elder brothers were opening the Old Boys' bowling! (A couple of years ago I went, in one of NZ's drenchingest, galoshingest winters, to cover a Lions' v All Blacks rugger match at Lancaster Park: any thoughts of cricket should have been a million miles away, yet all anyone could talk about was, not Laidlaw, Tremain, Meads, or Mourie,

78

but Richard Hadlee's latest performance for Nottinghamshire.)

By the early 1970s, Richard and Dayle were opening the bowling for Canterbury. Then for New Zealand on a few occasions, though at first the elder brother, more regularly than not, kept the nipper out of the national side. In 1975, uniquely, the three Hadlee brothers came to England in the Kiwi squad for the first World Cup competition. Thereafter, the younger brother eased himself into overdrive – and as his bowling became sharper and more controlled so, at batting, he was developing from a cheery slogger into a genuinely dangerous hitter. (He hit his first Test match century – against the West Indies – in just 92 balls.) He says his batting improved after being commissioned to write a children's coaching-book: the knack was to forget the frenzy and the drama of it all, and merely follow every time the art's very simple basic principles. To us behind the ropes, it seems that the only difference has been him staying there longer: when his Bob Charles's golfer's straight drives are not scorching the grass around long-on, they are peppering neighbouring rooftops and chimneys.

The unending daily disciplines of an English county season have obviously allowed him to shape and polish the natural gifts to such an extent that, this last 12 months, he has emerged as probably the finest and most lethel bowler of his type to play the game. Not without cost personally: like many perfectionists, he is also a bit of a worrypot. Behind that furrowed frown lies a furrowed frown. A couple of years ago, after a clamorous 'double' season at Trent Bridge, he admitted in a revealing interview on Tony Lewis's *Sport on Four* radio programme, how he thought he was near to a nervous breakdown: 'My mother told me to take a break from cricket, ''Mother Nature is telling you to slow down; if you don't you may not be with us for much longer.'' '

Even a holiday didn't stop the headaches, blurred vision and dizzy spells. He took a course to refresh his motivation: 'I learned there are other things in life besides cricket. When my career is over I'll be greatly relieved in some ways. I won't have to train. I won't have to pitch up at the ground. I won't have to tour. I want to go camping and shooting and fishing, lying in on a Saturday morning and coming home to a log fire in an open fireplace. I haven't had a winter at home for seven or eight years and it's something I miss. I want to become normal again. Being a professional cricketer isn't a normal way of life.'

As old Uncle Fred says, we don't know the 'alf of it, what's goin' on down there. Except that this week, under the gasometers, we will be applauding one of all time's superduperstars.

Silly Bid On

MCC are kicking off their 200th birthday summer by selling off a bit of the family silver. *Psst*, wanna ball that took all ten for the Gents in 1849? Or Gubby Allen's England cap? Or Plum Warner's tennis shorts; or Rhodes's sweater, or Ranji's blazer? Nearly a thousand lots go under Christie's hammer at Lord's on 13 April. But be warned, boxroom cricket is now booming big biz. Cricket junk is joyous jewellery to some.

I wonder how much the Gunn & Moore bat signed by W.G. Grace in 1900 will fetch? My first ever bat was a G & M (signed by me), given me by my Dad when I was about nine. Where is it now? And how much might it be worth? It remains succulent in the memory as the very best bat I ever had, long handle whippy as the headmaster's cane, and the thin-grained blade possessed of the richest red meat you could imagine. On 22 May 1949, it made me 75 not out in a house match at St Ethelbert's, Belmont, after which my career was never the same. I have the dog-eared scorebook in front of me, inscribed in childish, faint, un-Frindally pencil. Eleven of the last 13 scoring strokes were boundaries. Come to think of it, what price for that scorebook at Christie's? I'm not selling, pal; no way.

Around twenty years ago I answered a small ad in *The Cricketer* and took a deep breath, ready to withdraw £15, on the chance of buying an original Spy cartoon from Sir Leslie Ward's series of 'Men of the Moment' in *Vanity Fair*. I had heard that the estate of the celebrated *Manchester Guardian* cartoonist, David Low, might have been putting up for sale the drawing of Gloucester's whirring 'croucher', Gilbert Laird Jessop – which, apparently, he had bought for just £1 at Puttick & Simpson's sale-rooms in Leicester Square. No such luck, it went for three times my limit, but nobody laughed at my postal bid.

Just two decades later, in 1985, a Spy original of Jessop's level-eminence, F.R. Spofforth, the Australian 'demon', was hammered down by Phillips' gavel – at £2,300! Even Spy *prints*: I got mine of Sammy Woods for five shillings in 1967. I saw one on sale the other day – for £30. In the 1960s, too, I offered a fiver for T.W. Graveney's first England touring cap – and was beaten by just ten bob on the final bid. It would be worth tenfold today. Why, Peter May's *Surrey* cap fetched £105 last year, I'm told. Not to mention £750 for Sir Donald Bradman's 1936–37 blazer. Two years ago, Phillips valued a silk hankie, with which W.G. once allegedly blew his nose, at £30. It sold for £850. Lord's this week, I notice, have a few more hankerchiefs up for grabs. You can only presume that the good Doctor had a permanently streaming cold. One, a commemorative MCC-colours job, has a reserve on it of £5,000. Who could sniff at that?

There is among these latest Lord's lots, I notice, the almost statutory, faded old candy-striped I. Zingari blazer. No sale would be complete without one. There was, in fact, a real Mr I. Zingari – who was a daring Victorian boatman who promoted cricket on Goodwin Sands at low tide, but had no known connection with the club of that name which requires candidates for membership to stand in the nets without bat or pads and there to be bowled at by vice-presidents.

I crib that from J.L. Carr's classic *Dictionary of Extraordinary English Cricketers*, in which he also notes how Americans (as in other once amateur fields) were the first to this craze of cricketania big biz. For example, in 1911, the Chicago in-somniac, Karl Auty, had a joiner make him an under-bed shelf on runners, to accommodate his full set of *Wisdens*. Not to mention, in the 1850s, the New York millionaire, Hesketh K. Nayler, who derived sexual gratification by maintaining an establishment of ample women to play cricket before him with balloons and no clothes.

You can take it that a more narrow-eyed generation of Yanks will have their agents bidding at Lord's this week. They may not know about cricket, but they can bowl a nifty indipper when it comes to profit and loss, demand and investment. One of England's most appealing, genuine cricketing collectors is David Frith, the young editor of the splendidly devout and original *Wisden Cricket Monthly*. Against commerce's background of turbulent money markets and inflation, he reckons it is no surprise that hard-bitten businessmen with no instinctive interest in cricket should have invaded his province. I once observed the gleam of utter joy help moisten Frith's eye when D.K. Lillee took off his sweat-soaked, stinky old yellow headband and presented it to him. But suddenly, it's all changed, says Frith: 'Now items, which had changed hands for little or nothing, are passing under the auctioneer's hammer for what seem absurd sums. The sedate pastime of combing through the shelves in antiquarian bookshops became rather more futile as word spread, competition increased and dealers responded by marking up their prices. Vendors, too, placed much greater value on their offerings, pricing young beginners out of the market and causing established collectors, who had been used to buying at what they considered the right price, either to fight fresh battles with their consciences or to turn away.'

Sad – but in Frithie's case, you can't de-nut an obsessive, and he was most willing to admit last year in the sumptuous encyclopaedic *World of Cricket* that, midst all the commercial toing-and-froing, 'happy the youngster who, visiting Bert Oldfield's shop on yet another pilgrimage, was not only given, with all the warmth of a gentleman's heart, his 1930 Austalian tour blazer, but told he might as well have the New South Wales cap as well.'

Myself, I've never had much of this magpie instinct. I rather wish I had. In the West Indies in 1981, for a few weeks I carried round in a matchbox the grotty discarded bit of Elastoplast Geofrey Boycott had twined round his fingers under his batting gloves when he'd scored his Test century in Antigua. (A chambermaid threw it away in Jamaica.) I once thought of asking for a flake of hard skin from Jim Laker's spinning finger. And last August I did nick Phil Edmonds's *Financial Times* from the bench of the players' balcony at Lord's. I have kept a half-pint glass in which Arthur Milton once bought me a drink at a pub near Bristol Parkway Station, and some letters from Sir Neville Cardus – as well as one from the aforementioned Sir Geoffrey in which he signs himself, '*Your old Fruit 'n' Nut Case*'.

I wonder how much *that* would fetch at Lord's this fateful 13th? The nearest I've come to something that might have made me a bomb this week was the winter before last. One frost-hard morning I was strolling around Ian Botham's garden in North Yorks with the great man himself, when I half tripped on a bit of wood on the edge of the lawn. It turned out to be a now weather-ruined old cricket bat, forlorn and frostbitten with the rubber on its handle totally perished. 'Ruddy Liam!' says Ian, amiably cursing his son, 'the things he leaves out in the garden' – and he briefly examined the bat before leaning it on a fence, carelessly, and we went on our way. 'I got a hundred with that, last Test, Melbourne, Brearley's tour,' muttered Ian, matter-of-fact. I was, momentarily, stricken with desperation to ask him if I could have it. But didn't dare. I bet it's still leaning on that fence. Might have made my fortune this week. Surely the real thing would have made more than old wimpish Warner's tennis togs?

I haven't seen the catalogue yet but, sometime, the ball with which Fred Trueman took his world-record 300th wicket will surely come under the hammer and the Yankee dealers will begin the bids in telephone numbers. Now here's a true story . . .

Just before Jack Crapp died half a dozen years ago, I spent a soft and gently rewarding day with the old Gloucester and England hero. Jack had been the Test umpire at the bowler's end the very ball Fred had bagged his famous 300th. Jack's own philosophies had never gone overboard about FST's 'bullying' bouncers at young batsmen during his own playing career – and now, suddenly, here was a chance to get his own back. As they were coming back to the pavilion when the innings closed, Fred had, said Jack, asked for the ball so that he could get it inscribed. For once officious, Jack told Fred that he first had to ask the Oval secretary, Arthur McIntyre, for permission to hand it over and, if such was granted, the bowler could collect it from the umpires' room in ten minutes. Was old Jack, bless him, intent on taking a last twinkling bit of mischief with him to the grave – or was he getting off his chest the awful confession of his revenge on the great Yorkie fast bowler? We will never know, but he recalled of that day: 'When I got to the Umpires' Room. I just tossed the ball into a large box in which there were a dozen or so more balls, all worn about the same. Ten minutes later, Trueman has got his permission to have his souvenir and comes up to demand I give it him. I just go to the box, dip in and throw him the first one that comes to hand, don't I.'

So Jack, you old rotter, one of the most famous balls in all cricket history – worth a million at auction this week, at current Wall Street prices – may not be all that it seems?

'*It may be,*' said Jack, a serene smile just twitching the corner of his mouth, '*and then again, it mayn't.*'

Oval-Team Time

Hooray for The Oval Test. I'm much more a Kennington man. Agreed, there's *something* about Lord's – cathedral awe, hush in the close, best bib, best behaviour, decent tuck and all that: as well as ferocious, little grey gatemen in shabby, long grey macs, and haughty members looking down at you like something the cat brought in. At Lord's, for all the joy the old place has sponsored and witnessed, any touch of rumbustious human spirit has to be prised from the members. At the pavilion end anyway, you feel you're back at junior school again.

The Oval offers a welcoming, warm jingle-jangle. It is more of the people and for the people. Dickens went there, and Arnold Bennett, and so did Priestley when Yorkshire came down. The first Test that Wodehouse saw was Jessop's Match in 1902, when every clerk, boss and errand-boy evacuated the City and hared across the river to see the Croucher's fun. All of 101 years ago this summer, the Rev James Pycroft noted: 'At The Oval men seem to have rushed away with some zest from their City offices. At Lord's there is a dilettante look as if men whose work, if any, is still to come.'

You always seem to emerge from the grimy Northern Line escalator chute at The Oval Tube with a more carefree skip in you tread. The ineffable Cardus inspired, as usual, the modern thought: 'The proper way to go to The Oval is by bus; it is the democratic way. It is, unfortunately, no longer possible to go to Lord's in the proper way – for the Hansom Cab has become scarce in the land.' From the *Manchester Guardian* fifty-nine Augusts ago, and still holds good.

Present sadness at The Oval is that they've moved the Press-box down to the Prefab . . . er, Vauxhall end. Perched on the scaffolding in boxes we are, right next to the belching business-men in their corporate lunch huts. (At Lord's, they still call it 'luncheon'.) I miss the old Press-room in the pavilion, a raked, wide huddle of four ascending desk-strips, at which fusty, long-established, deadly enemies from rival papers worked and seethed, elbow to elbow, for whole careers.

But there is still no swank in the pav, nor outside round the great, sooty, shallow-banked perimeter of the vast old paddock, and there's no tut-tutting like at Lord's when you four-knot a handkerchief for your heat-waved head, or barrack the flannelled fools raucously – *C'mon Lockie, lad, stop throwing willya, and give it some air!* The character is not partially but wholly democratic and homespun. Sir Neville again: 'At The Oval, the atmosphere, the environment, is concentrated and characteristic. Bobby Abel batted with a Cockney accent; Sandham and Peach, too, belong unmistakably to Kennington. And even as the pavilion at Lord's is the embodiment of high-minded, select, and ancient authority, so is the gasometer at The Oval the very image of London's homely friendliness, its plain, tangible humours.'

The Oval has also, to my mind, the far better bookshop – and not only because, this 200th anniversary year, Lord's are shamelessly flogging every catchpenny knick-knack and tea-towel they can print with their logo. But you'd better be prepared to queue at The Oval Test this week – not so much for the cricket, but for one of the bargains of the bookshop year. The quirky questings of the Kennington Kid, the perspicacious memoirs of a cricketing man, namely *Percy* (Clifford Frost), is simply, a delight, with more smiles, insights, and honest-to-goodness revelations than we have presumed to expect from twenty such 'I tell all' sporting autobiographies. Pat Pocock's collaborator was the journalist Patrick Collins, but you cannot remotely see the join and the partnership gells to even smoother effect than such legendary ones as Laker & Lock, Edmonds & Emburey, Bedi & Chandra, or, should one say?, Pocock & Inti.

Pocock, who tweaked for England on twenty-five occasions (67 wickets, mostly bought abroad), bridged a vast gap – 23 years with Surrey from the ancient, seemingly timeless, dyed-in-the-wool era of the early 1960s, to the present manic age of the silver-plated cup and dyed pyjamas. The book, charmingly produced, could readily have been twice its 168 pages. But time enough for the endearingly chipper, South London suburban Perce to grow into the Test team's elder statesman and England's 'offie' eminence (he played Tests with both Colin Cowdrey and his son, Chris). Here are first-hand, first-rate, newly-minted cameos on the likes of Graveney, Sobers, Barrington, Stewart, Lock, Knott, Greig, Boycott, Jackman, Botham and Fowler, that anthologists will be feeding off ravenously for years.

Most of all, the tangy whiff of The Oval, and particularly that singularly quaint, claustrophobic, clobber-full Home dressing-room. Pocock first arrived on the bus from Merton in the spring of 1963, just six months after Lord's had announced the end of the age-old distinction between Gents and Players. In the season of 1962, for instance, Surrey's amateurs would change in an upstairs salon, away from the gnarled and horny-handed sons of toil. Or that was the general idea which had emanated from St John's Wood for generations.

Thus, it is exactly a quarter of a century ago this summer that the last Gents versus Players fixture was held. If you want another book to take on holiday as perfect companion volume to *Percy*, look no further than *Gentleman & Players* (Grafton), by Michael Marshall, Tory MP for both very safe and very 'cricketing' Arundel. Here is another little triumph, an indipper in the Imran class, and a certain, quality candidate for those *Books of Ye Year* paragraphs we drunken hacks are always asked for in December. This is one which I, for one, will actually have read.

Marshall has genuflected to cricket's classless anniversary of twenty-five years ago by the simple device of interviewing as many gnarled pros and nobby amateurs as he could lay his hands on. He has brought out the very best in them – and the very worst. The game in those days was peopled by a hell of a lot of goodies, as well as a fair number of prats. Far fewer twits now. There is a sting in most of Marshall's tales. They make for a real treat, and complement Percy's assortment perfectly.

Till Lord's (and, far more festively, Scarborough) hogged the fixture, The Oval played alternate host to the three-day, venomous Them & Us contest. I fancy Kennington always had a more decent, purpler-cheeked and well-rounded sort of amateur than prissy, pompadoured Lord's. The Thames is a meaningful divide here, and not many players (or gents) have transplanted. In recent times, the splendid John Emburey (a Peckham lad) left The Oval on the Northern Line 'up' platform, and another off-spinner, F.J. Titmus (sorry, Titmus F.J.) briefly came south from Lord's. In the 'Victorian Golden Age',

England had a mid-order bat, an Irish aristocrat moneybags called Sir Timothy O'Brien who moved from Surrey to Middlesex. His manner and manners in so doing upset the committee at The Oval and he was blackballed forthwith. A few years later, he was seen drinking in the pavilion at The Oval and the secretary was called to point out that he was no longer a member. 'Oh, that's all right,' Sir Timothy blithely replied, *'my man has signed me in.'*

Very Oval, that, and hooray for it! The clamour and the clutter. You can take your shirt off at The Oval and get down to real life – as we will see this week. At Lord's, you've only half loosened your tie and they call in the cops. Mark you, while the ghosts of good ol' O'Brien, and Fender, Hobbs and Peach, and Sandham and Surrridge, Loader, Lakerlock, Arnold, Jackman, Sandy Tait and Percy Pocock allied into one good fellowship under the (Cardus once more) 'companionable, comic, squat-shaped deity of the gasometer', we must not forget the Committee. Ah, the Committee. Do they ever change, anywhere?

I crib this from Jim Laker in *Gentlemen & Players*, though Marshall, for once weedily, hedges on the apocryphal. Stop me if you've heard it; but it's true: 'Immediately after the War, in the spring of 1946, Surrey were scratching around to find an amateur captain . . . and they had in mind one A.C.L. Bennett, who was a well-known club cricketer for the BBC and others. While they were debating the matter, news came through that Major Bennett was in the outside office enquiring about club membership. They invited him in and offered him the job on the spot. The only snag was that his name was *Nigel* Bennett, who had just left the Army with his gratuity and was wondering what he might do with it. His previous experience at cricket had mainly been with Wimbledon 2nd XI – but nevertheless he was delighted to accept the offer.'

Thus did Mayor Nigel Bennett lead out his Test stars on Day One in April 1946. He ruled with a rod of iron – and himself scored over 800 runs in his first season. It was his *only* season, mind you. Very democratic, very Oval.

Don't Rain on the Parade

Christmas Day, I agree, can tend to drag even round the homefire hearth. But not half as much as when tradition quaintly demands you put a match to brandied plum pudding when the temperature outside is 100° in the shade. I have nipped in and out of a few England cricket tours, but only twice been caught opening my cards on *the day* while sweltering around a hotel swimming-pool. Chlorine and Ambre Solaire does not, believe me, mix with scenes of snowdrifted stagecoaches, hollied robins, or Victorian crinolined crumpet ice-skating on ponds back in Blighty. Especially if you know you cannot get remotely near a place in the Test team any more. For 12th Men, festive mateyness on tour makes for even more melancholy.

Was it Mike Brearley who started the custom of appointing a 'revue committee' at the beginning of a tour, charged with writing and staging a concert for Christmas Day, preceded by a fancy-dress parade? On Tony Greig's ultimately triumphant tour to India in 1976 the team spent a miserable December 25 in the Grand Hotel, Calcutta. (Brearley was vice-captain.) They were between the first and second Tests. Christmas lunch consisted of cold, tinned, turkey mousse. A bottle of supermarket plonk cost £15. In the afternoon, Keith Fletcher came back from the doctor's to confirm he had chipped a bone in his ankle, so England's best unraveller of spin bowling was out for what could be a month. That was the last straw for the competitive Greig, and the drinks party that evening had scarcely started before the bellicose beanpole from Sussex by way of South Africa slung out the press to give his team (as one of them told me later) 'one of the fiercest rollickings since old Cratchit rebuked Tiny Tim'. It was the tour's turning point, and the series was won. Say what you like about Greig, he was a heck of a leader.

Half a dozen years later, we were in Delhi, this time with Fletcher himself as captain. The fancy-dress revue had by now become a tradition. The theme was 'heroes'. It was the rest day of the third Test, and the day before Geoffrey Boycott had overtaken Sir Garfield's all-time Test aggregate. Next morning, our Yorkie Prince of Plod took hours to dress up before emerging as a turbanned and bejewelled Prince Ranjitsinjhi. He took the prize, and his wonky grin was never wider. Botham's 'hero' that day, by the way, was 'Sir Geoffrey' himself – the great all-rounder turning up naked, except for a loincloth, peering little wire specs, and a tight, pink, rubber swimming hat, holed at random to allow a few sprigs of hair to poke out – a joke at the expense of Boycs's 'Elton John'. Across the huge chest, in lipstick, Botham had scrawled, MAHATMA BOYCOTT – 8,032, which had been Sir Gary's record of runs. It quite delighted Geoffrey. Botham got on with him far better than most.

Gatting's lot will have the fancy-dress party again this year. Whatever would W.G. have thought! At his Australian tour's Christmas break in 1873, he left Mrs Grace in Melbourne with friends – they had married only a fortnight before the team set off from Southampton on the P & O steamer, *Mirzapore*, in October – and went shooting near the North Cross Reef gold mine in the Victoria outback with his cousin, W.R. Gilbert: 'On the way in our hired buggy we came across an Irish settler, a wonderfully hospitable old man who, when we made ourselves known to him, could scarcely do enough for us. He showed us where to find the best sport, and then left us for a couple of hours, returning with a big basket of luscious peaches, which he had ridden over to a neighbouring squatter's to procure for us. Gilbert and I were in hopes of bagging a kangaroo, but no such luck came our way that day.'

On Boxing Day, Grace's XI played against 'the 22 of Stawell', lost by 10 wickets, and the Doctor's journal notes, by way of huffy excuse, that 'the ground was in deplorable condition, the greater part devoid of any herbage, so bringing all players, good and bad, down to one level. Our opponents were more accustomed to such wickets . . . (and) it is scarcely worth recording the progress of the play.' I've heard many excuses for a duck in my time, but W.G.'s always take the biscuit.

At least the great man kept a diary. Who does now? Except those with a publisher's advance and a tame ghostwriter in their baggage. Vic Marks, the Somerset all-rounder, published a cracking good, unghosted journal of a tour a few winters ago but, alas, in the end, his batting wasn't as good as his jotting. In the old days, they were all at it. After the victorious first Test at Sydney ended on December 17, 1897, Stoddart's team travelled by boat to Melbourne. The Middlesex bowler, J.T. Hearne, who had taken nine for 141 to wrap up the match after Ranji's 175 and MacLaren's 109, wrote little of cricket; his fascinating journal told of snakes, crocs, kangaroo hunts and plagues of flies, with far more relish each day than whether the pitches were taking spin. They had a sombre Christmas Day:

'*Saturday, December 25:* Spent travelling. Caterer aboard gave us real Christmas dinner and one might have fancied they were at home except for the beautiful green peas we had – not so at home. Joined train at Sale and left for Melbourne at 4 pm. Playing poker the whole journey and lost £2 5s 0d. Lost nearly all after dinner when I had an hour's run of most infernally bad luck. Arrived White Hart 11 pm.

'*Sunday, December 26:* Very, very hot day. Most indulged in extra turn in bed. Morning spent writing home. The chaps that have not been from home at Xmas before seem a bit down. Ted Wainwright especially. He remarked very feelingly at the breakfast table, "I wish I was in the little cottage turning the meat."'

They lost the next four Tests on the trot, though Hearne, by all accounts, continued to bowl decently. Wainwright's 49 in the fifth Test, helping to put on 111 with MacLaren for the first wicket, was the homesick fellow's best job.

Two hours later – the first to be chosen and sponsored by the MCC – Pelham Warner took as his reserve all-rounder (to Wilfred Rhodes), the then chirpy Sussex bits-and-bobs merchant, Albert Relf. Some year ago, the ever-splendid *Wisden Cricket Monthly* unearthed Relf's diary. Again, the side had travelled from Sydney to Melbourne for 'the festivities'. On Christmas Eve, Relf 'had a good bowl, got 4 wickets, they could not play well enough to touch me . . . Bowled very well, won match about 4 pm. Home to hotel and wrote letters and Xmas cards.' When would *they* arrive!

Later that evening, still full of the joys, Relf went to see *The Great Millionaire* at the theatre, but not before 'Mr Christie took us round the Chinese quarters in Little Bourke Street – interesting seeing the opium smoking and gambling dens – would not like to go again.' (Obviously no hordes of Fleet

Streeters were watching your every move in those days – else the *Mail on Sunday* would have beaten their shoddy 'Botham Scoop' by all of eighty years!) Relf's was a reasonable Christmas Day in 1903:

'*December 25:* Very hot. Busy packing, then did a stroll round just having a drink or two to old folks at home. Went to Menzies, the whole of our party sat down together and a happy and jolly party we were too. After dinner we all went to the drawing-room and had some singing and dancing. Left for Bendigo by the 4.50. Arnold, Lilley, Tyldesley and Bosanquet all resting . . .

'*December 26:* Very hot morning. Sat on balcony and watched people going off for picnics and drives. A fair crowd at the match. Fielder bowled well, made the ball bump at a good pace and I think frightened them out. Evening went to open air concert at the ground. Very good and a real crowd there. Got home and lounged about to get cool as the heat was frightful, the flies worse . . .'

Through his career, Relf's rival for England was not only Rhodes, but also S.F. Barnes. So he played only ten Tests, taking 25 wickets, 14 catches, and averaging 23 with the bat. He did the 'double' for Sussex eight times. He became coach at Wellington and committed suicide in the school pavilion on Good Friday, 1937.

Another diarist – and another self-confessed recluse: is it journal-writing or cricket that attracts depressives? – was the Cambridge blue and wicket-keeper batsman, Paul Gibb, who toured Australia with Wally Hammond's post-war MCC side some forty year ago. Gibb played in the first Test as No. 1, but was then replaced by the electrically-charged, raucous young Godfrey Evans. Thereafter, it seemed, the engaging worrypot, Gibb, did little more than play golf, write letters home, drink ice-cream sodas, and complain about the laundry. What a nice man he seemed, and, again, this crib (courtesy the editor-historian David Frith's researches for *Wisden*):

'*December 25, 1946, Sydney:* I had kept back letters from the family so I had a few to read when I awoke. It was good to think that the kids would be safely tucked up for the night, all ready to waken in the morning to perhaps the biggest thrill of their little lives . . . Cannot honestly be claimed that team Christmas dinner was a huge success. One or two of the boys managed to raise a gayish sparkle after they had swallowed several drinks but, for the most part, it was only too obvious they all wished they were at home. The skipper did his best to get plenty of liquor into me . . . I turned down all offers. Dick Pollard played a few songs on the piano before we all sat down to a quite nicely decorated table, put on paper caps, and ate our dinner.

'*December 26:* Laundry accumulating. Am in need of a seamstress to sew on buttons . . .

'*December 27:* Hutton and Washbrook scored centuries. At dinner last night Len had been wondering whether he might not catch a chill through sitting under a fan, but he did not appear to have suffered. Extraordinary how most of our professionals seem obsessed with the idea of catching chills. One might think there was danger in every little puff of wind. They seem dead scared, too, of eating an ice-cream or drinking a cold drink. After lunch at the ground I caught a bus back to the hotel and slipped out for a game of golf.'

That evening, the Duke of Gloucester, who was Australia's Governor-General, threw a party at Government House (the side had travelled up to Canberra by train: Hammond driving himself in a Jag). Gibb wrote that night that he had spent half-an-hour in conversation with the Duke, 'who had put one or two whisky-and-sodas away so was quite easy to get on with and frequently broke out into his somewhat high-pitched laugh, making the odd reference to Australian politicians, the discretion of which I could not help but wonder.'

On New Year's Eve, they were all back at Melbourne to begin the third Test. Just before the start (the batsman's match was to be drawn: centuries from McCool, Morris, Lindwall and Washbrook; Bradman only 79 and 49), the Duke visited the England dressing-room, shook hands with every player and asked *each* man, 'Have you won *your* toss?' The dear old regal eagle, badly briefed by his aide on the way, had misunderstood, thinking these cricketer chappies each tossed up to see where they were placed in the batting order.

Still, I dare say it momentarily livened up the England team's New Year. The real thing, too – and better than any fancy-dress charade.

Setting Sunny

In Bangalore in March 1987, the most prolific international batsman in cricket history waddled jauntily back to a Test match pavilion and took off his pads for the very last time. Sunil Gavaskar, of India and the universe, scored over 10,000 runs (2,000 more than anyone else) in 125 Tests, with more centuries (34 to the start of last week's farewell appearance) and half-centuries (44) than any other man. He stood less than 5ft 5ins in his little cotton socks.

Sir Donald Bradman scored a phenomenal 6,996 runs in only 52 Tests. That record was overtaken first by another genuine knight of the realm, Garfield Sobers, who reached 8,032 (in 93 Tests), a figure reached by 'Sir' Geoffrey Boycott only a fortnight before the last of his 108 Tests. In aggregate terms, India's diminutive demon has now left them far behind, and although there are many more Tests played these days, it is hard to see anyone overtaking 10,000. Martin Crowe of New Zealand, perhaps? He is only 25, and seems pretty greedy, but it will need a long, long slog.

You can appreciate the measure of Gavaskar's talent by looking at his record against the West Indies in his sixteen years at the crease. In that time, of course, the Caribbean has produced a successive string of lethal fast bowlers who have, not to put too fine a point on it, changed completely the leisurely grace and charms of Test cricket. In that time, against the West Indies, England's leading centurions have been Amiss, with four, and Greig, Gooch and Lamb with three apiece. Since he first took guard for India, in 1971, Gavaskar – an opening bat, don't forget – has hit this relentlessly venomous West Indian barrage for an astonishing 15 centuries, three of them double-100s. Since he saw off Wes Hall and Sobers, he has fed mightily off Boyce, Julien, Daniel, Clarke, Croft, Roberts, Holding, Garner and Marshall.

Yet the little fellow has never worn a helmet – only, sometimes, when the pitch might be none too good, a skinny, little plastic skullcap under his inevitable floppy, white sun-hat. If he is wearing it when he doffs the sun-hat to acknowledge another fifty, he looks like an apologetic, courteous and dapper mediaeval Pope. Of the countless whizzbangs that have whistled past his skull, only one has hit painfully – from Michael Holding at the Bourda in Georgetown in 1984: 'No, I didn't fall down; I might have looked groggy for a minute; it was a real blow; all the fielders rushed up, but all I could think of was, "Get away from me, you're stopping me going for a leg-bye," because the ball had ricocheted down from my temple to third-man. No, the blow did not throw me from my rhythm: I was about 38 or 39 then, and I went on to get 140-something not out.'

I was honoured to give Sunil a farewell supper in the summer of 1986 when he was making his final royal promenade through the English shires on the Indian tour. He agreed to come – only if I promised not to order him a curry. 'Everywhere I go in the world, my host offers me only curry,' he said, pained. 'It is the most bad in Australia where they even offer me an onion bhajee for breakfast.' In the event, he ordered roast lamb (well done), chocolate pudding, mineral water and one glass of sweet white wine. He wanted to be reasonably early to bed for he was batting first thing in the morning, and, on such occasions, he found a couple of hours watching late-night television from his bed made sleep more conducive – *Miami Vice* (pronounced *Wice*) was on that night. Then he might read a few pages of his massive Robert Ludlum novel before switching off the light and preparing himself for his innings in the morning.

Sunny by name, and sunny by nature. The first time I had cracked a popadum with Sunil was at Kanpur on the MCC's tour to India in 1981. It was a famous dinner for my all-time diary, for two other previous captains (and kings) of Indian cricket were also at the table: Sunil's brother-in-law and another marvellous midget bat, Gundappa Vishwanath; and the one-eyed wonder, Mansur Ali Khan, alias the Nawab of Pataudi, 'The Tiger', son of a Prince, and coached at Winchester by the great Frank Woolley himself.

I was mesmerized by the conversation, and seem to remember I dared to ask only two, pathetic, hack-like questions. Why, I asked Sunil, is it said that many of your mountain of runs have been scored because your Indian umpires are afraid to give you out? Sunil smiled with those bright brown eyes, and said nothing. I had looked it up, I said, and *Wisden* never lies, 'You have been given out lbw only four times in your (to date) 66 Test match innings in India, a remarkably low proportion.' Sunil smiled on, but his brother-in-law, Vishy, looked sad for the slur on his friend, grabbed a record book from the shelves and began to count. In 59 Test innings *abroad*, it transpired, foreign umpires had given Sunil out only five times.

Touché, with knobs on. 'I knew it would be very few times,' said Vishy, 'for you always have to realize how perfectly positioned are Sunil's feet – and hence his bat – whenever he plays a stroke. This is also why he never gets hit by bouncers – if your feet are in the correct position, then so is your head.'

The other question I ventured was to the 'Noob', who had lost an eye in a motor accident at 20, yet a year later was captaining India. He went on to score over 3,000 Test runs, including six hundreds and a double-century against England. Tell me, I asked, how long after your accident did you first realize you had a chance to be a Test match batsman? 'As soon,' said the Prince, 'as my good eye could focus on the state of the English bowling!'

Pataudi is ten years older than the two little masters. Sunil and Vishy were both born two years after Salman Rushdie's 1947 *Midnight's Children*, but both, like the Booker prize-winner, were brought up 'listening to Polly Umrigar scoring centuries on All-India Radio'. Umrigar was assailed by the likes of Trueman and Statham, and Pataudi by Hall and Griffith, but both retired before the pace of things to come, in the unrelenting, non-stop head-hunting shape of the West Indian battery (not to mention the extremely bitchy Ms Lilian Thomson) that Gavaskar has faced up to throughout his career. Say Sunil: 'It is the odd ball that takes you by surprise which is the danger. You must never jerk your head back without thinking.'

But you are 5ft 4½ins and this blur of a missile is coming from less than 20 yards at well over 100mph?

'Scared? You can't be scared. Thank God, I have never been frightened. I might go out there feeling worried – but only about my form, about my feet moving in the wrong way, about being certain to get behind the line of the ball. But scared? Of course not. Cricket is my love. It is my fun.

'In my time the most noticeable thing has been how the art of playing back has changed; not many batsmen these days go back and across, sideways-on, as the textbooks would have us do. And many pitches are not up to scratch. I was lucky; I learned on good wickets. Now people at the crease open up their guard – and suddenly these West Indian fellows are upon you and you are in big, big trouble.'

While I could name you at least eleven Englishmen who still have nightmares about batting in the West Indies, Sunil has found it, incredibly, most satisfactory. Well, 15 centuries and three double centuries!

'The Caribbean is a lovely place to play cricket for a batsman. I love the light there, and the sun on my back, and the crowds, ah yes, they are all so involved and passionate and understand fully the game. And all the West Indian players, too, they're all such very friendly chaps.'

Of all his legendary innings, history will probably log, indelibly, the greatest as being his 221 against England at The Oval, on the last day of the final Test in 1979. Brearley had set India 438 to win in 500 minutes. It would have been the highest winning score of all time by a side batting last. Gavaskar led them, with a rampant glory, to 429 for eight. Nobody who was there will forget it. Yet he himself can remember only one split second of the entire innings: 'The only thing that ever recurs when people mention that knock was just one delivery – from that good fellow, Botham. He comes charging up at me and bowls a slower one. His varieties are sometimes the very devil. What is coming next? But this one was the most miserable slower one that has ever come to me in all my life. I just whack it past point for four, and grin at the big man. It was so miserable a ball that I can never forget it. I dream about it still. But of anything else in that innings I have no memory whatsoever.'

Our memories, fortunately, are much sharper. Now, alas, they are all we have left. He will be much missed – for it is quite possible that we will not see his like again. Ever.

Action Replay

Mornin', Ma'am, Mornin', y' Highness

Ah, the season! In the corner of the room, and from the corner of your eye, you will by now only *sense* the gringoes and dagoes battering on at their World Cup soccer. By this stage, surely, the nation has turned the sound down on that relentless nasal snuffle, as it continues to label its unending list of ludicrous foreign names. Those of us who matter in midsummer England have other things in mind. Anyone for tennis: for Wimbers is on the way. Clink of croquet. And the pukka are into their chukkas. Villages are cricketing, genially; and there's still another Lord's Test to come. Which ribbon shall I bind round my boater at Henley this year? And they've unravelled the bunting at Cowes, where there's water, water, everywhere and an awful lot to drink.

Clement Freud is taking me to Ascot. Treatsville. What will he dream up to put in his wickerwork hamper? We're bound to have strawberries, and eye up the hats and the hoorays and horses, and wink at the twinky starlets, and doff our toppers when the Queen goes by. Last century, in the season, the whole *Punch* magazine office would have a day off for an outing to either Ascot or Epsom or Henley. The following week's account of the picnic would be titled 'Mr Jingle on the Jaunt'.

The smooth, unending flow of major sporting jaunts in England's high summer has been part of the ordered scheme of things since any man alive can remember. Dropped, haphazard, into the calendar, you can now tell the time and the date by them. Men in the outposts of a sweltering Empire would turn up the fan a notch or two, shout 'Boy, another whisky an' soda!' and crack their boots with a riding crop and think themselves accurs'd they were not there – for a million miles away, the Test match was starting at Lord's, or 'good ol' Teddie' was at Ascot, or the Eton v Harrow, or, dammit, at happy Henley, down by the breeze-blessed, blissful, dragonflied riverside.

More often than not, mind you, the Empire was left to run itself when England's summer season was in full swing. From India and the colonies the steamships would head for home, gunwale-packed with imperialists sniffing some sport as it should be staged – and if there was time, between the clatter of hooves and the bounce of balls, they would sort out their stocks and shares, be charming to Mama, toy with a tart or two, perhaps take a wife, get used to the sound of gunfire again on the August moors, before sailing from Tilbury in September to continue to garrison the world.

Freud's treat will be my first Moss Brossed Ascot. It will be different for sure to be on the side of the toffs in toppers. Paul Callan, one of Fleet Street's favourite gossips over the years, once warned his young-Trot readers in the old, much lamented pre-Maxwell *Mirror:* 'Do not bother with Ascot unless you remember to raise your topper to the Queen's racing representative, the Marquis of Abergavenny (and make sure you pronounce him *Abgenny*), and to remove your hat to below the shoulder if a member of the Royal Family happens to pass by. But don't cheer, please.'

Nor, I fancy, should you mutter a tip to Her Majesty. A minion will have placed her bets soon after the arrival of that morning's *Sporting Life.* Margot Asquith once got a winner for the aforesaid Teddie, Prince of Wales. It was the first time she had ever met him. In her 1920 *Autobiography* she recalled: 'He asked me if I would back my fancy for the Wokingham Stakes. We walked down to the rails and watched the horses gallop past. One of them went down in great form; I verified him by his colours and found he too was called Wokingham. I told the Prince that he was a sure winner; but out of so many entries no one was more surprised than I was when my horse came romping in. I was given a gold cigarette case and went home much pleased.'

I wonder what sort of hat Margot wore? At Ascot, the millinery is more important than the mounties in their silks. Apparently, one year in the paddock a starlet in head-to-toe scarlet, with a parasol to match, made one of the nags buck and rear as she made her spectacular entrance. 'It is perfectly *scandalous*,' she remarked to her agent, 'that they allow horses in here!'

The aim sometimes, it seems, is to get turned away from the Royal Enclosure for wearing what the old Duke of Norfolk used to refer to as 'inappropriate garments'. About ten years ago, an unknown American film actress, Linda Lovelace, sent round a press release that she would be going topless to Ascot next day. In the event, she chose a see-through blouse. As her entrance was barred at the gates of the regal sanctum, the beringed doyenne of Fleet Street, Miss Jean Rook, who had not read the handout, was among those keeping her out. 'Right, lass,' said the no-nonsense Yorkshirewoman, snapping open her notebook, 'name, age, and where d'you coom from?'

Next morning, the whole nation had heard of the porny film *Deep Throat.*

Nor have men escaped censure from the fashion rules at Ascot. Teddie set the tone, much to the displeasure of his mother. One year, the Prince came across Lord Harris, owner of the famous tweed-making firm, who had turned up to the races in a suit made from that cloth. 'Mornin', 'arris,' the future King greeted him loftily, 'goin' rattin'?'

England's high summer season was founded on the Prince of Wales's diary appointments. Before Victoria died, it was estimated that her eldest son worked on just 27 days in the year – and that includes calling such official functions as public dinners, 'work'. This left him 337 days per annum for 'play'. The retinue would spend the winter hunting and shooting. By May, he would be in his private quarters at Newmarket for the spring sales. After Ascot in June, Lord's for the Test match (there is the classic painting of him promenading the boundary rope under the present day Warner Stand, in conversation with his wife, but eyeing up Miss Lillie Langtry in the crowd). Nor would he ever miss the Eton v Harrow. He attended his first Henley in 1863. Early June, he moved to stay with the Duke of Richmond at Goodwood, for the races, and so be en route for Cowes to preside at the Regatta until the middle of August. Only then, England's season over, might he take in some Continental fillies and frolics.

Eton v Harrow was a right winking-neon asterisk of the summer's procession in those days. Indeed, the very first Wimbledon final was postponed for two days so the spectators would not miss the 1877 match at Lord's (the Hon Ivo Bligh was playing for Eton, and the match was drawn). Those early championships at Wimbledon sum up the point. For instance, the second man to win the title was Frank Hadow, a young pioneer of the Empire, back for the hols from his coffee-plantation in Ceylon. Jeremy Alexander has culled the files of *The Field*, the Englishman's most enduring sporting mag, to bring out the inspired, snippety little *Field Story of Wimbledon* (Associated Magazines). Of Hadow, he writes: 'Returning on leave, he found his sisters playing this new game, tried it himself and was persuaded to enter Wimbledon.'

In so doing, he not only won, but also invented the lob. Hadow said later: 'I was told the lob had not been introduced before; certainly I had never tried it. It was only natural, though, with a tall, long-legged and long-armed man (Mr Spencer Gore) sprawling over the net ready to reach over at the ball before it had even reached the net.'

At the end of 'the season', Hadow went back to Ceylon, and though he lived to 91, he never played the game again.

As well as his lob, Hadow had to have dress sense. It is, as we gather, the most necessary part of England's sporting season. Before the first Wimbledon final, the editor of *The Field*, James Walsh, had pinned a notice on the pavilion board that morning of July 9, 1877, starchily ordering: 'Gentlemen are requested not to play in shirtsleeves when ladies are present.'

Things have changed, I'm afraid, down in SW19. Only a few days ago, I met a marvellous old lady, Myrtle Maclagan, 75 and a former 'Queen Bee' in the WRAC, who also happens to be the first women ever to score a century in a Test match – for England – in Sydney, January 1935. She prefers tennis now – or rather watching at Wimbers, what. Standards are slipping, alas, says Myrtle: 'A chap last year, on a very hot day with very big crowds, tapped me on the shoulder and said, "Miss, would you please move your handbag, 'cos it's sticking in my chest." I turned round and looked at him. He didn't even have a shirt on! Ugh, just a big, bare, hairy chest. I didn't only move my handbag. I moved myself off as fast as I could. How ghastly! At Wimbledon, I ask you. It made me absolutely mad ... They put notices up about no litter as well as no shirt removing. Who bothers? There's just one answer – throw 'em out!'

At Cowes, they don't seem to mind what you wear. The few times I have been there for the week, it's seemed my gumboots are more filled with spirits than Solent. Yacht racing must be the only sport in which you can carry around your own cocktail cabinet. As well as, come to think of it, you own portable bunk. The women hangers-on seem to hate the sailing; but they love the bunk bit, I fancy. As that jolly sooper punster, Jilly Cooper, remarked after her first rough rendezvous at Ryde: 'I never liked sailing men. They yell blue murder at you all day, but then, when the boat is moored, the whisky comes out, Captain Bligh turns Casanova and is all ready to seek out your jolly erogenous zones and play deck coitus.'

For those exact reasons, I suspect, did the Prince of Wales revel in his patronage of the Royal Yacht Squadron's August shindig. Indeed, when his schooner *Hildegarde* won the Queen's Cup in 1876, Watson's contemporary report noted, 'So popular was the victory that even the cast-iron rules of the Squadron were relaxed to allow ladies to rush excitedly on the platform to witness the exciting finish.'

The bluff old fellow was also keen on croquet, doubtless, again, because the newish sport, with its appealing garden-party attitudes, positively encouraged participation by the fairer sex. Lt Col Prichard's classic history of the game says the future King was 'neither a good player nor, it was rumoured, a good loser'. But the click of the mallet and the scent of summertime grass was very much part of days off from the official season. The body at Wimbledon, of course, was officially called the All England Lawn Tennis and *Croquet* Club, and the championships for the latter were staged even before the first tennis event.

To be sure, the croquet-lawn had long been a, shall we say, fertile ground to forward any marriage plans. There was many an Empire loyalist who took a fancy to his mate at a game of croquet – and by October, she was packing for Africa or the Orient. Clunk-click went the mallet – and so did the strings of his heart. The sport represented a sort of crinolined dating-agency. Before the club moved to Wimbledon, it had enquired about the possibility of laying out lawns at, among other sites, Lady Holland's estate in Holland Park, Kensington, and in the grounds of the Royal Horticultural Gardens at Kew – but the latter committee snortingly rejected the idea with a letter saying, 'Our institution was established to promote horticulture, not husbandry.'

In my slight experience, a dashed good game of croquet can

still get the juices going: a sunny, drowsy, bee-buzzing day, some springy, nail-scissored grass, and a soft-chuckling, long-legged gel in a white summer frock . . . Clunk-click. The nicest players all seem to look like Princess Di, from a heat-hazed, Pimm's-induced distance anyway. It is good, too, to see the game establishing a revival of late. It's even been on ITV. It has fought back well since the Croquet Association some time ago wrote to *The Times* to state that 'as the sport needs a high degree of skill and intelligence it is not, therefore, going to attract the lower income groups.'

Lady Diana's husband has, I suppose, jacked up the interest in another of the summer season's passing fancies – polo. I saw him play once. He really gets stuck in. He seemed to be enjoying it so much that he even waved to us Press hacks in the brown ale tent at Cirencester. He dismounted and told us, breathless and exultant (him, very definitely not us), 'I can honestly say that there can be jolly few team games in existence to rival polo for sheer, jolly excitement, speed and fascination.' In the second half, he fell off – probably due to the laziness of one of us hiccup of boozy hacks, for, at half-time, we were among the hoi polloi riff-raff dragooned into treading-in the hoofmarks and divots on the field. Very feudal, polo. Anyway, one of us rabble spent the interval venomously using his heel as if he was preparing for an extra long place-kick at Twickenham.

Hey, but steady on, now I'm going to Ascot, I've got to change my tack. Toppered and tailed. *Mornin', Ma'am. Mornin' y'Highness.* As Mr Jingle on the Jaunt wrote a hundred years ago after a *Punch* outing in London's summer season: 'Henley hospitality proverbial – invitation to sixteen lunches – accept 'em all . . .'

My friend Mr Freud's *one* lunch at Ascot will do me. Treatsville! The Season Starts Here.

Down Under and Out

The world's one-uppers have been Down Under of late. *C'mon, Aussie! C'mon!* Yawn, yawn. The waters off Fremantle are boiling up as the purgatory-long America's Cup at last catches a glimpse of its finishing line. The Davis Cuppers of tennis have just left Melbourne, and this week Sydney stages the final Ashes cricket Test. Rugby Union's first World Cup is straining to take the stage. *C'mon, Aussie! C'mon!* – the boastful chorus has been a grating New York theme, enjoyable nevertheless when it dies drunkenly away in yet another defeat for the homesters. They really do fancy themselves, these days, do the Aussies – unless it's just their television commentators.

Their most singular, muscle-rippling threats, of course, are reserved for opponents from Britain, or more particularly, England. (In the case of the yachting semi-finals this week, the astonishing crew from New Zealand are being lumped in as English – that is, take your pick, pale-faced, upper-class cheats, twits and whingers.) John Snow, England's eloquent and hostile fast bowler who, with Geoff Boycott and Raymond Illingworth, was in the process of winning back the Ashes sixteen years ago, told me one of the most revealing tales of the Aussie approach to sport, from that tour's Melbourne Test. John had taken a hatful of wickets by way of peppering a few green-capped craniums, and then retired to the third-man boundary for a rest: 'I became annoyed when a ten-year-old boy kept calling out to me, "Snow, you bastard!" His father sat beside him apparently approving of such behaviour. Having taken a stomachful of this treble's voice chirping, my school teacher's instincts came out. I strode across to him and said, "You have far too much say for such a short bloke." Whereupon his father spoke up for the first time: "Give the kid yer autograph, yer mug!" he ordered, between large gulps from his can.'

Such an attitude is – according to one of Australia's best students of the native psyche, the writer Keith Dunstan – perfectly acceptable. It shows the kid's manly will-to-win

104

attitude, for sport is an Aussie's ultimate super-religion, the one thing every true Oz believes in with passionate fervour: 'Sport is wholesome. It can do no wrong. It builds stonger Australian men and women and, best of all, it spreads the fame of Australians overseas. It helps unify Australia as a nation. Not to be keen on sport is, therefore, unclean, unmanly, even homosexual, and definitely contrary to the ethics and super-religion of the nation.'

To be sure, a bit of me will miss being in such a social battleground when the alarm goes off on a cold and frosty pre-dawn, and I finger out a frozen mitt to tweak the bedside radio and hear the worst from Christopher 'It's a lovely day here: beautiful blue sunshine' Martin-Jenkins. I will think of my first trip to The Hill at Sydney, when I went to the Test match to watch one of Brearley's teams take them on in the late 1970s. I had heard so much about The Hill over the years of boyhood that my approach to the ground that first morning had something of the pilgrimage about it.

It is more of a hillock than a hill. It was a bit of a disappointment. The crowds in their denim shorts, predominantly teenage and student layabout, through the day became the more raucous in direct ratio to their drunkenness. There was not much of the legendary wit I'd heard about. ''Ey, Brearley, f'gawd's sakes, y'make Mike Denness look like Don Bradman!' or ''Ey, Willis! Call yourself fast? Y'Dad wanted a daughter and y'Ma wanted a son, so they're both happy, eh?'

In his beautiful essay, in Michael Meyer's original and undernoticed anthology *Summer Days* (Methuen) around that time, the Oz novelist, Thomas Keneally, wrote of the change his lifetime had seen in the Australian appreciation of their sporting culture: 'We may be a small and callow race but there is a divinity to our cricket . . . Cricket was possible! We knew why it was. We had more sunshine, we ate more protein, we washed more regularly than the Poms! In the manner in which soccer is the great way up for the children from the economic sumps of Brazil, so cricket was the great way out of Australian cultural ignominy. No Australian had written *Paradise Lost*, but Bradman had made a hundred before lunch at Lord's . . . Now all the urgency and all the ecstasy were gone. Even Kerry Packer, who avenged some forgotten school cricket team slight by buying the game for himself, must be aware of this. That despite the big money, cricket in Australia has become merely a game. And when that happens, we're in trouble.'

Keneally was observing the generation gap between Bradman and Border. I wonder if the yachtsmen's might have changed similarly – but in a mere four years since Alan Bond's outrageous and vibrantly cheeky victory in the America's Cup off Rhode Island, when his wing-keeled *Australia II* and jovially swaggering crew made surly fools of the New York Yacht Club diehards? What a win that was, even to a hitherto disinterested landlubber.

I was only in Cornwall the evening the news came through, in 1982, chatting up a blonde in that over-expensive riverside restaurant off the creek at Helford. Next to us in the pink-tableclothed, knife-clinking hush were two Aussie tourists. One of them got up to make a phone call. There was a whoop from the booth. He returned to order champagne. Australia had, he said, won the Cup. He was an Australian dentist visiting his great-grandfather's grave. Great-grandad would have been proud of him that night. And mine of me. We must have cleaned out the Helford cellars and, our women long gone (mine only to be seen again for one short, sharp, terminal discussion), we rolled up that winding hill above the river at dawn, ropey-legged and arm-in-arm like storm-caught matelots rehearsing the hornpipe. Then I collapsed in the first bus to Manaccan and never saw him again, either. But we had celebrated a famous victory.

Nothing like that spirit now, say friends who have dipped in and out of Fremantle these past interminable months. The 'sport' over there has been totally dominated by big bucks and narrow-eyed big business – and business is business. You can't buy a key-ring that isn't quadruple-priced for the Cup. When the racers aren't too butch, they're too bitch. When England's over-hyped but under-helped *White Crusader* was still at Earl's Court's Boat Show, surrounded by collecting-tins in the autumn, you knew its card had been marked and the lack of preparation would prove fatal for qualifying. And so it did. For the rest, only four years later, the world looks to another underdog, this time in the glass-plastic shape of *New Zealand* to make the bleating big-timers squirm.

I fancy defeat in the America's Cup will be an even bigger blow to the Aussies than loss of the Ashes (or the 'World Cup' pyjama one-dayers that follow it). But *C'mon, Aussie! C'mon!* – at least they've seen off the Brits on the water. Poms never did really twig sport, anyway.

One of Australia's legendary opening bats was Clem Hill. In his dotage, he enjoyed classical music. Not long before his death in 1945, the English conductor, Sir Malcolm Sargent, was doing a stint with the Melbourne Philharmonic. After a performance one night, the theatre manager asked Sir Malcolm if he would do them the honour of seeing Clem Hill in the morning.

'Love to,' replied our vigorously charming smartyboots. 'Tell me, how high is it?'

Gentleman and Players

Somewhere in Europe, 1940. Hotfoot from sugar-lumping Grimmett's field for Hammond at Old Trafford in *The Lady Vanishes* two years earlier, Basil Radford and Naunton Wayne are now aboard the *Night Train to Munich:*

Caldicott: That German officer looks a lot like old Dickie Randall. You remember, used to bowl slow leg-breaks. Played for the Gentlemen once – caught-and-bowled for a duck, as I recall.
Charters: You think he's a traitor then?
Caldicott: But he played for the Gentlemen!
Charters: Ah, yes, but only once.

They churned them out in those days, and no film was worth releasing unless it had a couple of slack-chinned, stiff-lipped Brits chuntering on about cricket. It was probably allowed because Hollywood at that time was still being enchanted by the likes of Sir C. Aubrey Smith (Sussex and England), Mr Boris Karloff (formerly W. H. Pratt, Esq, of the Uppingham XI and Surrey 2nds) and Charlie Chaplin (born under the gasometers at Kennington).

Sir Aubrey played frequently for the Gentlemen. He captained Sussex for a number of years, and, in 1888, took the first English XI to South Africa. He was an accomplished stage-actor – Shaw once said, 'No man on earth could play better the Duke' in *As You Like It* – before he fell for the blandishments, blossoms and booty of Hollywood in the 1920s, where he played the archetypal Anglo in over fifty films; every contract stipulated that he be allowed the month off when the Australians were playing the Test match at Lord's.

Another theatrical knight dear to Hollywood was earmarked by his father at birth as an undoubted No.4 for the Gentlemen. But Laurence Olivier had no talent with bat or ball. Oliver *père* had been a celebrated Oxford sport and played for Hampshire and MCC. Alas, little Larrykin's top score in life was two (bowled by his master, Douglas Bader). He was No. 11 in a school house match at St Edward's, Oxford, and only four had been needed to win. Oh, the shame of it! Many, many years later, Sir Laurence confided: 'I have often thought what a pity it is – how much better a life I would have had, what a better man I would have been, how much healthier an existence I would have led, if I had been a cricketer instead of an actor. But it was not to be. I don't know what it was – the finger of God had not touched me with a stump or something. It just wasn't there.'

One of the world's most famous cricket-nuts/actors was the great and good Trevor Howard. I once spent a marvellous day with Trevor talking about his cricket (best bowling six-for-two for MCC *before lunch*), and his driving offences (with cars, not bats). The first time he was nicked was the day England won the Ashes in 1953. His producer, Euan Lloyd, was called for the defence: 'Your Worship, Mr Howard and I were driving along Piccadilly with the car wireless on. It all depended on two final runs. When finally someone hit a four which won the game, Mr Howard jumped out of the car in front of Fortnum & Mason, danced on the pavement, let out a roar, then jumped on to the bonnet of the car, peered at me through the windscreen and yelled, "We've done it! We've done it!"'

Throughout his life, Trevor richly deserved honorary qualification for both the Gents *and* Players. So, perhaps, did Richard Burton. The Welshman was a nifty rugger player in his youth – indeed played his last game at 28 when he was playing Hamlet at the Vic. Such an opponent was, almost literally, meat and drink to the rugger buggers, as Burton would recall with that hilarious, but pained relish of his, savouring the flavours in every word if not the memory: 'I was elbowed, gouged, dug, planted,

108

raked, hoed, kicked a great deal, sandwiched, and once humiliatingly taken from behind . . . I was gardened, mowed and rolled. Their prop with whom I shared cheek and jowl for the eternity didn't believe in razor-blades since he grew them on his chin and shaved me thoroughly. By the end of the game my face was as red as the setting sun and the same shape. I stuck it out because there was nothing else to do, which is why on Monday night in the Waterloo Road I played the Dane looking like a Swede with my head permanently on one side and my right arm in an imaginary sling.

'I was intermittently crooked and cramped with severe shakes and involuntary shivers as of one with palsy. I suppose to the connoisseurs of Hamlets it was a departure from your traditional Prince but it wasn't strictly what the actor playing the part had in mind. A melancholy Dane he was though. Melancholy he most certainly was.'

Richard continued to enjoy the game, at a distance. To his death, he would have videos of the Welsh international matches flown out to him – as does his Celtic co-star, Richard Harris, still, when the greens have put up a dandy performance. Burton also enjoyed boxing, and would often be seen at the ringside for a really Big One. The fight game threw up the same sort of gruesome glitter as Hollywood. Of all the boxers who got up from the floor and into the celluloid, I suppose Max Baer, one-time heavyweight champ of the world, transposed best. (Like when Rodgers or Hammerstein or somebody auditioned Rocky Graziano once, the Rock opined, 'Yeah, the singin' was easy; memorizin' the words was the difficult bit.')

The Harder They Fall was Humphrey Bogart's last picture. It was also Max Baer's last. The night after the opening, Baer woke up in the Hollywood Roosevelt Hotel with a sharp pain in his chest, and fumbled for the bedside telephone.

'I need a doctor,' he whispered.

'A house doctor, sir?' enquired the operator.

'No, dummy, a people doctor!'

At which Baer, the most 'human' and witty of all the great fighters, died. He was 50. Had he been English, he would unquestionably have played for the Gents.

Bop Till You Drop

Sometime ago, battering on (yet again!) about Ian Botham's glorious resurrection in the final Test match against New Zealand at the Oval, I remarked something to the effect that it was a pity the editor of *Boy's Own Paper* was obviously otherwise engaged and could not be there to report it. No sooner do you have such passing thoughts and penned them as throw-away lines, than you forget all about them – till first post the following day. This time, it was an eight-letter bombardment from people still in grieved mourning for *Boy's Own Paper*. Did you know it had been dead for well over forty years? It was cut down one week in wartime active service. One Wednesday it was there. The next, it was gone. Or was it?

I don't why, but I presumed it was still being churned out somewhere. No, alas. Old men just sit in the suburbs weeping quietly over their pile of back numbers. Shame, no one sent me a copy. I'd love to borrow one for a few days. Certainly, I could imagine its editorial staff being peopled by men with names like Arthur Rumble. As so it was. Wrote the same, from Tower Road, Epping, with kindly strictness: 'As a loyal reader of dear *Boy's Own Paper* for many years, and a member of its editorial staff from the time I left school in 1927 until shortly before call-up in 1940, I am often amused – and, sometimes, irritated – by journalists' and other writers' references to the *BOP* as if it were a magazine for namby-pambies, usually in a derogatory manner. Few mention it with real affection. Certainly it was the best magazine of its kind, and it enjoyed a wide readership throughout the world, as I should well know, having been responsible for, among other things, the organization of the *BOP* "Pen-Friends Club".'

Of my obviously sacrilegious reference re Botham, Mr Rumble chides: 'Well, well! The last editor of the *BOP*, Robert Harding, who used to commute to Bouverie Street (just off Fleet Street) from his home in Leigh-on-Sea, has been dead these many years. Black mark, Frank!' Mr Rumble adds a plaintive

110

PS: 'There has been no attempt to resuscitate *Boy's Own*, as far as I know. There is room for a magazine of its fine quality in today's world. Who will start the ball rolling?'

And yet, what's this? Mr Rumble is definite: 'The magazine became a war casualty in the early 1940s.' But on the doormat that morning lay another letter, from Mr David Cox, of Carline Road, Lincoln: 'It is remarkable how mention of *Boy's Own Paper* continues to crop up, in spite of the years now since its untimely and unwarranted demise. My father, Jack Cox, was editor from 1945 to the end. He always claimed that the tag of "larger-than-life-glory-stories" was a relic from pre-war days, rather than its post-war image. Certainly my definitive collection of *BOP* volumes, which we retain in the family, proves the point. Sadly, my father, you were right, was not available for comment, since he died suddenly five years ago, but he would certainly have revelled in Botham's splendour.'

It is odd, to say the least, that Mr Rumble returned from his war quite convinced that his beloved organ had been a casualty. Were all his string of pen-pals round the world living in the same delusion? For certainly the *BOP* came up with shining morning face each Wednesday for a number of years. For another generous correspondent, reacting to my mention of *Boy's Own* Botham, sent me – anonymously, in a plain brown envelope – a true delight: a biography, by that very same Mr Jack Cox, of H.D. 'Donny' Davies, who died in Manchester United's air-crash on the slush of Munich airport runway on that fateful February 6, 1958, when he was, says the blurb of the Sportsman's Book Club, 'association football correspondent of both *The Manchester Guardian* and the *Boy's Own Paper*'. So *BOP* was obviously still going strong in 1958. I dare say I'll be inundated tomorrow morning with copies of this very week's issue!

Anyway, thanks to someone out there, I have in my hot little hands a real gem. Donny Davies is still a legend in the now very sparsely populated offices of *The Guardian* in Manchester. Whenever I go up there, old men with rheumy, soft-boiled eyes talk of him lovingly and with longing for the once Corinthian days of sports-writing. And when he had finished his essay for the *G*, he'd put in a clean sheet of paper and tap out his weekly thoughts for the *BOP*.

Vaguely, on Saturday tea-times in my youth, I remember Eamonn Andrews on the wireless *Sports Report* calling up Donny

Davies in Manchester to tell us what went on that afternoon at Deepdale or Burnden Park or Turf Moor, and for a minute or two his amiable voice with the Lanky chuckle in it, and the Al Read observation, would tell it like no other on the programme. He was dead before I could have read him in *Manchester Guardian*, but I wouldn't have put two-and-two together for, there, he wrote under the by-line 'An Old International'. (Ah, where are all these names now? Even in my time, I was once 'Ajax' for the *Slough Observer*, and 'Edgar Street Wanderer' for the *Hereford Times*.)

'Old International' (he had played as an amateur for England, as well as for Lancashire at cricket) would have been 94 last March. I never knew there was a book. It cost 6s 9d, post-free to members, and in it, Mr Cox quotes Davies's obit written by Cardus: 'He always wrote with his eye on the ball. But because he was more than one-eyed, he also saw the drama and the scene, the crowd spending its passion, and the players, now masterful and god-like, now impotent, cast down and comic in their sudden exposure of mortal fallibility. The younger school of sports-writing is almost insulted if you suggest that now and again they might make literature out of a report . . . "Old International" was not only the best of soccer reporters; he was also something of a poet, and very much a Lancashire poet.'

The little book quotes Davis liberally from *The Guardian* and the *BOP*. Nobody before or since could surely have got away with this intro to a soccer match: 'Happy is said to be the family which can eat onions together. They are for the time being separate from the world and have a harmony of aspiration. So it was with the scoring of goals at Old Trafford on Saturday . . .' Or, from another United game, against Sheffield Wednesday: ' "Ah'll noan grumble if hoo's nowt but bread and jam for tea," boasted one elated Manchester supporter on his way home after the match. "Them were five of nicest ah've seen 'i youn sin' Johnnie Morris took is 'ook." Few would disagree with him except perhaps to add that the two Wednesday goals were not to be sneezed at either . . .' See, he even manages to observe the rule, Get the Score in the First Paragraph.

A few more snippets at random: ' "Sneke Hips" Colman, of United: one of these days, when he is in the mood, we shall have the Beswick Prize Band to accompany him with snatches of reasonably tuneful ballet music, say, from *Swan Lake*. Then we shall see the little fellow at his best.' United v Tottenham: 'From the remote eyrie of my seat it appeared as though Robb had fallen over a concealed door step or into an open grave. Perhaps that was the referee's view also, for he turned a deaf ear to all appeals for a penalty.'

Another intro, this time to a piece about a Cup-tie prelim: 'An elated bus driver, off duty, yesterday addressed a rapt and crowded bus load from the rear platform. In his opinion, City will skate it in today's third-round game at Newcastle provided only ''(a) that Joe Hayes pulled his socks up, (b) that Roy Little found out that he was coming or going and (c) that Dave Ewing didn't require a week to turn round in.'' Given these adjustments, I am inclined to agree with him.'

Or Raich Carter: 'It was said of Whistler (probably by himself) that he mixed paints with brains. So Carter does with his football.' Or young George Eastham, on his first appearance for Newcastle: 'He comes of good stock; his father was a good ball player, second to none, but dogged throughout his career by a secret sorrow, for he could not bear to part. The son, happily, knows better.' Or Wilf Mannion: 'A Mozartian in his exquisite workmanship, with a style so graceful, and so courtly, that he would not be out of place if he played in a lace ruffle and perruque.' And John Charles – still, for some Italians and Welshmen, the best of them all: 'We take for granted his strategic grasp, his seductive pass, his bursts of speed, his taming of the ball, his violent shooting, his gentlemanly self-control, however shabby the provocation . . . he is a giant who can leap and sprint and shoot, and shake off opponents as a dog shakes water off its back.'

I could go on for reams. The very last match he covered of Manchester United's before their fatal last performance in Belgrade, was a 6-2 victory by Busby's Babes, 'our young hopefuls, our happy warriors, made Old Trafford on Saturday like Mrs Fezziwig, ''one vast substantial smile'' with their blend and balance, freshness, gaiety of mind and physical resilience.'

A week later, half of them lay dead, the 'Old International' with them in the Munich mortuary. His last words of his last report, cabled from the Red Star Stadium, Belgrade, were: 'played magnificently throughout'. I wonder, during that re-fuelling stopover at Munich, if he might just have been setting down his thoughts for his weekly readers of *Boy's Own Paper*? By then, in mourning, the old magazine itself could certainly not have had much longer.

Knock on Wood

August is the clunk-click month. The bowlers are bending to their task. Black on green. White flannels and home-knit cable stitch – and the imperceptible mushy hush of brothel-creepers. *Oh, good wood, Wally! Nice bowl, Perce!* There always seem a lot of Walters around on the bowling-greens of Britain. Also Percivals, And Miriams and Mavises on the ladies' rink. *Oh, I say, Miriam, meticulously done, ol' gel!*

There are also, of course, David and Tony. In spite of the enthusiastic embrace of television, bowls remains short of recognizable performers. For almost three decades, bowls has meant to the public consciousness absolutely nothing – except David Bryant's curly Peterson pipe, glinting spectacles, bank clerk's haircut, and flying-legged follow-through. Now Tony Allcock has appeared – young, blond, bustling, and when he swaggers purposefully up to his little rubber mat you quite expect to hear that rousing signature tune from that old Amsterdam detective series, *Van der Valk*, for Allcock uncannily resembles the actor, Barry Foster, who played the part.

Competitors at the 1987 English national men's championships this week and next, at Worthing (the women play at Leamington Spa), will have their soft, faraway eyes more fixed on the distant horizons than usual for it is a 'world's' winter this time, with the world championships being held in Aukland in February 1988. Bryant, 56, and Allcock, 32, have already been chosen to lead the English challenge.

Both are Westcountrymen: Bryant from Clevedon on the Somerset coast; and Allcock from Bussage, perched on one of the blissful valleys that tumble down into Stroud. Someone once told me there was a Wessex saying which went, 'Naught can rival Bowles for sport save good ale and a comely wench' – though I've never asked the game's two modern high-fliers,

114

Allcock and Bryant, if they'd care to comment (though I bet she's called Mavis).

The thing that gets bowlers' goats of both sexes is to suggest their sport is just an old folks' fancy. After he'd won some long ago Commonwealth Games' title, I suggested to Bryant that his victory was a nice encouragement to the middle-aged. He remained polite, of course, but more than momentarily miffed: 'We're awfully competitive, you know. Soccer men can work off all their heat and adrenalin by charging about kicking things. Cricketers can either bowl a bumper or start swiping every ball that comes down. We blokes have to rely on nothing else than concentration and self-discipline. But, oh yes, do believe me when I tell you that six jacks have been smashed at these Games, and one or two of them hit forty feet into the air. There's an awful lot of pent-up emotion wafting around a bowling-green.'

Bryant is a schoolmaster. His grandfather was a founder member of the Clevedon Bowling Club, and his father, Reg, skipped Somerset. He says he learned tranquillity by watching them play on their dozy, seaside green – but the young man preferred cricket and tennis till his eyesight deteriorated. He joined the club in 1947, won his first English title in 1960, his first Commonwealth in 1962, and was Champ of the World by 1966. Since then, to bowls, he has remained the Bradman, Piggot, Pele, and Ali all rolled into one.

'I'm not an athlete, more a gymnast and golfer soldered together. All I know is that I've got to be supple. Every morning, around 7.30, I leave the wife sleeping and slip out of bed to put in half an hour's yoga on the carpet. Suppleness is all – especially with my dodgy back.

'I've always enjoyed table-tennis – and I used to play skittles in a pub league, but I was no better than many of the locals. I've gone tenpin bowling twice. Well, there's an extra dimension in our bowls, isn't there? In golf, you play a decent shot and the other fellow has to match it – he's not allowed to knock your ball out of the way. Nor in darts – you just tot up a score and the opponent tries to beat it, he can't do anything to disrupt your flow. Same at snooker: you can only do anything when you get to the table.

'But in bowls, you can roll down three perfect-looking things – and your opponent can suddenly wipe them out with one bowl and you're sunk. Altogether a whole new ball game, isn't it?'

Oh, good bowl, Wally! Nice one, Dave!

Whatever happens this week, Bryant has been selected to team up with Allcock in February's world championships. They first came together in the 1984 championships at Aberdeen when they won the pairs' silver medal, since when they have won the indoor world title in successive years. If Bryant was the first bowls player to become a national figure since W.G. Grace (yes, he was captain of England at bowls, too), then Allcock could yet be the most famous since Francis Drake. This summer, he turned full-time pro, giving up his job as headmaster of a school for mentally-handicapped adults. It was a wrench, he says, but in big-time bowls a man's gotta do what a man's gotta do.

In fact, though Gloucestershire claims him, he comes originally from the other side of the Cotswolds. His parents were both leading players in Leicestershire, and after flirting a little with Pony Club gymkhanas, he joined the Fosseway BC in Syston at 14, and immediately won four club titles. He was on his way: 'I do not remember ever having a coaching lesson – but perhaps that reflects on my delivery! I think a lot of my delivery and quick ''snatching'' derives from the number of bowls I used to deliver as a lad on my parents' long lawn beyond their bungalow, where I would play dawn to dusk, even in frost and snow.'

Now that same chubby Leicestershire lad with the angelic curls of a Gower has followed Bryant in dragging the game out of the suburbs and into television's voracious sights. There is now a Tony Allcock Bowling Centre at La Manga, a ritzy sports complex in Spain. The publishers, Stanley Paul, have even brought out an attractive, heavily-researched, 300-page anthology on the game, *The Story of Bowls from Drake to Bryant*, edited by the television journalist, Phil Pilley. He has left no bias unturned – a whole chapter, even, on Shakespeare's references – but I particularly liked the crib from a pre-war bowls magazine which essentially sums up the soft and amiable appeal of the game to my generation. Well, the times you have passed by a bowling-rink on the train, everything trying to be prim, and trim, and white; engrossed in inaction; and the silent slither of the brothel-creeper... 'Tidy suburban greens, squeezed between the privet and the 8.30 railroad to Town; flousy greens as untidy as a theatricals' landlady's parlour; greens apparently full of spivs and pin tables; seaside greens where you get sprinkled by salt

116

spray when the wind is in the wrong direction; sleepy, good-natured village greens where nobody cares if you dent the council's woods and you help with the roller; old school-tie greens, with the Western Brothers and the prefects standing aloofly around . . . and, oh yes, those restricting greens on which you feel like some new candidate for an appointment visiting the prospective employer, all dolled up in your most impressive suit . . . How I hate those collar-restricting greens!'

Collar-restricting, good phrase. Like the time the distinguished Victorian amateur, George T. Burrows, reported his challenge of the celebrated northern Crown Green professional, William Taylor, who was known as '*Owd Toss:*

' "How does tha' play?" asked Toss.

' "Same as you," I replied in my best Cheshire accent.

' "Clever, aren't ye? Does tha' tak' coat off?"

' "Yes, when I'm keen."

' "Does tha' tak' waistcoat off?"

' "Sometimes – if it's hot weather."

' "Does tha' tak' collar off?"

' "Very often, if I'm out to win."

' "Oh, tha' tak's collar off, does that? Then tha' can only have three start in 21!" '

Nice one, George! Nice one, Dave! Oh, good bowl, Tone!

Anthem Is As Anthem Does

The Commonwealth Games' boycott has deprived us of some of the world's most exotic and unlikely tunes. Up the Anthems! A by-product of this sort of sports day is its Global Song Contest, and as the patriotic, proud pouter on the podium fights back the tears, Adam's apple a-quiver, all you need is Terry Wogan's mascara'd French side-kick announcing the musical merits in reverse order: *Sierra Leone nul point. Sierra Leone no points.*" And the superimposed flag twines up the flagpole.

Grande Bretagne aussi nul point, for while the Union Jack may be the best flag, the National Anthem is surely one of the dreariest. That's what I love about the Commonwealth Games. The only other one I have been to was at Edmonton in 1978. A medal was presented to the first Brit and, as usual, we old sweats in the cursing Press box shuffled to our feet – but instead of playing *God Save the Queen*, out roared a record of a 500-strong male voice choir with *Land of My Fathers*. Was it for good ol' Berwyn Williams? Suppose so. Later that week, a tearaway tiny tot called Barry McGuigan, in the green vest, beat the splendidly named boxer from Papua New Guinea, Tumat Sockolik, and they strung the little golden biscuit round his neck and there were moist eyes in the Press box, as well as on the podium, as the whole hall, it seemed, gave lilting voice to *Danny Boy* –

> *But come ye back when Summer's in the meadow*
> *And when the Valley's hushed and white with snow.*

I thought, again moistly, of that night in Alberta when, eight years later, Barry boy committed GBH at QPR and won the professional world title against Eusebio Pedroza. That evening under the West London stars was prefaced with Barry's Dad, Pat, silencing 30,000 by crooning the same song before the first bell. *'Tis I'll be there in sunshine or in sorrow.* Pedroza never had a hope after that. Pat was third in the Eurovision Song Contest in 1967, behind a Spanish soprano and Cliff Richard. The title of his song was *Chance of a Lifetime*.

Offhand, the best English victory anthem I remember was at Moscow in 1980. That time, you will remember, Mrs Thatcher had done her best to boycott the British team's entry on account of Afghanistan and Joggin' Jimmy Carter, but most of the team turned up on the promise that, in the event of any victories, the Union Jack would not be run up, nor the National Anthem played. Instead, up fluttered the five-ringed flag and they played the weirdly wonderful Olympic Hymn – all involuntary trumpets and composed in 1895 by the Demis Roussos of his day, Spiros Samaras.

I was at the poolside when Britain won its first Moscow medal – and by marvellous fluke the Union Jack *did* shudder up the pole. For the bronze medallist to Duncan Goodhew's gold was an Australian, Peter Evans. And Goodhew himself, bald as an egg and still a most singular one-off, had himself premeditated victory by clambering out of the pool and into a home-made red, white and blue dressing-gown. In a stone-faced city, that was all warmly emotional for us Brits.

118

Differently dramatic, a few days later at the athletics stadium, was the evening they blared out old Spiros's shanty once more, this time when Steve Ovett beat the hot favourite, Sebastian Coe, in the 800 metres. When Seb, shattered, leaned up to shake Ovett's hand on the podium, Clive James classically described the 'look on Coe's face as if he'd just been handed a turd'. In his memoir of those Olympics, Seb reckoned that a bit much: 'I was just blank. I didn't hear the Olympic hymn as the flags were raised . . . it was nothing to do with Steve. I was just totally disconnected. I knew I had run appallingly in what was meant to be *my* event, and the numbness would have been the same whoever had won. That rostrum was no place to be smiling after tossing the race away.'

A few days later, heroically, Sebastian went out and won the 1,500 metres, with Ovett third.

Mary Peters, of the melon smile and the Veronica Lake hairdo, had her first little weep at the *Londonderry Air* when she won the pentathlon at the last Edinburgh Commonwealth Games in 1970. But hers was a real double handkerchief job when she topped the podium at the Olympics in Munich two years later. Mary once told me that she was the only one in the house with a dry eye that night: 'The old tear ducts were beginning to start work as they began to play *God Save the Queen*. Doubtless they would have done, but down on my left poor Burglinde Pollak [of East Germany, who was third] started gasping and sobbing and almost choking, and I was so concerned about her that my own tears wouldn't come as they raised the Union Jack slowly to the masthead. My mind should have been filled with visions of green hills far away and the familiar streets of home, and yet there I was worrying why Burglinde was crying so. I thought perhaps that, being an East German, she was mortified at losing – but afterwards I discovered that she had been simply ecstatically overwhelmed at the sheer joy of coming third! So bang went my own chance of some emotional reverie.'

It was in Germany, at the original Olympic Stadium in Berlin, that there had almost been a major diplomatic incident thirty-six years earlier when the English soccer team was ordered to give the Nazi fascist salute to the 'Royal' Box when they played the anthems before the match. In his autobiography, *Back in Touch* (Barker), Stanley Matthews recalls how the England team was appalled: 'Sir Neville Henderson, the British

Ambassador, came into the dressing-room, on the face of it to wish us luck, but rumour had it that he had been involved in the decision to make the salute . . . Goebbels, Hess and Goering would be watching the game from the Distinguished Visitors' Box. I looked at the other players. There could be no mistaking their feelings, but we were virtually under orders. Finally Eddie Hapgood, our skipper, shrugged and the decision was accepted – but it was a team of angry players who made that long walk down the steps and on to the pitch of the stadium, which was a mass of blazing red swastikas, thousands upon thousands of them. We gave their precious salute, and then settled down to play football.'

England won by 6-3.

Another political salute that stirred up a sporting occasion was on the Olympic podium at Mexico in 1968 when, after the 200 metres, the gold and bronze medalists, the black Americans Tommy Smith and John Carlos, heard *The Star-Spangled Banner* strike up, bowed their heads and raised their gloved firsts in a Black Power salute for American civil rightists. They were banished from the 'Olympic movement', though as we know this week, sport and politics have become a heck of a lot more collectively disruptive since then.

I'd like to think that the gesture in 1968 might just have had something to do with the tediousness of *The Star-Spangled Banner.* We Brits are lucky with *God Save Our Gracious TEAM.* It is only played before soccer or rugby internationals or at Cup Finals. The poor Yanks have to stand rigid at their *Banner* before every conceivable Saturday night or Sunday morning event – from an under-12s ice-hockey fixture to a stock-car meet in the desert, from a two-bit prize-fight to the Super Bowl Final. In one main league baseball season it will be played 2,500 times. It was written after the Battle of Baltimore in 1814, but only adopted as the national anthem after President Woodrow Wilson said it was his favourite all-American song.

In their domestic sports day spectacular, which they called the 1984 Los Angeles Olympic Games, we were having to stand rigidly to attention (phones at one ear, fingers in the other, as we were hustling copy back to London deadlines) every five minutes through the day in the Coliseum, as yet another US medal winner had his homely patriotic little blub on the podium. Halfway through the interminable refrain, there is a

120

15-second passage which, we gleefully discovered, you can accompany perfectly with the words, *We wish you a merry Christmas, we wish you a merry Christmas, we wish you a merry Christmas – and a Ha-a-ppy New Year.* It did not go down well with the homesters. Nor, come to that, had it four years earlier in Moscow when, in similar circumstances, we gave full throat in English to the unending East German national anthem, which fitted as near as dammit to the carol, *While shepherds wash their socks by night, all seated on the ground.* We have missed, this week, putting words to the anthem of Papua New Guinea. Now there, if my memory's correct, is a real humdinger.

Question Time

Name the heaviest tonnage a boxing ring has had to endure in a world title bout? Oh, easy-peasy, 465½lbs, Larry Holmes (211) versus Leroy Jones (254½) in 1980! *Way out, idiot! 488¾, Primo Carnera (259½) v Paulino Uzcudun (229¼), October 22, 1933.*

Who was the first substitute sent on in a soccer Home International? A cinch: the very lately late Jimmy Mullen, of Wolves and England in 1950. *Dunderhead! I thought you were meant to be in the biz? It was at Wrexham in 1889, Pugh (Rhostyllen) taking over in goal for the injured Gillam (Shrewsbury). I thought everyone knew that!*

Now you can't possibly fail on this one. Which was the last completed father-and-son Test match pairing? And don't give me that stale old answer "Miandad". Walter and Richard Hadlee. *Years out!* Oh yes, sorry – Colin and Chris Cowdrey! *Are you trying to be funny?* No, I give up. *You must be the only imbecile in the whole world who doesn't know it's Hanif and Shoaib Mohammad, of Pakistan.*

Just one more chance. Please. To save my reputation. Please. I've a wife and two cats to support, and there's a kitten on the way. Just one more, I beg you. *Okay then, this for your life. Any babe in arms could get this. Ready? Name me the most players from the same club who have turned out for England in the same soccer international.*

Oh thank you, sir, thank you . . . 1953, v Hungary, the four Tangerine Seasiders, Johnstone, Taylor, Matthews and Mortensen. *Miserably wrong.* Oh, yes, I remember . . . 1970-something, the Red Quintet, Clemence, Neal, McDermott, Keegan and Kennedy. *You're as good as dead, dunce!* Of course! Last year . . . Steven, Stephens, Stevens, and Stephen! *You're rubbish!* A clue, I implore, gissa clue! *A London club.* I've got it! Hoddle, Waddle, Doddle, Sodall!

Screams followed by a dull thud. They announced the answer at the memorial service . . . November 14, 1934, v Italy at Highbury, Moss, Male, Hapgood, Copping, Bowden, Drake, and Bastin; all seven from Arsenal.

Variations of the nightmare have been recurring three or four times a week, doc. Ever since the first edition reports from ringside of the night-before's all-action area eliminator – between Kid Cain and Sugar Ray Abel – hit the streets, it has been amiably presumed by the populace that sports-writers know nothing about sport. Certainly nothing about sporting facts. It didn't matter much: you could flannel and flather with adjectives. But now it can be painfully *proved*. Those blithering millionaires who invented the tedious parlour game, Trivial Pursuit, have not been content to loll on their yachts, languidly counting and shuffling their pack of green cards, each one of which says $100,000. Oh, no! The clever sods have brought out an exclusively Sporting Edition for Christmas. It will be the end of back-page journalism as we know it. (Perhaps the *Mail on Sunday* heard about it first, for in the summer they appointed as their new No.1 cricket *writer* that beaming barbate boffin and sniggering sliderule swot, Bill Frindall. Oh, my Cardus and my Glasgie long ago! Or can you punch-up purple prose on a pocket calculator these days? Perhaps you can on the *Île des Chiens*.)

I am not looking forward to the old Yuletide loggery this year. My father-in-law not only thinks he knows it all. He does. He can recite without a breath the claret-jug winner, say, of every Open golf championship since Young (or was it Old? he'd know) Tom Morris at Prestwick in 1872. He can parrot-fashion not only all post-war Cup Final goal-scorers, but each of the ruddy *referees*, for heaven's sake. He can even tell you the date and hour Steve Davis was born – though there I don't believe him; surely the pinch-lipped pale loiterer of the pockets was simply de-mummified by Sir Mortimer Wheeler during his excavations of the chalk cupboard, at the Romford Locarno c1950?

My father-in-law knows that 1987 is the centenary of the highest ever Minor Counties score (F.E. Lacey, 323 not, Hants v

Norfolk at Southampton); that Bolton Wanderers are the only side to have won the Cup four times without conceding a goal; that the late Scouser comedian named himself after the 1912 Open winner at Muirfield, Ted Ray. He thinks I should be jailed for false professional pretences. I concede only that he has a point. Certainly he is going to rub it in this Christmas when the board comes out after the brandy.

I was away at the time (possibly watching a soccer match, or game of rugger, or at any rate something of which I've completely forgotten the score, let alone the scorers, not to mention the name of the referee *godammit!*) when the smirking Trivial Pursuit people unveiled their new edition by way of a pudding-proof wheeze – a TP match between the Fleet Street sports-writers. It was, by all accounts, a fiasco. Scarcely any hack knew anything. Actual *facts* remained sacredly secretive. Especially when answers were asked of the so-called quality press. *The Times, Guardian* and *Observer* were apparently totally humiliated, and could hardly drum up even The Don's career average between them (95.14, by the way: or was it, blast it, 99.94? Or was that his Test average? Or his tally on wet Wednesdays in Worcester? Ah, me, hang on a tick while I look it up. See what I mean?).

At least the *Observer's* sports editor was big enough to concede the decision – and then come out punching. Peter Corrigan's spikily splendid, ruminating column cheered me up more than usual that Sunday. I already have a photocopy for father-in-law. Wrote perky and unapologetic Peter: 'The main thrust of our mission is to relay to you the information, the emotion, the analysis, and the meaning of sporting activity around the world. Facts and figures involved are obviously important but they flow so quickly through the enquiring mind that most of us possess the memory-retention power of the common gnat. It is therefore no disgrace that *The Observer* was knocked out in the first round at Trivial Pursuit . . . Beware, there are sporting smart-asses everywhere. And their day has just dawned.'

Put it another way. When your card comes up enquiring, say, *Q. Who was floored most times in world heavyweight title bouts? A. Floyd Patterson, 17,* I can tell you that when I had tea with him once a the Regent Palace Hotel in Piccadilly, nice, soft-spoken Floyd fingered his jaw, shook his head, and explained amiably: 'No man, it never hurt; it was a relief really; you just float off like a baby going to sleep; or like taking dope, I guess, and just floating down to the mattress all comfy like.' They are the facts I want to know.

Unlike my father-in-law, who doubtless knows that 48 Joneses and 40 Daviesies have played for Wales at soccer, not to mention 53 Joneses and 51 Daviesies at rugby. But does he know that *one* Jones-Davies turned out in the scarlet (London Welsh, 1930-31)? Well, *I* do. Isn't that more interesting – also, that he dropped a couple of sitters against Scotland and the boyos called him Hywell Hyphen.

I did once catch out this knowall-by-marriage I've been lumbered with. Or rather, I think I did. *Name me the left-handers who have scored centuries for England since the war?* I was at the time mulling pleasantly over a possible piece of meaningless, infill waffle (just like this) about the sinister, southpaw trends in Test cricket. He rattled them off, just like that . . . Broad, Edrich, Gower, Barber, Subba Row, Watson, Parfitt, Pullar, David Lloyd and Watkins.

'Ha! Gotcha!' I said, triumphant. 'You've forgotten Peter Richardson!'

He didn't even blush. 'Oh,' he said, 'you mean the Worcester and Kent stalwart, of course – 2,061 runs in Tests, five 100s, and only man in history to be caught out, 8 times, all behind the wicket in every one of his innings of a Test series; of course I knew it, but presumed that was going to be your supplementary, ol'boy.'

It's no trivial thing, being married to the daughter of a smart-ass. How many swotting days to Christmas?

Grandstand Tour

All around are enticements for the most esoteric, eccentric, not to say concentric, holidays. Perhaps we wouldn't fill more than a rusty Dormobile full of nuts, but if I was a travel agent I'd give some thought to just one Grand Tour of the world's great sporting stadiums. It could be called *Erewego Erewego Travel* and the price could include hourly hand-outs of lager six-packs. I'd sign on like a shot.

Matches need not necessarily be in progress when you visit. Funnily enough, there is a particularly eerie magic (good sporty word that: as in *Yeah, Bry, Shane give a magic cross, dinney?*) in standing alone and silent in an empty, cavernous stadium where you know great deeds had once been done to the real-life accompaniment of an erupting, passionate and primitive roar from tens of thousands of throats. Perhaps now, as you stroll around the deserted, vacant, pin-drop lot, your travel company would provide a Walkman cassette-tape of commentaries of all the fleet-footed feats that had taken place on the famous field.

Your guidebook could direct you towards, say, the north-west corner-flag at Wembley. Not a soul in the place except you – but 15 yards in from touch and 35 from goal, for instance, you could break into a baggy-trousered, soft-shoe shuffling gait as the tape in your ear would replay Raymond Glendenning's epic 1953 commentary, its crescendo reverberating through every hair of his RAF handlebar moustache . . . *Here comes Blackpool again . . . right-half pushing the ball through . . . Fenton to Taylor . . . through to Matthews . . . Matthews on the edge of the Bolton penalty area . . . dribbling right in . . . past his man . . . two yards out . . . squares it . . . Perry coming . . . yes, it's there! . . . it's there! . . . Perry has scored number four!*

From north London's seedy old dustbowl with the velvet turf, *Erewego Inc.* would tour the world. We would start, of course, at the Colosseum – the MGM lion superimposed over human screams? If you could manage to cross the road, that is. As you know, I have just come back from Rome. The incredible old pile still stands sentry – the most ancient traffic bollard in Christendom. Tens of thousands of Fiats snarl around it each day and, beneath it for good measure, an Underground train each minute. Yet still it gapes down at you, hoarding sporting secrets from its twenty centuries with a grey and knowing solemnity. Will the Houston Astrodome celebrate one single century? I doubt it. Certainly, I bet Wembley won't.

I have been to one or two places the itinerary would have to include. I'd readily go again. I've sat on The Hill at Sydney, and seen Botham get a ton at Melbourne. But I've never been in on a Test at the Gabba, the WACA, or at Bourda. I've been enthralled when Holding's paced out his run at Sabina, and when Gavaskar's beguiled Bombay. But I've never watched cricket at Newlands, just Lions being mauled by Springboks.

125

I've seen Pelé at the Aztec, but never at Maracana. I've cheered Viv at St John's, McGuigan at the King's Hall, and Sugar Ray at Caesar's, but never yet been to Madison Square. I've cringed at All Blacks unChristian at Christchurch, but never seen them put the wind up Wallabies in Wellington. I've sat at the polo at Cirencester, but never been near a ballgame at the Polo Grounds. I've walked round The Ovals at both Kenningtn and Kensington. I've sung at the Arm's Park, been blotto at Ibrox, and drunk vodka in the Stadioski Whatsitsname in Moscow. But I have not yet made Bernebeau.

But I have been to Bislett. Not that anyone was running there at the time. That makes my point, and after the Grand Tour's start at the Colosseum, all roads lead from Rome, but the first stop, I think, would have to be Bislett by moonlight. Bislett's secret is in being tiny, intimate, claustrophobic. Fans can almost touch favourites as they fly past.

Bislett's atmospheres are also helped, to my mind, by it being, not plonked on some scrubland pasture way out of town, but pretty much in the very centre of Oslo (from the Colosseum itself to, say, St James's, Newcastle, this communal core seems crucial). Anyway, in 1981, I was in Oslo for one of England's World Cup qualifying soccer matches. The game itself was played on some smalltown, nondescript paddock out in the suburbs, but that's by the way, as is the fact that poor old Ron Greenwood's England team played like drains and got well stuffed by Norway's pretty inept part-timers.

Except that the result caused a rabble of raucous Anglo-klaxon yobbos in Union Jack T-Shirts to provoke a series of skinheaded affrays in the vicinity of the 'stadium', which meant me having to stay on the telephone to London long after the match had ended, up-dating arrests and ambulance casualty figures (all part of any sports hack's duty in those days). The upshot was that I missed the last bus back to our downtown hotel. So had to let it in the moonlight, dodging or talking myself through as "friend", the odd roadblock set up by various posses of the youth of England.

As I neared the centre of the city, I was accosted by a particularly tanked-up, half-naked cadre of fellow countrymen, who enquired of me what I had thought of the game. On being informed gently of my opinion, that Mr Greenwood's lads would have had the match in the bag if they had simply been able to project the spheroid with their feet for no more than ten yards from A to B in anything like a reasonable straight line, my compatriots began to menace closer around me. I then noticed, in the moonlight, the twinkle-bright glint of a jagged, newly broken beer bottle.

I pinned my ears back and ran like hell. *Get 'im!* It was very scary. They were gaining. I knew I wouldn't quite make the hotel. Round a corner, I dived into an alley, panicked painfully over a fence, and hurled myself down into a huddled ball, retching with fright and breathlessness but doing my best to look like an innocent sack of potatoes in the dark.

It worked. After a truly frightening five minutes, the shouts and footsteps of the searchers died away in the distance. *Erewego! Erewego!* faded into the night air. Norwegian grannies were probably more their cup of tea, anyway. Safe now, I stopped shaking and stretched full out – and, suddenly calmed, started counting the pinpricks in the great canopy of sky-laden darkness above me. The moon was like football-ground floodlighting and I was on the centre-circle.

No, I wasn't. I was lying on a sort of rubbery-red surface, striped with wide white lines; and I had dived for cover against a plyboard sort-of-fence with writing on it. It read CAMPARI.

I sat up and looked around. I was on a running track. Not only that. By absolute fluke and by acting the scared rabbit that I had been only minutes before, I had thrown myself for holy sanctuary on the very *finishing line* of probably the most famous athletics track in the history of the modern world. Where only the year before Sebastian Coe (a different standard bearer for the youth of England) has astonishingly broken three different world running records in as many months – for the 800 metres, the mile, and the 1,000 metres.

Thus, had you chanced to glance down from the window of a high hotel in Oslo, well past midnight, as moonlight bathed the finishing straight of the 8-laned track, you would have seen a raincoat, old brown sports jacket, typewriter and briefcase piled on the infield grass – and a tubby, middle-aged figure in his braces and brown brogue shoes haring exultant, but breathless, towards the line. All around would be a deserted , eerie, late-night northern stillness, but in the fat man's head would be bursting a cacophony of cheers almost drowning David Colman's apoplectic *Has Coe gone too soon? . . . No! . . . It's Coe! . . .*

127

Coe! . . . Now! . . . The astonishing young man has done it again!

After that, *Erewego Tours* would proceed, say, to Zurich's *Weltklasse* track where, later that year, Sebastian broke the world's 1500m record. Then on to the Olympic Stadium, Berlin, where we holidaymakers could pace out Jesse Owens's 1936 long jump run-up. Then, possibly, on to Vienna where the Lion called Lofthouse did his stuff . . .

Whatever the cost, count me in. Cheap at the price.

Shooting Times

To 'win Wimbledon' meant something completely different to the Victorians. The tennis championships at the end of the last century were very small fry indeed – and every schoolboy knows that the first winner of the gentlemen's singles in 1877, the Harrovian Mr Spencer W. Gore, thought the game dull in the extreme and its 'monotony would likely choke off any promising player before he had time to excel in it.'

No, when the guys and gels who guarded the steamy sentry-boxes of Victoria's Empire announced their intention to travel home 'for Wimbledon in July', they meant only one thing – the National Rifle Association's Grand Imperial Meeting on Wimbledon Common. It is now held at Bisley Common, Brookwood – and this weekend the crack and splatter of gunfire reaches its 127th annual crescendo across a paddock of Surrey scrubland. That's an awful lot of sandbags sieved.

Exactly a century ago, the NRA were forced to move from Wimbledon. So many scores of thousands thronged the Common each summer – let alone the 25,000 or so soldiers detailed for duties during the fortnight – that some residents bravely ganged up and demanded restoration of their commoners' rights. Among other inconveniences, they were also in fear of their lives from the inaccuracy of drunken marksmen – witness *The Wimbledon, Tooting & Merton Temperance Gazette* of July 1886: 'Cannot something be done to stem the tide of drunkenness and immorality at the Wimbledon Camp meetings? I am quite sure, from long experience, that alcoholic drinks do not assist any man hitting the target . . .'

By no means did Mr Punch avert his beady eye. He always relished his annual trip to Wimbers . . . 'Wind-driven Wimbledon . . . who does not know the white tents resting on the fragrant heather like a nest of poached eggs shining in a dish of verdant spinach?' Ah, where are they now, the great sports-writers of England? Exactly a century ago, too, our esteemed Mr Punch noted his *Nine 'Whys' of Wimbledon* with such perspicacity that I dare say many of those who are huddling under canvas this very week in another part of Surrey might echo 'aye' to his clairvoyant's list:

'*Why* is the Camp situated between two Railway Stations, and near neither?

'*Why* must you to get to your destination, either puff up a high hill or pick your way over a rutty common?

'*Why* must you live in utter discomfort in a bell-tent with a lot of other fellows for a couple of showery weeks?

'*Why* is the Staff permitted to revel in boarding, carpets, elaborate furniture, and flower gardens?

'*Why* is the Members' Camp permitted to assume the appearance of a collection of Stock Exchange boudoirs?

'*Why* is the shooting so badly managed?

'*Why* is the marker invariably asleep when a fellow clearly makes a Bull?

'*Why* does one's rifle, so good at practice, always go wrong when it comes to competition?

'*Why* do all the earwigs take my tent for a trysting place?'

Wise whys, the hundred years' whys. I'm afraid I can still sigh roughly the same sort of thing for any of the olde established events in England's social, sporty season, from Lord's and Henley, and back to Bisley. But we paupers still turn up as gawpers, don't we? And, deep down, as proud as Mr Punch to be there.

In fact, once the NRA moved from the excesses of Wimbledon to the more 'county' environs of Bisley, it seemed determined to clean up its act. The boozing competitors and the snoozing markers were weeded out. In 1869, one Wimbledon caterer's picnic order for just two days had been: '8,000lbs of bread, 16,000 rolls, 5cwt biscuits, 600 quarts ices, 780 gallons tea, 100 tongues, 100 hams, 5cwt salmon, 156lbs eels, 480 lobsters, 900 heads poultry, 6 tons meat, 80 hogsheads ale & stout, 760 gallons claret cup, plus sundry wines, spirits, liquors & aerate water'.

Nowadays, alas, a guzzler's Wimbledon means £1.50 for five sad strawberries on a paper plate, and £20 for a warm bottle of bubbly.

Mr Punch did not take to Bisley at first. On the week the meeting moved down ye anciente M3 to the Hants borders, he wrote in his issue of 19 July, 1890: 'Why, it is twice as large as Wimbledon . . . But where are the fancy tents, and the luncheon parties, and all the etceteras that used to be so pleasant at Wimbledon . . . Bisley is more like Shoeburyness (where the Artillery set an example to the Infantry) than the Surrey saturnalia. And is it all to be *all* work and *no* play? That will be the general idea. Of course, in the evening, when nothing better can be done, there will be harmonic meetings round the camp-fires. But while light lasts, the crack of the rifle and the ping of the bullet will be heard in all directions, *vice* the pop of the champagne corks superseded.'

Crack and *ping* indeed. The noise, when the wind's in the wrong direction, can be as excruciating as the sound-tracks of a Silverstone Grand Prix and Isle of Man TT laid on top of each other. My first visits to Bisley were in the late 1950s when I was a cub reporter on the old *Surrey Times* group and had to turn up on the two Thursdays of the shoot to get the results-so-far for the *Surrey & Hants Weekly*. It was so noisy you couldn't hear the Brigadier-type stewards telling you first to '*duck*' and then to '*clear orf!*' It was scary, and I did not take to it at all. They never even offered the Press a brown ale.

Susie Cornfield's new history for Pelham, *The Queen's Prize* –the fortnight's premier competition: the Empress pulled the first trigger at the inaugural 'Wimbledon' in July 1860 – makes amends for those inky-fingered humiliations of mine. It is one of the best little sporting social histories of its type I have come across for some time; breezy and bright-eyed and insisting that the shooting fraternity is a crackshot one in every way. Perky all through, Susie at one stage saucers her big, beguiling eyes and asks the NRA's present chairman, Sir Roland Gibbs, and the secretary, Brigadier Peter G. A. Prestcott, what Bisley means to them. Ah, dear girl, what times we've had . . . and the soft-boiled eyes get rheumier. If he could only take one memory away with him to heaven, Sir Roland would plump for 'a picture of Century Range, with every target engaged from 300 back to 600

130

yards: the whole range a mass of humanity, lying down and shooting: I think that is such as wonderful sight'. And while the Brigadier admits 'I am a sufficiently bad shot to have never got to Bisley', which is an awfully decent way of putting it, he 'did shoot regularly for the battalion – perhaps it was the others who let me down . . . but I have nevertheless killed a stag from the back position.'

Is that good or bad? Is the Brig. brilliant or a bounder? Susie offers no comment.

And Eton be blowed – the British armies' battles have been more likely won on the butts at Bisley (or Wimbledon). Mr Punch's picnic on the Common in 1862 inspired him to return to the office with a poem for his issue of 19 July:

'Woe to the foe who dares our shore,
When, side by side, those rivals pour
On horses, guns, and men,
Such bolts of fire as those that tore
The air in Surrey's glen.'

Surrey's midsummer gun-slingers are still pumping lead into their jolly old sandbags. But, I trust, drinking a little less.

Anyone For Wireless?

On the last Saturday of June 1926, the Head of Programmes for the fledgling BBC wireless station, Gerald Cock, visited the Wimbledon tennis championships for the first time. He loved all games. He watched Kitty Godfree and her husband become the only married couple to win the Mixed Doubles, then insinuated himself into the All-England committee room for tea. It had been an entrancing day, and as he walked in the evening to Southfields railway station, he determined to have a crack at organizing a running commentary by wireless the following year.

On the Monday morning, in his office at Alexandra Palace, he wrote to the All-England secretary: 'Dear Sir, Would you and your associates view the possibility of carrying out by this Company a running commentary of some important matches next summer . . .'

In his enthusiasm, the estimable Cock might have cocked it up there and then. For he had written to the wrong man, and by return he received a frosty letter from the new secretary, a Major Larcombe: 'Sir, The man to whom you addressed your letter resigned from this club three years ago. I have noted your enquiry and my Committee will be advising you of their decision in the matter in due course.'

And so it began the following summer. Cock chose his friend, Capt Teddy Wakelam (who was to become the Brian Johnston of his day) as commentator, and the Club insisted he was accompanied at the microphone by one of their senior members, Col R. Brand, to make sure that the newfangled gimmick would not lower the tone. Just as they do to this day, for at every press conference during Wimbledon fortnight, a suited, po-faced member in his green-and-purple necktie sits alongside the various whingeing brats as they air their unformed views and let their hang-ups hang out.

I can find no reported mention at all of exactly the first match to be broadcast live on the wireless. The experiment for England's little band of crystal-setters must have been successful enough, however, for Cock to send the two commentators a typed memo praising their 'tiring work, especially as there is very little ventilation in your hut and as I know your voices had to be hushed as not to affect ticket holders in adjoining seats.'

By the next summer, a ventilator was provided in the hut and, also, Cock agreed with the Committee to pay for frosted glass to be put on the outer window of the Gentlemen's dressing-room, of which the two commentators had had a perfect view the year before. The Committee also accepted Cock's advice on the installation of a microphone on the umpire's high-chair. *Quiet, please!* – and by 1929, the BBC were budgeting £100 for the fortnight, with two hours of transmission each afternoon.

Wimbledon's wireless commentaries very soon became part of the summer's fabric. Wakelam and Brand were helped out at the mike by a Major Cooper-Hunt, and then followed a list of increasingly well-known voices, like Freddie Grisewood, John Snagge, Rex Alston, Stewart Macpherson, and Tommy 'The Fleet's Lit Up' Woodroofe. 1986 was the fortieth anniversary of

132

by far the best of them all: Max Robertson first commentated from Centre Court in 1946, the year the elongated French waiter, Petra, won the title. His machine-gun, firing-squad volleys remain a quite thrilling hark-back to the great days of steam. He once told *The Guardian* how the game had speeded up – 'that it's now like playing yourself from both sides of the net – and at the end you have all the elation of the winner and all the exhaustion of the loser.'

Meanwhile, Gerald Cock had turned up to the 1936 Wimbledon with an extra bounce in his tread and gleam in his eye. He had just been appointed first Director of BBC Television. Indeed, only six weeks after the Championships had ended with Fred Perry's hat-trick win, Cock assembled his tiny staff in a bare room at Ally Pally and told them the new service would start in *two weeks'* time! (The first show was a 'magazine' programme called *Here's Looking at You.* Estimated viewing figures – between 250 and 300.)

By this time, of course, Cock was on most cordial terms with Major Larcombe. In the New Year, he wrote to the Secretary: 'Could television carry out experimental transmissions . . . We would be tackling unknown quantities and the apparatus has not yet been used over such a distance, we do not know whether we can achieve yet a satisfactory link between Wimbledon and Alexandra Palace.'

But they did – even though, two days before the 1937 Championships began, a BBC engineer's memo reported that: 'Cause of interference for our mobile transmitter at Wimbledon has been traced to Hornsey Central Hospital, who have agreed, so far as is possible, to suspend diathermy activities during times we are transmitting.'

Hornsey kept its word and, on the afternoon of June 21, an unbroken passage of 25 minutes was relayed from a match between the British champion, Bunny Austin, and a Mr G.L. Rogers. Less than 2,000 Londoners had television sets, even though sales had been boosted by the Coronation of George VI the month before. (At least part of the Championships nowadays are watched by over 350 million people in 90 countries.)

Next morning came the first ever TV crit, in the *Daily Telegraph:* 'Televiewers . . . could observe every movement of the players. Even the passage of the marks of the lawnmower over the grass were distinctly visible. There were also scenes of spectators in the stands and their faces could be seen clearly. The television pictures were accompanied by a commentary by Mr F.H. Grisewood.'

Eat your hears out, Clive James and Julian Barnes!

It so happens that two whole years before that first excited visit to the strawberry fields of SW19 by Gerald Cock, a 16-year-old, raggedly-trousered laddo from Fulham went to watch tennis at Wimbledon for the first time. He had already long left Everington Street Elementary School to become a general duties' ballboy at the riverside's salubrious, upper-crust Hurlingham Club. For a ballboy, he had always been an intent listener when a member was being given coaching lessons and soon he would be appointed an assistant on the coaching staff of twelve.

That midsummer afternoon in 1924, he and his friend, another ballboy called Ernest, went to watch the ladies' final – Kitty McKane (soon to be Mrs Godfree) beat Helen Wills 4-6, 6-4, 6-4. He was enchanted. And still, moments before Dan Maskell is cued in to begin his commentaries to the whole wide world, he never fails to focus his eyes on that very same corner seat where he and Ernest sat that day, 'the third row back, seats four and five . . . ooh, my goodness me, little did I know then . . .'

For Dan Maskell's been watching Wimbledon even longer than the BBC.

134

Passing Shots

Protection Racket

The lights are going on all over Europe. Summer hols over, scowling sadists in shorts are popping their francs, lire, pesetas and pound coins into the dreaded courtside light-meters and squaring up to each other for another wicked winter of GBH and torture on the T. The squash season has begun.

On August 31 1986, Jahangir Khan, the 22-year-old prodigy who is already to his game what Grace, Bradman, Pelé, Ali, Laver and Barry John were to theirs, won the Pakistan in Karachi for the umpteenth time as the traditional signal to the Western world that the awful nine-month mad-eyed mayhem can begin all over again. *The Times* correspondent in Karachi reported that the astonishing young man's 34-minute victory over the Australian champ, Ross Thorne — who won only four points of the final's 31 — was 'cool and predictable, yet beautiful and fascinating', four adjectives which, in my experience, it is impossible to pin on any squashman. The report continued that 'Thorne oculd only smile, for that was all that was left to do.' Smile? When did you last see a squash player smile? Unless it was that crooked, evil, lip-licking de Sade job when he's in-hand at 8-nil up.

Even in Mrs Thatcher's Britain, it seems, we have run out of recruits in ruthlessness. The British squash boom is over. But Europe is catching the disease. Figures in *The Guardian* the other day showed how the UK's 1970s squash explosion has quietened down to about three million registered players (which I dare say could be doubled by a similar amount of occasional and totally unclubbable racket-owning thugs). Meanwhile, through the 1980s, the number of players in France has doubled to 98,000 with 700 courts and 300 clubs; Spain, which had a few thousand players at the start of the decade, now has 60,000 and one of the largest centres in Europe, *Castelana Squash*, opened in Madrid this year. Germany has half a million pouting, pain-inflicting

136

Becker types who prefer to hate a small black ball than a fuzzy white one. The sombre, suicidal Scandinavians have, as you would expect, taken to squash with an icy-eyed and rotten relish.

If these new recruits to sporting sadism are able to read English, there is no knowing what depths of spiritual or physical violence they could sink to if they get hold of Barry Waters' latest survival guide, *Squash Balls*, (Roger Houghton Ltd) a pretty cheap murderer's manual. Of its type, apart from Wat Tyler's classic and revolutionary *Garrotter's Guidebook*, I cannot think of a more awesome book detailing man's necessity to vanquish at any price since the urbane and wonderful Stephen Potter published *The Theory and Practice of Gamesmanship, or The Art of Winning Games Without Actually Cheating*, all of forty years ago. I trust Penguin still have it in print.

Each of these sporting notes of mine inspires a handful of letters — mostly, it must be said, to put me right on cricket scores or soccer spellings or boxing books. (Sorry, I seldom reply, but all points are usually well and swottingly made and always have me miserably contrite.) A couple of years ago I wrote about the day I gave up playing squash. It prompted just about the most sympathetic postbag I've ever had. Even two months later, the letters of condolence were still coming in from Kuala Lumpur, Brisbane and Brasilia. Condolence *and congrats*, I might add. This is what I wrote: 'I have finally kicked the habit. It was a dramatic withdrawal: 7-7 in the fifth and retching for breath. I went for the ultimate, unforgivable pass. My regular opponent was a best friend, and another gasping slob of middle-age. We were pals anywhere but on this parquet-floored snakepit. Robert was in the very wind-up of his crucial service, when I croaked the command, "Hold it!" He allowed the wretched rubber onion to bobble, unbouncing, to the floor and he turned his blood-shot eyes to mine, aggressively. "I am not," I said as firmly as I could while attempting to focus my glare on his brow, "I am not going to continue this match with you looking like that. You win, Bob ol' friend, I concede the game and set. Let's go and have a drink on it."

' "What do you mean, you swine?" he said through heaving gulps of breath.

' "The last time," I lied, "I beat someone with that blotchy, purply-mauve forehead I see on you, he died in the showers even before he had squeezed out his Vosene."

' "I don't believe you, you bastard!" he said. But the poor fellow's defiance lacked conviction.

' "Be it on your own head and sickly brow," I told him, as he turned to serve for the match. He ran not a step for either of my returns. I won 9-7. Game, set and match. He never played again. But neither did I.'

Stephen Potter invented purer ploys. Squash, he wrote, offers no problem; aim to play your important games when it's rainy weather outside: 'It will usually be possibly to find a small patch (on wall or floor) on to which water is dripping. When opponent is winning, *particularly if he is winning his service*, become suddenly alarmed for his safety. I, Make futile efforts to remove water with handkerchief or by kicking at it; 2, Talk of danger of slipping, and 3, If necessary call for sawdust which, of course, will be unobtainable.'

Waters is almost as wily. First you must realize no one takes up the game for fun. You might enter a squash club, buy a drink and presume that everyone's human. Suggest a game — and suddenly the meekest of them has invariably turned into a blood-lusting monster: 'Almost without exception, squash players, deep down, are power-crazy egomaniacs, with a profound inner need to dominate at something. Don't believe any of that nonsense they give you about playing the game for exercise, or to forget the office, or to get away from the wife. Fact of the matter is, they come to the club in search of a *victim*. These are the people who, if they weren't executives, or housewives, or taxi-drivers, would probably be public executioners. They don't just want to kill the ball: they want to kill *you*.'

Pope Potter the Great, mind you, was first to realize that the squash court itself was not the true gamesman's hunting ground. Most of the hard work had to be done beforehand — ploys in the changing-room, even, are leaving it a little late. In my day, a useful start was to set tactics into motion during the very phone-call at which you and your opponent were arranging the game. Mention, in passing, that you are carrying an injury sustained in a *League match at the weekend after another club* (and name it) *had asked you to help them out*. This immediately gives you a host of obvious advantages, not least a loser's excuses. In Potter's more leisurely days, he was able to employ 'lunchmanship' to effect. At luncheon, before a game, he would sometimes casually produce from his pocket 'an old and even slightly punctured ball, which I always refer to as the "new, specially slow ball, recently authorized," and I add that it is in general use now because "otherwise rallies would never end."' The opponent, somehow, is less confident.

One regular opponent years ago would always beat me though his beer-pot was more evident and his general co-ordination and ball-sense seemed, in modesty, less sharp than mine at the time. He would always wear, even in the hottest and most torrid of last set battles, a shrunken, creamy old Cambridge University cricket sweater, to which he had no right (he was very red-faced redbrick) but, I thought, we all have our foibles. I started winning with ease only after coming across Potter: 'At Oxford, though never a Blue, I used to wear a Blue's tie, particularly when playing games against nice men who knew I had no right to wear the honour. This simple trick, which is said by psychologists to induce the "pseudo-schizophrenic syndrome", or doubt, is most effective in moving ball-games.'

Waters agrees totally about the gamesman's need to get in his retaliation first, for once locked into the awful, windowless dungeon, the knackering effect of match play can scramble all suave judgment. Only talk to your opponont on court, he says, if the stratagem tends to distract him. If answer comes there none, don't let this inhibit you. At the last resort, 'always feel free to offer a running commentary on *his* game. Either lavish praise on *his* efforts, calling out "shot!" to all his best flukes and making *apparently* flattering remarks like, "Interesting, that grip of yours!" Or you can even be a bit more ironic, calling out when he hits into the tin, anything from "What rotten luck!" "Nice one, Cyril!" "Thank you very much, Squire!"'

But the most useful remark is the early one which implants doubt in his mind about his game. You must get him worrying for the rest of the match: 'I know some people do play that shot off the wrong foot, but . . .' At the very last, try, 'Your forehead's giving off a terribly purply hue . . .' but only when totally desperate.

Like Potter, Waters insists on style: 'Any Survival Squasher must make it clear that for him squash is very much a survival activity. Only then does it not matter whether he wins or loses.' In other words, a squash survivor must understand, right from the outset, that the correct clothing may mean wearing his

Ralph Lauren polo shirt, say, or perhaps turning up in what is basically a tennis outfit, or in rugby kit, thereby implying that squash is not really his game at all.

Potter would have agreed. Should you be losing, stress inferiority of squash to rackets, which in turn, of course, is so inferior to tennis. Thus Potter's sequence of talk might run as follows — 'I was playing tennis at Lord's yesterday. This game's all right, but you know, after tennis, squash seems — well — you do feel rather like a squirrel running about in a cage, don't you?'

Jahangir Khan, only 22 still, has not been beaten by anyone in nearly six years. With the unquenchable spirit of Potter in his corner, perhaps we should put Barry Waters in with the astonishing young Pakistani. I can see it now: Barry, of course, would be first into the dressing-room to change. His bag will be open, so as to make sure that when Jahangir arrives he will notice the bloodstains on our boy's spare shirt. And the Indian clubs will be visible, too, from a corner of the bag: wrist exercises are crucial. As he hears the door, Barry will already be in position on the bench and as the champion enters he will begin his sit-ups — counting loudly '. . . a hundred and eighty-one, a hundred and eighty-two, a hundred and eighty-three . . .'

Jahangir could be beaten before he starts.

A Load of Bolero

A stampede it ain't — but even the most unlikely TV gawpers could be hurrying hastily home through British city rains every tea-time till the end of the month. The Winter Olympic Games begin at Calgary on Saturday, and seeing wealthy smart-arses fall down mountains represents compulsive viewing for some.

The five-ring circus's four-year cycle relentlessly karate-chops whole wedges of your life away. Can it really be forty-eight months ago since we Brits clomped our fur boots through the slushy streets of Sarajevo, humming through chilblained lips the opening strands of Ravel's ruddy *Bolero*? How jingo, jangly boastful we were. Now Yawnvill and Preen have skated smoochily away for a lifetime of ice pantos, so, at Calgary, Brits will be back to being 37th out of 40 in all the sliding and sledging events, and the only fun is to swop the unerring quality of David Vine's patriotic excuses.

Actually, my highspot at Sarajevo in 1984 was not Torville and Dean's doleful diamanté duet. It was the night the British Olympic Association threw their party. Guest of honour was the Princess Royal, herself a previous Olympian, of course. Her stay in town was but a brief stopover on the way from London to Africa, where she had urgent engagements pertaining to her Presidency of the Save the Children Fund. Indeed, she had to leave the party early and go straight to the airport. Only a select handful of the British press were secretly invited to the do — certainly not the Fleet Street pop paparazzi. But one of them got to hear of the gathering half-way through the evening — and he burst in, breathless, angles and headlines all aquiver, to be told Her Royal Highness had already left for her next engagement.

'Where to?' he implored. 'The Gambia,' he was told — and, before anyone could elaborate, he charged out, to spend the rest of the night whipping and tipping his bewildered local taxi-driver over most of Bosnia, insisting he deliver him to a nightclub called *The Gambia*.

Nor have the Winter Olympics ever really been my scene. My first were at Grenoble in 1968. This was the life, I thought, as I contentedly lounged over the *après-ski* bar with all the beautiful people the night before racing began. Only a few hours later I was rudely wakened in my draughty chalet in the press village with orders to *Raus! Raus*! and board the battered old bus which would take us to the top of some nearby Matterhorn, there to watch the start of the Downhill heats, or somesuch.

I have never had such a scary hangover cure in all my life. It was sheer on both sides, and front and back — sheer drops and sheer terror. The snaky mountain track was shimmering glass in the headlights of the wheel-spinning little jalopy: the driver was as carefree as he was obviously mad. We made it to the top. It was absolutely perishing. I had none of the gear. Everyone else was colourfully quilted in the full, expensively trendy, Klosters thermals. With my threadbare, two-toggled, 1959 Milletts blue duffle wrapped around me, I must have looked like the French Lieutenant's Woman waving forlornly, not for the Frog on the sprayful Cobb at Lyme, but for Cap'n Scott in the blizzard at Base Camp Two.

141

The racers got ready. I watched them start till the freezing snow sealed my eyelashes. One by one the whole field of skiers hollered suicidally into the mists — and then our bus skidded all the way down the mountain. It was even more nightmarish than the ascent. I vowed there and then that if I ever had to cover a Winter Olympics again, I would always do so from the TV corner of the press tent — with a glass of warm wine in my hand. In twenty years, I never broke that resolution. The vine goes well enough with the Vine.

This time, at last, they've got the message, and said not to bother to go. So I'll be watching Saturday's opening ceremony in the, comparatively, blazing tropical heat of a serene English winter. I might even find myself enjoying the Opening Ceremony. These are convoluted, tedious and nationalistic, not to say nutty, things. Don't let me spoil Saturday's curtain-up for you, but it must be said that winter Openings each four years are worse even than those of summer. The forced smiles really freeze to the faces of the marching ranks of ruthless competitors — for, baby, it's cold down there.

Half the teams will march out, swathed in blankets like mountain terrorists. The Canadian hosts, I bet, will all be in Mounties' scout-hats; the Americans will swirl by in stetsons. That will be the end of the bravado. The Brits, if previous uniforms are anything to go by, will be muffled up like frost-bitten beekeepers and look beaten from the start (which they are); the Soviets will have fur-hatted heads buried deep into their shoulders, like so many Gorky Park gardeners arriving for the dawn shift; the French will be their usual sullen squad of moping Michelin men; the Italians' ears will be mummified into layers of scarves; and the Swiss and Austrians will look glumly frost-bitten already. Only the Scandinavians and Norsemen will seem warm and in the pink — and, of course, they will win everything.

I will be cheering just one fellow in his beekeeper's bonnet of olde England. Eddie Edwards, representing the Gloucester Artificial Ski Slope Club, has made the team in — of all things — the Ski Jump event. He bears a slight resemblance to Mister Magoo, but he answers to the name, 'Fast Eddie'. His is an heroic achievement.

A couple of winters ago, just after his 22nd birthday, Eddie raised some subsistence sponsorship from his local Cotswold

Printers, and announced he had forsaken his ambition to get into the British slalom team — Gloucester's nylon slope was none too wide for practising swerves — and henceforth would devote all his energies to jumping. Gliding, he reckoned, was cheaper than sliding.

Eddie begged, borrowed and hitched his way to Lake Placid in America's Adirondack wilderness. The US Olympic team were training there — and they came out to watch the loopy Limey have his first jump. *Wowsey!* They adopted him on the spot, for he hit the ice at an astonishing 40 metre mark. Within weeks, he had smithereened the British ski-jump record of 61 metres, set by Guy Dixon at Davos back in the mists of 1931. Hoverspeed Eddie landed at 77metres. He was weraing boxing boots, the back of his catsuit was torn and flapping and his spectacles steamed up.

In the racy little Christmas indipper, *Bedside Skiing* (Stanley Paul), Eddie told John Samuel about his record: 'I just kept flying. The best feeling I've ever had. So smooth, so good, so confident. It can depend on luck. An extra gust, that sort of thing. Then you go on floating and floating. I'm a bit obsessed, I suppose. Technically, my arms and head are still wrong. My takeoff is really good and so is the flightpath. Someone said I had my arms too close to my sides in flight. You need them six inches out to catch air, twisting the palms face out when you're going, the image of a boy on a dolphin.'

Eddie should be last next week — but, in his case, the last shall be first. Wish him luck in Saturday's parade. He'll be the one with his glasses fogged up. Skiing is a whole new fall game all right — and for the like of Eddie Edwards, the sheer exhilaration is obviously worth the sheer terror. For me, hooray, no more uphill for the Downhill. I cannot tell you with what relief I'll be watching David Vine and his team of David Colemans this time. Happy days, no more *Boleros* on the brain.

Photo Finish

I take it you've noticed a pretty dramatic week on the sports pages. Not all that much to write home about for the hacks. But oh, my dears, the *look* of the thing. The world judo championships, the RAC Rally, and the ice dance finals have given the boys with the Box Brownies a blinkin' bonanza. Flash, bang, wallop, what a photograph! Every one a Michelangelo. Or, as the old American pugilist, Mickey Walker, opined on Rembrandt, 'He can paint like a Dempsey with a left hook!'

Fleet Street's confounded new technology may have done an awful lot in even further unhinging tthe mental stability of the grubby trade's pen-pushers, but it has sure done a most handsome job on the quality of newsprint pictures. You can now, quite simply, *see* what a photograph means without having to match it up, squintingly and furrow-browed, with the caption, and thus come to an approximation of what the muddy blob above might mean.

It is just as well, for sports photography is considered a high art form now. Once upon a time, those huddled masses snapping away behind the goal at any League footer match were — judging by most of their results next morning — all competing for the job as ace snapper for the *Spot the Ball* competition. Not any more. Now, as often as not, the man behind the lens is more of a superduper star than the show-off in front of it. And there are an increasing number of swish, swank coffee-table books to prove it.

I have a hunch as to the exact $\frac{1}{100}$th of a second that it all changed. The evening shadows were lengthening on the Gabba cricket ground at Brisbane just before Christmas of 1960. An exciting cricket match was coming to an end: Australia versus West Indies. High up on a gantry behind the bowler's arm, hunched over their ancient bazooka-like 'Long Tom' plate cameras were two deadly professional rivals — Ron Lovitt, of the *Age*, and Harry Martin, of the *Sydney Morning Herald*. The excitement of the closing overs of the Test match meant that they had used up all their glass plates. Thus, with one ball left to be bowled by the Caribbean demon, Wes Hall, Australia needed one to win, with one wicket standing — and, more to the point, the two opposing snappers up on the faraway rim of he stand had only one plate each left for the final delivery.

Big Wes fingered the gold crucifix which dangled from his neck, and turned nervously at the end of his run-up. The last Aussie batsman, Kline, settled uneasily into his stance at the distant crease. Up at their station, the two photographers looked at each other with helpless shrugs. At last, in the long history of Oz newspapers' dog-eag-dog hatreds, the *Age* looked at the *Herald* and decided on a compromise. They had one plate each, and four results were possible.

They had been weaned on the bitter rivalry from the first day of their respective apprenticeships in the darkroom. Now they came to their agreement and tossed up. Martin would photograph the stroke no matter what happened: he would thus take the winning run, Kline being bowled or leg-before. Lovitt would take the action following the stroke — catch, run out or victory salute.

Hall bowled. Kline pushed to square-leg and ran. Martin still waited. Joe Solomon swooped in and threw the wicket down. The umpire's finger goes up, and — *snap!* — Lovitt of the *Age* takes the most famous cricket picture of all time. It went round the world and for the first time a sports photographer became a household name. The breed has never looked back.

Britain now has a cadre of crack snappers. Scribblers who go on a job with one of them feel their accompanying 1,500 words or so are, in the editor's mind, no more than just an extended caption which he can take or leave. The pic is the jewel in the page, these days. Cricket has been supremely well served in recent years by Patrick Eagar, a devout student of the game with a mesmerizingly sharp and searching focus, and Adrian Murrell, racy and emotive, with the ability to put a grin or a grimace on the game with a single freeze of a frame.

The lamented *Sportsweek* magazine (conceived, safely delivered and then strangely strangled almost at birth earlier this year by Robert Maxwell) illustrated, literally, the emergence in glorious Technicolor of such spectacular talents as Norman Lomax and Christopher Cole. They have a hard act to follow, for the maestros over the last couple of decades — in evocative black-and-white anyway — have been Chris Smith, now of *The Sunday Times,* and the young man who succeeded him when he moved from the *Observer* ten years ago, Eamonn McCabe.

The coffee-table books are now coming as fast as it takes a WI hen party to get through a small jar of Nescafé. I'd be very surprised if Eagar wasn't polishing and cropping another of his outrageously cool, calm and colourful albums for the Christmas market — on the sub-continent's wonderful World Cup capers, perhaps? Certainly, Murrell's *Cricket Impressions* (Kingswood) was worth waiting for and, as an amateur 'art shot' Instamaticite, I found the accompanying text, in his own write, quite fascinating. It's fun, of course, but not $\frac{1}{500}$th as easy as it seems.

Kingswood's go-ahead set-up also publish *Eamonn McCabe: Photographer.* All the sporting classics and quite a few more genuine art jobs that could be heralding a change of tack to more geometric landscapes, urban and rural. (Let's hope it's only a phase, stark and dramatic as they are. To me, it's a bit like Botham taking up embroidery.) McCabe will tell you that he has been lucky with the number of major news photographs he has got. But this is, of course, an example of the Gary Player Law: the more I practise, the luckier I get, says Simon Barnes in his good and typically original intro to the artwork: 'McCabe becomes emotionally bound up in the event, and has an intuitive understanding of what is happening and, crucially, what will happen next. That is why, time and again, pictures happen for him, the timing of the comedy is perfect and the people seem inevitably to form into patterns for him.'

But the dandiest doyen of the monochrome is Mr Smith with his portfolio, *Sport in Focus.* Partridge Press has done him full justice with some rare quality printing by BAS, of Over Wallop, Hants. Dudley Doust, Hugh McIlvanney, Brendan Foster and Brough Scott provide some enlightening commentary in their different, muscular styles — most memorably by Doust in elegant tribute to Smith's golf work.

As I say, a good week to launch the '87 Christmas coffee-table creakers. Not a hairy forearm in focus, or a bawling, toothless centre-forward in celebration. Clear the back page, and use 'em big. The ice dancer's long, long legs. Skidmarks on the round Britain whizz. And judo's mauling matmen — as McCabe says, 'a very tricky sport to shoot; if you don't get it right it looks like two pillow cases having a fight.'

Courtly Loves

THIS new year gives us a nice little centenary. In 1886, good ol' Teddy, the Prince of Wales, had his first horse-racing win as an owner. The nag was called Counterpane. It dropped dead after its next race — but the Sport of Kings was off and running.

I fancy its next century will not be so regally patronized. I have no confidential evidence for this of course, but have a hunch that Royal Appointments on the Turf are on the wane.

After the Queen and, of course, her beloved Mum, what likely apprentice is natural heir to assume patronage of the silky, snooty, topper-doffing game? Horses, as such, have no need to worry, mind you. Nags themselves remain part of the regal fabric. But three-day eventing is as far away from the Mug's Game as cricket is from baseball. Who have we got? Prince Charles seems genuinely fired by a missionary zeal that might even take him from the polo fields. Anyway, neither Himself nor His sister have ever shown much enthusiasm for Epsom or Ascot, let alone the 3.45 at Wincanton or Market Rasen, whence results, apparently, still keep Granny beaming spry. Nor has the Duke of Edinburgh bothered overmuch about being seen stifling a yawn at the said Ascot *gavotte*. Matelots don't twig nags — though he enjoys his carriage-driving round Windsor Great Park.

Who else is there? Prince Edward likes rugger and acting and, presumably, helicopter driving. Prince Andrew would prefer being in the Press Tent swopping yarns at f8 and 500th of a second with Ed Byrne or Gerry Cranham, racing's two celebrated happy snappers. The Kents prefer tennis. So does Princess Diana. And she also likes cricket.

At Wimbledon a couple of years ago, I watched Diana closely. McEnroe was playing at, for once, his most benign and entrancing and when, at dead on four o'clock, the Royal Box flunkey called them downstairs for tea, the Princess was loathe to go, really wanting to see the match out. She also spurns, so far, to learn the Royal Tennis Handclap as patented by the Duke of

Kent — a bored manual hurrah in slowtime, which looks as if he's laboriously trying to swat an imaginary bumble-bee about six inches above his forehead.

Princess Diana's elder son will not, I guarantee, be a racing man. He is accounted for, I'm pleased to say. When Prince William was born, all his delighted grandfather, Lord Spencer, would say is, 'I hope and pray he plays cricket for Gloucestershire.' End of quote. Princess Di has since become President of dear old Glos CCC, and one of the first Christmas cards the club received last month was one from the good lady, with the PS that she had noted, with warm pleasure, the dramatic advances the county had made up the Championship table through the summer. It was noticed, by the way, that in that obsequious royal television interview last autumn, the fawning ITN newsreader who conducted it felt obliged to talk to her about polo. With all his researchers, why didn't he ask about cricket?

I digress . . . In the summer of 1886, the Prince of Wales's first winner as a racehorse owner made, at a stroke, the whole raffish pursuit legit and respectable. True, his mother had occasionally attended the Ascot Gold Cup, down the lane from Windsor, when Prince Albert was alive. But that was deemed to be no more than part of the royal duty, like going to the Cup Final today might be for Princess Margaret. After Albert's death, Victoria never went racing again. She found its society dubious and disreputable. Her son, however, took to it with a will, once he had been taken to watch Hermit win the Derby in 1867.

Rakish coves like Charles II and the Prince Regent, of course, had enjoyed a flutter and all its attendant thrills — the like of which Queen Victoria warned her son against in a letter from Osborne when he was 28 years old:

'Dearest Bertie,

Now that Ascot Races are approaching, I wish to repeat *earnestly* and *seriously*, and with reference to my letters this spring, that I trust you will . . . as my uncle William IV and Aunt, and we ourselves did, *confine* your *visits* to the Races to the *two* days, Tuesday and Thursday, *and not go on Wednesday and Friday* to which William IV never went and neither did we . . . your example can do much for good and a great deal for evil . . . I hear every true and attached friend of ours expressing *such anxiety* that you should gather round you the really good, steady, and distinguished people.'

Racing was one matter on which the Prince stood firm: 'I fear, Mama, that no year goes round without you giving me a jobation on the subject of racing ... I am always anxious to meet your wishes, dear Mama, in every respect, and I always regret if we are not quite *d'accord* — but as I am past twenty-eight and have some considerable knowledge of the world and society, you will, I am sure at least I trust, allow me to use my discretion in matters of this kind.'

I crib that correspondence from one of the season's most stylish and genuinely enjoyable books, *The Fast Set* (Deutsch), which, along with other high-grade stuff probably, got buried and unnoticed in the welter of humdrum Christmas catchpenny dreadfuls. It is George Plumptre's story of Edwardian racing with, as you can imagine, the Prince of Wales in the starring role.

Although his first winner came home in 1886, I daresay the Prince had owned quite a few unofficial ones in the preceding years (but didn't want Mama to know). He had registered his racing colours eleven years earlier, in 1875. The famous chocolate-box confection of purple, gold braid, scarlet sleeves, black velvet cap with gold fringe is, unless I'm mistaken, the very same favours which the Queen's jockeys sport today — though if I am slightly out, don't all write in at once. Ten years after leading in Counterpane, the Prince won his first Derby with Persimmon, by a neck. The Brough Scott of the day logged the reaction thus: 'With what throbbing pulses the Prince had watched this thrilling contest of giants can only be guessed. As for the spectators, the cheers had swelled to a hurricane which must have been heard for miles around. The Prince of Wales had won the Derby! After years of patience and ill-luck at last he had his reward. It was a spectacle such as had never before been witnessed on a racecourse. Members rushed down from the stand to the enclosure, waving their hats as they gazed to where His Royal Highness stood, pale but with a delighted smile on his face ... winning the Derby always meant much; in the history of the race it had never meant as much as this.'

Ninety years on . . . and might the Queen be the last of the royal racing line? It would be just if cricket got a look-in at last. Much depends, I suppose, on where Prince William is sent to school. At Gordonstoun, the wild-eyed German educationalists, clambering up and down crags in sandals, cannot be expected to understand the delicate intricacies of the memerizing googly, or the charms of the wrist-rolling late-cut, as it ripples past third-man's stretching left arm.

For it is about time Royalty patronized our finest national game. Quite possibly Princess Diana would. Come to think of it, I wonder if she named Prince William after Gloucester's W.G.? Or even Bill Athey?

On the Ropes

AFTER all the hoo-ha it was, as most of us had expected, a pretty gormless evening when we gathered to present Joe and Marlene Bugner with their exorbitant retirement cheque at the Tottenham football ground. I bet there were ten better fights going on in pub tap-rooms or street corners within a square mile of White Hart Lane's square ring. Certainly, Dave Mackay caused more seriously hurtful mayhem on that particular centre-circle every other Saturday for years.

For his whopping windfall of a quarter of a million quid, podgy Joe had only to feign a furrowed brow for just over twenty minutes. Somewhere inside that heart of his ('the size of a garden pea' — H. Cooper), the brand-new Australian must have been exultant at pulling off this last trick for such a bundle of booty. All he had to do was bite off a little more than he could maul. It was comparatively painless, and cheap at the price.

The inelegant hippo dance was totally devoid of menace for young Frank Bruno, forehead even more lined in concentration, simply tromboned out his left glove, seemingly scared to use his right in case, in cranking it up, it exposed his own very meltable mandible to Bugner's famed flurries of powder puffs. And so they stank out the joint — the whole elaborate itinerary reaching a merciful conclusion when Joe, squatting near the ropes as if on a pile of cushions, was not so much punched but pushed over, as if a drayman was absent-mindedly toppling a sack of spuds. The towel fluttered in. Joe picked it up, wiped the grin off his face, and waddled up to the head of the pension queue.

150

I quote: 'It wasn't a crashing knockdown, the kind that leaves the recipient limp, like a wet hat, or jerky, like a new-caught flatfish. This appeared to be a sit-down and think-it-over knockdown, such as you might see in any bar-room on a night of full moon. Joe might have begun the process of ratiocination right away. But the conclusion at which he was arriving was not instantly apparent. Like a drowning man in stories, he may have been reviewing his whole life . . .'

Nothing new under the moon. That passage, in fact, describes the way another 37-year-old Joe — the Walcott fellow from Jersey — picked up a similar pension thirty-five years ago, when Rocky Marciano beat him in just two minutes 25 seconds at Madison Square Garden. The crib is from one of all sports-writing's classics, *The Sweet Science*, by A.J. Liebling, who used to ruminate racily on boxing, and much more besides, in *The New Yorker*.

At last, books like *The Sweet Science* are on the shelves of England — thanks to a brand-new enterprise which is to be wished extremely well. A few years ago, an engaging young New Zealander, John Gaustad, opened a little book-shop devoted entirely to sport just off London's Charing Cross Road. He called it 'Sportspages'. It went well enough, and I remember saying to him one day that if only he could find a bit more space, he could even think of stocking a few second-hand, precious out-of-printers. He has done much better than that — and recently teamed up with the American big-timers, Simon & Schuster. Sportspages now has its own publishing imprint and the first batch of a dozen or so books should be filling a heck of a lot of stockings before the end of next month.

Says Gaustad: 'The idea behind Sportspages is very simple — to make available a range of the best in sportswriting. They may be new books or reprints; fiction or non-fiction; the work of a writer or a player. They will be sometimes passionate, some-times judicious, and often both in turn. The ground rules for choosing books for the series are also very simple — they must be about some sport or another, though typically of course the best sports books are as much about life as about sport; they must be honest; they must be well-written and enjoyable reading; and I must like them.'

The straightforward paperback reprints — in grand, large, readable type, by the way, unlike some of the original editions

— mostly come in at £5.95, a bargain for such as Roger Angell's *The Summer Game*, John Moynihan's *Soccer Syndrome*, and Thomas Boswell's *How Life Imitates the World Series*, each of which in their differing ways bulge with humour and savvy, vim and romance. Hurry, hurry, while stocks last. Every one a winner. Angell's 300-word panegyric to the day the demolition men moved into the Polo Grounds in 1964, for instance, is worth the price of the whole glorious book. It corresponds, also, with the cursing whimper that is given out by Londoners of a certain generation each time they pass, nowadays, the recent balled-and-hammered dereliction of the White City or Harringay, those two celebrated centres of excellence and dreams, muscle and memory. Just scrubland now.

Similarly, in New York in '64, in the place that Farr squared up to Louis, what depressed Angell most about the decease of the bony, misshapen old playground was the attendant, irrevocable deprivation of habit — the amputation of so many private, repeated, and easily renewable, small familiarities: 'The things I liked best about the Polo Grounds were sights and emotions so inconsequential that they will surely slide out of my recollection. A flight of pigeons flashing out of the barn-shadow of the upper stands, wheeling past the right-field foul pole, and disappearing above the inert heat-heavy flags on the roof. The steepness of the ramp descending from the Speedway toward the upper-stand gates, which pushed your toes into your shoe-tips as you approached the park, tasting sweet anticipation and getting out your change to buy a program. The unmistakable, final *Plock*! of a line drive hitting the green wooden barrier above the stands in deep-left field . . .'

Or how about Boswell on Reggie Jackson, baseball's George Best or Ian Botham? For what, pray, distinguishes the great player, the man caressing his plaque in the Hall of Fame? ' "The pride," says Jackson, "that makes a player believe that he's better than the rest." Reggie Jackson says these words like a boy bringing home a drawing from school, one that has "A-plus" written in the corner. Perhaps he doesn't really mean to boast. What he wants, and still so seldom gets, is a measured, unhysterical response. Neither the rabid cheers nor boos that are supposed to be his fuel, but rather a friendly, honest appraisal that indeed his hard work has been found worthy.'

Let's put it another way. Also from Gaustad's enthralling first pile, is Sam Toperoff's homage to *Sugar Ray Leonard*, which was first published just before the pale, oystery-eyed sprite gave a pasting to the hitherto gruesome Marvin Hagler. Nobody gave him a chance, confident in come-uppance of cockiness, 'certain that Narcissus would fall head first into the pool and drown, and not, like Prometheus, steal the fire.' But Toperoff, for one, triumphantly roots for the fire stealer — 'I love the daring, the recklessness, indeed the arrogance that challenges all restrictions. Yes, almost always hubris gets slapped down, put in its place, and the conventional I-told-you-so explanations of the chalk-players are handed down as great profundity.'

Ah, but every once in a while . . . like Bestie and Botham long ago.

Though not, alas, Joe Bugner, who came, never thought of conquering, and then ambled off in his green-and-yellow, demon king's dressing-gown, cheque in one hand, blonde on the other. Not carried out on his shield, like poor Joe Louis at the very last: 'When Louis got up, Marciano hit him with two more left hooks, which set him up for the right and the pitiful finish . . . The punch knocked Joe through the ropes and he lay on the ring apron, only one leg inside. The tall blonde was bawling, and pretty soon she began to sob. The fellow who had brought her was horrified. ''Rocky didn't do anything wrong,'' he said. ''He didn't foul him. What you booing?''

'The blonde said, 'You're so cold. I hate you, too.'''

They don't write 'em like that any more. Or didn't. On second thoughts, thanks to Sportspages' revivals, now they do.

50 N.O.

This Sunday — October the Fourth, 1987 — is the thirtieth anniversary of the launch of the first Sputnik. It would have been Buster Keaton's 92nd birthday and St Francis of Assisi's 761st. Sir Michael Hordern will be opening his presents this Sunday morning in his best absent-mindedly enthusiastic manner; and so, in his altogether more languid, lordly way, will Basil D'Oliveira, who will be only (he claims) 56. This Sabbath,

I, too, keep holy. For I hit the big Five-O. A half-century, sir! Agreed, not chanceless and not at all pretty to look at, but a fifty is a fifty in anyone's scorebook — and now, like Hutton used to, forget the sheepish cap-doffing and bat-raising, just take a new guard from the umpire and get your head down for the full three figures.

Every year at this time I keep meaning to send off for a reprint of *The Times* of October 4, 1937, but I never remember till it's too late. Wouldn't be the same if it didn't come on The Day. Not that very much happened in 1937 — in terms of my bag anyway. It was a very boring ballgame year. All rather predictable: Don Budge and Dot Round shot everyone down at Wimbers; Henry Cotton won his second Open, at Carnoustie; silvery-haired Raich Carter silkily won the FA Cup for Sunderland at Wembley; and teenage Tommy Lawton took over the No.9 jersey from Dixie Dean at Goodison. Only the second jet-black nag of the century won the Grand National — Royal Mail at 100-6 — and Sydney Wooderson, a Surrey insurance clerk in wire specs, cut the world mile running record to four mins 6.4 secs. He wouldn't have been round the last bend if he'd have been racing Aouita today.

On the *very* night that I was born, the British lightweight champ, Jack Kid Berg stopped the ditto welterweight, Jake Kilrain, the Bellshill Belter from Lanarkshire, whose real name was Harold Owen, in the tenth of their scheduled 15-rounder at Earl's Court, London. Now there were some bells to be rung in by! Info courtesy a revealing new biog, *Jack Kid Berg, The Whitechapel Windmill*, by John Harding (Robson Books). The Kid, born Judah Bergman in 1909, is still whizzing round London, full of the joys in his little red car. Between 1924 and 1945, he won 157 out of 192 contests, many in America where every Jewish quarter in any city he fought in looked on him as their totem and superstar. He was what they still call 'an all-action crowd-pleaser', a head down, Terry Downes-type, egg-whisk over-armer. When he beat Kid Chocolate at the Polo Grounds in 1930, Paul Gallico wrote in the *New York Daily News*: 'I don't believe Kid Berg is a great prizefighter . . . when the thing is over his opponents discover they are not injured, their haircombs are a trifle dishevelled, their beezer a bit red, perhaps, and they are considerably out of breath, but of vital injuries they have sustained none. However, they always find

154

they have lost the decision . . . (and) the whole thing was just round after round of getting cuffed and slapped hither and yon. No hard punches, no knock-downs, no cuts, nothing but constant annoyance. And, drat, it, the loss of the decision.'

Just like, I dare say, the soft Scottish curses of Jake Kilrain through swollen lips in that Earl's Court dressing-room dungeon after the fight on the night that I was born — doubtless being more gently cuffed and slapped into life by the midwife at the Herefore nursing-home, right across the road from the Edgar Street football ground. It was only a paddock-extension to the cattle-market then, and United shared the pitch with the soon-to-be bankrupt Hereford City. I was already two years old before United even made the Southern League.

A few weeks earlier, down the Ledbury road, that autumn of 1937, Tom Goddard had rounded off his summer season by taking all ten against Worcester at the Cheltenham Festival on a real sticky. Was that the evening that the tall, nut-brown, insecure old off-spinner had come back to the pavilion feeling understandably chuffed with himself, only to have the surly, ungenerous genius, Wally Hammond, dismiss the feat as 'not so much good bowling as rank bad batting'?

Any half-decent batsman, challenged Hammond, could have played Goddard with a walking-stick. Tom, seething, took the bait, presented Hammond with a walking-stick and, in the evening murk, the two cussed and defiant England players strode out to the match pitch. The stumps were put back in and Goddard bowled an over of his most sharply fizzing devilishness. Every ball, Hammond played back to him with massive certainty off the very middle of the stick — and then tossed it away, snorted derisively and marched off without a word. (And, next day, while only two other Glos batsmen managed even double figures, Hammond made 178 against Perks, Howarth and Jackson to win the match.)

On the face of it, 1937 was a pretty crummy cricket year to be born in. There was only a weedy Test series of three matches against the club cricketers from New Zealand, who included the pipe-smoking Walter Hadlee, father of you-know-who, Patsy Hendren retired from Middlesex, leaving the stage clear for the 19-year-old D.C.S. Compton. Denis's first taste of the representative big-time was that July — a duck for the Players v the Gents (*st C.R. Maxwell, b F.R. Brown*).

Only a fortnight earlier, also at Lord's, there was another auspicious first-innings quacker in his debut Test against New Zealand: *L. Hutton b Cowie 0.* The pale, frail, concentrating Yorkshire boy was only 21 that month, The next day, Sunday, the shy sad boy had mooched all by himself around London, dropping into the news cinema near Charing Cross when it opened at tea-time. The newsreels kept playing his humiliating duck of the day before and, in the dark, the audience around him kept sighing and tutting. It doubled the lad's depression so much that he made only one in the second innings — and thought he'd blown his career.

Not a bit of it, as we all know now. Indeed Sir Len, and Denis Compton too, are among the shortlist of legends who have garlanded my paltry half-century. It has been a tumultuous Five-O, come to think of it. I saw Bradman only play golf (from behind a hedge at Adelaide when he was a sprightly 72), but I had laughing long drinks with Gary Sobers one night after he'd won a Test match on his own; and I've since got drunk with Ian Botham more than once on the night before he's peppered the pickets for a power-crazed century inside the hour. I've had supper with Fred Perry, lunch with Lew Hoad — and on the night after he was beaten by Rosewall, in what is still reckoned the all-time epic indoor singles five-setter, in the WCT final at Dallas in 1972, I found myself placed right next to Rod Laver at the Championship banquet. He spent an hour explaining the topspin lob.

Just as Ali once patiently explained to me, one afternoon in Munich, how to hit southpaws with short left hooks. Ali, I reckon, really was the *greatest*. More so even than Barry John in tandem with Gareth. Or the two cavalier JPRs- the Welsh Williams and the Gallic Rives. I was about 15 when I first saw Jackie Kyle slice through a three-quarterline. Was he, perhaps, the greatest? Or was it Piggott going for the post? Or Coe ditto in his prime? Or Pelé at the far post? The most sublime thing I ever saw Pelé do was in the 1970 World Cup final in the Aztec, just before the whistle, when he caressingly rolled the softest of balls thirty yards to his right and exactly, millimetre perfect, into the path of his captain, Carlos Alberto, so he could ice the cake with a celebration clincher.

There has been, of course, one quite cataclysmic development that exactly spans my fifty years. In 1937, that Raich Carter

Cup final was the first ever transmitted live by BBC television's infant service. There's a half-century anniversary for you, and that alone, in hindsight, makes 1937 a heck of a famous year. And continents began to speak unto continents, too: exactly five weeks before I was born, they got through on the landline they had laid along the bed of the Atlantic Ocean, and the first international live commentary of a boxing match, all seashell static and crackle, was broadcast, when Tommy Farr, of Tonypandy, lost to Joe Louis, of the Universe. They heard it, as it happened, in Wales — live from the New York Polo Grounds on the night of August 31, 1937. No more waiting for bloated Fleet Street sports-writers to sail back on the *Queen Mary* before reading all about it.

Fifty years — and the baby has come a long way. By the time Bobby Charlton was letting fly his whizzbang specials at goal, the whole TV nation, whether in hovels or palaces, was able to exult as one. By the way, Bobby isn't fifty till Sunday week — October 11 1987. Happy birthday, Bob. And Basil, too, of course. Thanks for the memories. It's been, as they say, a pretty ding-dong first-half. All-action, crowd-pleasing, knockabout stuff. Just like Kid Berg when he answered the bell fifty October the Fourths ago.

Still Live

Deedum, deedum, deedum, deedum, dee diddley dum dee-daaah!

'They turned down Sloane Street, and the warm windows cast light patches on the pavement between blobs of the street lamps. The same tune muffled through the walls as they passed from house to house, fading then swelling between the space of each lighted window. "Hey up, Dad, that *Sports Reports*, I'll race you!"'

Deedum, deedum, deedum, deedum, dee diddley dum dee-daaah!

That 5 o'clock winter's Saturday evocation is from Barry Hines's rich and rottenly under-rated 1960s novel, *The Blinder*. And still each succeeding generation scurries home to tea, to 'the results' and to *Sports Report*. Come in, Donny Davies from

157

Manchester; are you hearing me? Or Bill Bothwell, Larry Canning, Bill Lowndes, John Arlott or Geoffrey Green? And a further cast of thousands. Ahh, they don't make programmes like that any more. Oh, yes, they do! Same time, same place, same Saturdays as ever were. Hey up, Dad, I'll race you!

The generation gaps converge this week for we are all getting dolled up in black ties and the full works to attend the Hilton Hotel in London for a dinner of celebration for forty years of the Saturday radio institution as well as the sixty years of sports commentating itself (first 'wireless' Cup final, 1927). Terry Wogan is MC, one of the chief guests of honour will be the elder blarney-boy who blazed the trail from Dublin for Terry, old Eamonn hisself, and the cabaret lead will be the man who makes Mike Yarwood sound like Mike Yarwood, the young and only Rory Bremner.

These mutual backslaps, of course, are always thick with thanks to the production's tea-ladies and sandwich-makers. Deservedly, too. This week laps of honour will be taken again and again by the unsung back-up team in the dug-out who get the show on the road each week, the *AveyougotBothamontheline; andcuttherugbytape; andcheckedtheTorquaykickoff; and clearedthetapemachines; andtimedtheforeignnews; andwrittenthetenniscue; andwhythehellnot*' brigade. BBC Radio's erudite enthusiast, Bryon Butler, the soccer correspondant, who has been coming up refreshed and refreshing most every single Saturday for two decades now, does those honours to the devoted dungeon drudges generously in the book he has edited to mark the forty years, *Sports Report* (Macdonald/Queen Anne Press).

With each copy is included an hour-long sound tape, compiled by Peter Griffiths and Patricia Ewing, which rummages through the archives of breathless broadcasting since the time that Bradman was batting when I was a boy. Alas, not much survives from theose earliest pre-tape recording days, but when it does, hooray for the old disc and drum. The first live commentary you hear is one of Fanny Blankers-Loen totally hyphenating all the dried-milk opposition at Wembley in 1948, and the first voices that shriek through the crackly static like excitable schoolboys are the Aussie Max Robertson, the Canadian Stewart McPherson, and that most perfect plummy Englishman, John Snagge ('I can't tell who's leading, it's either Oxford or Cambridge!')

158

Like the man said, 'Come in, Barry.' Shame, no Barrington-Dalby inter-rounders seem to have survived (*'Both boys stood toe to toe in a classical exhibition . . .'* was all very well when you'd heard, moments before, the stricken, belching grunt of a poor sod as he took another wallop in the solar plexus while Eamonn or Stewart was taking a rare breath at the ringside). From Barrington-Dalby to Stuart Hall, it is all here, posteritied and unchangeable.

The tape ends, appropriately, with a recent match report by Stuart Hall from Manchester: 'So, chilled with expectation, the faithful supplicants arrive at the shrine, and . . . as the snow-flakes whirl in the wind, United immediately generate a hot rhythm.' *Deedum deedah*, indeed, though as Butler says, this unassailably longest running sports programme of all is (with 1,500 editions) 'nimbler on its feet, more flexible, broader based and certainly a touch breezier than it was in 1948; but unmistakably it is a chip off the old block.' The format endures.

Forty winters ago, Raymond Glendenning saw the red light, tweaked his soup-strainer moustache, and said: 'Hello there, sports fans, and welcome to *Sports Report*, a weekly programme on the air at this time every Saturday, with a roving microphone to bring you not only the football results, but up-to-the-minute accounts of the major sporting fixtures from all parts of the country, and an ''open'' microphone to bring into your home, wherever you may be, a half-hour coverage of sport, wherever it may be taking place. How well we have succeeded in this very first edition, you will be able to judge after the next 29 minutes . . .'

Or forty years, as the case may be. As the school song says, *'Forty years on, this field will ring again and again with the tramp of the twenty-two men'*. Quite so.

From Bradman by Arlott, and Turpin by Barrington-Dalby, all down the years to Maradona's infamous goal (by the *hand of God*) described so memorably, as it happened, by Butler himself: 'Shilton is incensed . . . and the ball bounces with a little sigh of apology into the English net.'

The founder of the feast and onlie begetter was Angus Mackay, an Edinburgh journalist who joined the Corporation in 1936. He ran the show severely and commandingly from 1948 till the early Seventies and had, say, Stuart Hall offered him one of his larks' tongue reports back in the old days, writes Butler,

'Then the lean Scot with slicked hair, trim moustache and eyes of wrath, would almost certinly have reached him in seconds, wherever he was, and garrotted him on the spot.'

The book, to all intents, is an affectionate memoir of Mackay from all his 5 o'clock *alumni*. Of many good tales, I enjoyed particularly Peter Bromley's from a long ago Cheltenham when Mackay ordered a one-and-a-half minute piece from the racing commentator looking forward to the imminent Gold Cup. However, the race before it, the Champion Hurdle, provided what they thought on the course to be a good little story (won by a one-eyed nag and ridden by an amateur), so Bromley mentioned this for twenty seconds before going on to deal with the Gold Cup. Next day he received a rocket from Mackay for departing from his brief, after which the following correspondence resulted:

Memo to A. Mackay
From: P. Bromley

I acknowledge that I departed from my brief and spoke for 0'20" on the Champion Hurdle, and apologise if it spoilt the impact of the piece about the Gold Cup. however, I would like to point out that:
1. I was convinced there was a news story in the Champion Hurdle.
2. I suggested the 20 secs on the Champion Hurdle to the racing producer before the programme and he accepted it.
3. I did not over-run.
4. I *did* tip the winner of the Gold Cup.

Memo: to P. Bromley
From: A. Mackay

1. *We* weren't.
2. He didn't.
3. You're not expected to.
4. You are expected to.

Dee diddley dum dee-daaah!

Oh, and It's a Beautiful Catch!

Vernon Scannell, broken-nosed poet and lyrical pugilist, has laboured long in his library to present Oxford University Press with a rich anthology of *Sporting Literature*. It is a comparatively big book at 354 pages, and certainly an enjoyable little triumph as the anthologist jabs and weaves and piles up points, always moving nicely and familiarly, but occasionally stopping you in your tracks with a cracking one-two.

That brilliant Argentinian oarsman of a decade or so ago, Alberto Demiddi, once solemnly said to me in a seeming boast, 'I am the greatest single skuller in South America.' Then a pause, and a sudden wide grin, and, 'I am the *only* single skuller in South America!' Same with Scannell's new collection; it is not so much the best of its type, but the only one I have come across by a student with so broad a reading-list and so enthusiastic a range. It is very good to be going on with and, to my mind, anyone seeking to do better will have to burn a heck of a lot of flickering night-light oil.

A number of sports, of course, have been decently looked after by a string of either fast-buck or slow-browsing anthologists — notably cricket, with a fair few on golf and fishing and matters equine (and a rewarding new collection on rugby union, by the way, from David Parry-Jones). Scannell culls and collates the lot of them, but there is no question of a cribbing job — indeed, in many ways, this new catch shows up a number of the one-sport specialists for the hoary hundrum hoarders they are.

The Mantovani effect is the one to strive for in this task — old ones, new ones, loved ones, neglected ones. That good chap, Anon, naturally leads Scannell's index of authors, followed by Arlott and Auden, and then, in a torrent of delights, a whole alphabet of brand-new discoveries (to me, anyway), speckled about among the friendly familiars — Bennett, Betjeman and Byron, Cardus and Coleridge, Darwin, Dickens and Doyle, Egan and Hazlitt, Larkin and London, Macdonell and Newbolt, Pepys and Pope, Sillitoe and Storey, Surtees, Synge, Walton, Wodehouse and Yeats.

It always jars when the anthologist dots his own stuff about his published collection, leaving the reader to think that either they were included by mistake when he was gathering up his papers to take them to the publisher and, although he was mighty embarrassed about it, it was now too late to ditch them barring a reprint; or that the fellow has such a high opinion of himself that he feels he has a right to proudly prop up his own index, a self-preening *Bloggins, Joe* sitting smarmily between *Blake, Wm, and Byron, Ld.* Usually, the answer is, I'm afraid, that if a hack is willing to do the work for the pittance, then the publisher is happy to turn a blind eye to the perk of self-promotion.

Fearing such charges, Scannell comes out punching from the opening bell, Honeyghan — intent to get in his retaliation first, and well he might recall with premonitory trepidation a review of *A Little Treasury of Modern Poetry*, compiled by an American, Oscar Williams. A compatriot, the critic and poet, Randall Jarrell, in his assessment of the book, mentioned that Oscar Williams had included nine (presumably treasurable) poems of his own, compared with five from the pen of Thomas Hardy. 'It takes a lot of courage to like your own poetry almost twice as well as Hardy's,' reflected Jarrell.

Scannell excuses himself, and allowably I suppose, for the inclusion of three of his own pieces, 'not because I like them twice as well, or even half as well, as anyone else's, but because they deal with a sport about which I know quite a lot (I am willing to take a substantial bet that I am the only published poet who has owned a professional boxer's licence from the British Boxing Board of Control), and I hope that something of this knowledge of a game, the true nature of which few people who have not practised it even begin to understand, will convey to the reader at least some sense of authenticity. In other words, 'Big Frank' Scannell's 'know what I mean, 'arry?', as in:

The same with poets: they must train,
Practise metre's footwork, learn
The old iambic left and right,
To change the pace and how to hold
The big punch till the proper time,
Jab away with accurate rhyme;
Adapt the style or be knocked cold.

As you would expect, in fact, Scannell's boxing selection is outstanding. I bet his offcuts and rejects in that section would tot up to another whole volume. That gruesome roped-off square they misname a 'ring' has inspired some classically ripe overwriting all down the centuries — and even today, the muscular adjectives on fight-night still show no signs of becoming battle weary. For the rest, Scannell's net is weighty, wide and handsome. He takes the term *sport* to include all those physical or non-sedentary activities which involve some kind of competition or the pursuit of a quarry. The lot, in fact, though with apologies to motor-racing or skiing — not because he is indifferent to the attractions of the neglected sport, but simply because he found no literature of any real merit which was suitable for anthologizing. Shame, for a new edition he might look up some of the marvellous motoring metaphor-necklaces strung together by the Americans, Posey and Moses, or even that very fast and capable first-hand reporter, Jackie Stewart.

He makes amends for his omission of skiing with some quite electrifying stuff on mountaineering — which is the same hairy thing anyway, except slower, downhill, and on slats. Or that's the general idea — sometimes it's the other way around, as in this, from Edward Whymper's *Scrambles Amongst the Alps*, when the daredevil Victorian nut notes his 200-ft fall, head first and in seven or eight bounces, as he ricocheted down the icy rocks of the Col du Lion: 'I was perfectly conscious, and felt each blow; but, like a patient under chloroform, experienced no pain. Each blow was, naturally, more severe than that which preceded it, and I distinctly remember thinking, "Well, if the next is harder still, that will be the end!" Like persons who have been rescued from drowning, I remember that the recollection of a multitude of things rushed through my head, many of them trivialities or absurdities which had been forgotten long before; and, more remarkable, this bounding through space did not feel disagreeable. But I think that in no very great distance more, consciousness, as well as sensation, would have been lost, and upon that I base my belief, improbable as it seems, that death by a fall from a great height is as painless as end as can be experienced.'

Thanks, Ed, I feel better for that.

Arnold Lunn, grand old man of the mountains, chillingly pursues the same. His rapid descent was a mere hundred feet, with only four bone-crunching bounces: '. . . and each time I somersaulted off into space I simply felt the same angry disappointment that my fall had not finally been checked. An impression of the mountain apparently hanging upside down in the sky etched itself in my mind. I remember keen disappointment every time I struck the rock and failed to stop, but perhaps the basic reaction was one of indignation, almost of injured vanity. *"You can't do this to me . . . YOU CAN'T DO THIS TO ME!"*

'If the last enemy is death, the last friend and ally is vanity. The vanity motive, so much more important in history than the profit motive, persists in the most discouraging circumstances.'

Dear Arnie, surely the world's most philosophical fall guy.

But such nightmares sidetrack. So, too, does this whole book, for the fact is, almost every page in this grand get-together diverts. As a bedside book, it's an indipper in the Dilley class — pithy and quick, sometimes lulling, sometimes surprising, always deserving of attention. And, by the nature of our calendar of sports, always seasonal. It deserves to be still selling well at Christmas — but in the meantime, with the rugger hearties preparing to do (probably) grievous bodily harm to their first-ever World Cup, how's this on the pleasures of rugby, from wimpish Wupert Brooke:

When I first played I nearly died,
The bitter memory still rankles –
They formed a scrum with me inside!
Some kicked the ball and some my ankles,
I did not like the game at all.
Yet, after all the harm they'd done me,
Whenever I came near the ball
They knocked me down and stood upon me.

But rugger be damned for a sixmonth! For here comes summer — as Mr Kipling quoth:

Thank God who made the British Isles
And taught me how to play,
I do not worship crocodiles,
Or bow the knee to clay!
Give me a willow wand and I

With hide and cork and twine
From century to century
Will gambol round my shrine.

So into the nets, my boys! Hooray, hooray! Hurry, hurry, while stocks last.

Mad Dogs and Businessmen

We are in the middle of 'The Season', and any genteel, self-respecting Brit (who hadn't already hotfoot an escape from the election) is heading fast for faraway hills. Things are not what they used to be for the price of a rented suit. The languid days when it was in to be out and about are long gone. The six weeks or so that starts with, I suppose, the Chelsea Flower Show or the grey-brick May Balls and ends with the last hoorays at Henley or Wimbledon, or the dying screech at Glyndebourne, has now, alas, been lock, stock and barrelled by City sponsors and big business. And business is business. Imperceptibly through the 1980s, Mrs Thatcher's brave new world of macho money has turned England's timeless, grand and stately old summer into a corporate charabanc outing. 'On the ball, City,' is a sporting chant with a singular difference.

See all the small ads in the personal columns this month: *Desperately Needed* — two tickets for . . . Ascot, Wimbledon, Glyndebourne, wherever. Not inserted by genuine sporty or operatic buffs, nor even these days by *Psst, 'oo's gotta spare?* spivs. The plaintive appeals are paid for by company liaison officers whose miserable jobs are on the line unless they can lay their hands on 'just the two', so their managing director can wine and dine some uncomprehending Johnnies, Japs or Germans at the big one. These corporate upstarts and foreigners presume they are muscling in on the age-old traditions of the English at play. They aren't, not any more they aren't. *Real* Englishmen don't eat strawberries any more.

Cringe, if you have to, at Royal Ascot next week. The poor Queen still has to, bless her, as her once favourite paddock in her

165

Castle's very back garden is taken over by the new jet-set's frightful, freebie Phils and their mindless millineried molls, who know not a jot of difference between a fetlock and the formbook. They are only there for the gear. And to do a deal or three.

Even modern founder of the faith, the *Daily Mail's* Nigel Dempster, has run shrieking from his own recent creation. He used to host a party for over 130 in the roped-off car-park, catered by Scott's, the Mount Street restaurant, but last year he told his readers he would in future be watching from home on television: 'Ascot is just rabble everywhere nowadays . . . just a great social-climbing gathering and it's just ludicrous. You can't walk anywhere because there's no room. If you get up off a seat, someone else sits on it . . . Even Dukes don't go any more because they don't want to be in a freak show.'

In olden days, The Season was dropped into England's high summer calendar as if ordained by heaven. It was a cloudless, daisy-fresh dalliance meant to restate Victorian virtues to colonizers home on leave from administering the Empire. In between a month's steamboat sailing from India or Africa was six weeks of socializing calm on the manicured lawns of Blighty. Chelsea for the blooms, Lord's for the second Test, or the Gents v Players; regal Royal Ascot; and they'd have a day off before the challenge round finals at Wimbledon, so everyone could take in Eton v Harrow at Marylebone. It re-fired faith in Mother England, and thus all went well with ye world.

Obliteration by big bucks has been as sudden as it is total. I have been reading Simon Brett's collection for his *Faber Book of Diaries* (fairly tasty as curate's eggs go, but why no ballgame sport? Even a couple of cricketers' journals by such as Gibb, Relf or Roebuck would have been well worth scissoring, I'd have thought). In the early summer of 1954, Frances Partridge exactly catches the mood of The Season's olde tyme timelessness: '. . . crowds of variously elegant and dandified young men, many wearing beautiful snow-white flannels, straw hats and huge buttonholes. A great feeling of youth, high spirits and pro-miscuous élan; also a lot of pretty girls with peach-like complexions and ugly clothes. Drizzle fell sparsely, the river glittered like tin under a grey sky flaming with sunlight at the horizon; the races created intermittent moments of excitement and roars of ''House! House!'' like a cheerful dog barking. Ralph wore his Leander tie, and in the boat-house we saw an oar with his name painted on it. An afternoon of youthful glamour and gaiety.'

In 1987, alas, while the old, leisurely Thames still amiably twitters by, the men in the marquees on the bank laugh not with glamour or gaiety. They are dressed the part by the brothers Moss, and they throw not a glance as the oarsmen pass by with rhythmic, symmetrical grace. Having been rude to their wretched over-dressed wives, and the waiters, they guffaw down another brandy or two, before resorting, rudespeak, to their Vodafones. *Get me Zurich, and pronto!* A day without a deal is not a day that dawned. Relentlessly, the Thames-side tents of such as Barclays and Shell, the Norwich Union and Plessey, are gathering on the other bank at Henley and, all too soon, will be swamping the Stewards' Enclosure itself. You mark my words, business is business — and business is booming. The Battle of Plessey indeed. The client is England's new cosseted king.

Witness Wimbledon: the tennis tournament has been totally ransacked and routed by the corporate corps. Simply, by the beginning of the second week of the fortnight's Championships, there will be more of mammon's marquees on the grounds of the All-England Club than there will be players still competing. Last year, there were 47 of them, each with their own big top, and corded carpet, and Renta potplant, and cringing waiters and champagne corks and strawberries to follow. Wimbledon has been won in straight sets these past few years by ICI, and BAT, and IMG, and BP, and IBM and all that lot. Literally, they surround the tennis courts. The forementioned alphabetical conglomerates press their canvas cafeterias hard on to the very stop-netting of the prestigious Court 14 itself. The slightly smaller-fry dish up prawn cocktails to their arriviste clientele in a tented village, behind the BBC ops-room, on the old cricket pitch at Aorangi Park; and the really *nouveau* companies with pretensions — who still call clients, customers — make do on the golf club car-park. Game, set and match.

There is a helipad somewhere. Last year, early one morning, I joined the all-night queue as the pavement-sleeping, bleary-blanketed, tennis-loving *hoi polloi* were waking up and crossing fingers they might get in to see some decent sport. This was one hippie army the establishment of commerce was not going to move on. For it proved the very point of their privilege, money and access. Them and Us. The Havenots and the Freebie Folk.

The huddled masses in their queue straggled down the South-fields Road. The gates don't officially open for them till noon — and a Centre Court view is out of the question anyway — but by mid-morning the choppers are clattering in over them, the occupants scornfully looking down at the bedraggled rabble. This different breed of men (and their molls) have been flown in from Berlin or Bonn, or even Birmingham, Milan, Madrid, or even Manchester. They have an assured seat on Centre Court, though, of course, they need not be able to differentiate between a backhand pass and a tennis elbow.

The tennis begins. *Ping . . . pong . . . plunk . . . plick . . . Thirtay-Fortay! New balls, please!* and all that stuff. Still, half the seats are empty. But if you cup your hand to an ear, you can, between the oohs and aahs and smatters of handclaps, catch on the wind the tinkle of glass and the guffawing belches and farts of privilege. In the canvas palaces, the captains of industry have finished guzzling, have put the Vodafone briefly on 'hold', and are preparing for their parade.

Out they come at last, a bulbous, wet-chomped cheroot in one hand, and, invariably, a parasoled Poll in the other. (It's one thing to be the client of a captain of industry: it's their dimwit dolls I feel sorry for.) The sad, swanks' parade has them stepping briefly and blinking into the real world of unshaded sunlight, sweaty armpits and concourse crush — just a couple of hundred yards (unless you're a johnny-come-lately from the golf-course tents) till they make their reserved seats at Centre Court. They stare, uncomprehending, at, say, half an hour's tennis — before they nudge their mournful, mascara'd mates, and suggest it is surely time for tea.

So back, haughty, through the harassed throng to their tented sanctuary. Three large brandies, and the freebie is done for another day. The helipad is humming — and the client liaison officer loosens his tie. He has kept his job for another season.

Ah, The Season. Back to Brett's diary selection, and a portent. Perhaps there is nothing new under the sun of an English summer. Nigel Dempster's world-weary predecessor was Charles Greville, who took himself early to bed on the night of July 3, 1838, to write: 'Was at the Ball at Court to which hundreds would have given hundreds to go, and from which I would have gladly stayed away: all was *very brilliant, and very tiresome.*'

It is, verily, the season for cynicism.

168

Hooray Henley

Pull your finger out, Clare! C'mon Jesus, f'Chrissakes! Trin-Trin-Trin-Trin-Trinity! Oh, top hole, Tradesmen! Well rowed, Balliol!
The hollers and heaves and hoorays of Henley will have less of a domestic Oxbridge ring about them this year. It will be even more of a global gathering of the clan down by the riverside this week, for the old regatta plays pipe-opener to the busiest, most rowlocking summer that Britain's oarsmen have ever staged. The fellows in their badged, shrunken, prepschool caps, and striped and straight-jacketed wetbob blazers, are disembarking from all points — for the week on the Thames is being followed fast by the matey Commonwealth Games, which reintroduces rowing into its programme, and the high-powered World Championships at Nottingham in August.

If you tip your boater to Henley's pastoral anachronisms, and then proceed to the steely-eyed, unsmiling, bigtime stuff at Nottingham, you will get a fair idea of the ruthless competitive advance of modern sport. Henley is a joke. But a jolly nice joke. If gracious Olde Englande is dead and buried, it is certainly not forgotten at Henley. The sponsors' marquees for the *nouveaux* sergeants of industry are kept well out of sight and on the far bank at Henley.

The outside world cannot gate-crash the Stewards' Enclosure. You cannot even take in your trannie to keep in touch with the Test score. 'Is that a portable wireless receiver?' asked a spotty young upper-crust Fogey, who was manning the gate last year. 'No, it's me trannie,' I said. 'This,' he sneered, 'is a portable wireless receiver. Please leave it in that tent with those confiscated perambulators.' Babies' pushchairs, I gathered, were treated with even more scorn than radios at Henley, though once inside I did see a few senile, slack-chinned old buffers being wheeled around in wheelchairs. Most of them looked like one of those characters Robert Morley might play in his grandest moods of acting. At Henley, wheelchairs are not perambulators.

No radios. No babies. Nor is Henley too keen on women who

might want to be something other than decorative, parasoled appendages in pastel-printed frocks. Rowing is a fine sport for women and they have a long history of being good at it. In the Olympics, they now row the same, gut-gasping distances as men. Not at Henley, they don't. The Stewards allowed 'experimental' races by girls at Henley in 1981 and '82, but obviously did not like what they saw and fast reimposed their 140-year-old ban, saying there was no room in the Regatta's over-crowded programme. Oh yeah! They have this year upped their 'week' from four days to five — but still no women can row down the sacred sexists' stretch of stream. The only happily-tolerated woman at Henley was Ivy Batty, who, a couple of years ago, celebrated her silver jubilee as caretaker of the ladies' loo.

Kingston Rowing Club still smarts from the severe reprimand it received from the Stewards eight years ago, when it sent in an entry for the Double Skulls in the names of A. Hohl and P. Bird. At the starting line they were discovered to be the maiden names of the leading British women's crew of the day, Mrs Astrid Ayling and Mrs Pauline Hart. The blazered Robert Morleys were not amused.

Women, petite and demure, are allowed to cox, of course, and one or two have steered Boat Race crews recently. But a certain type of gent cannot stomach the idea of a gel pulling an oar. At Henley, one of the oldest races is the Ladies' Challenge Plate, first rowed in 1845, but it is definitely rowed by men, though I can understand the Dublin sub-editor on the Irish Times who once headlined a Trinity College victory in the Ladies' Plate with TRINITY GIRLS WIN HENLEY PRIZE.

Henley's male chauvinists, mind you, could well feel vindicated when they witness the sweat-soaked, straining women sploshing and grunting up the course next month in the 1986 World Championships. Such competitive dynamism, to be sure, might well have surprised Lucille Eaton Hill, who in 1903 published in *Athletics and Out-Door Sports for Women*: 'The physical benefits which women derive from rowing cannot be exaggerated, provided they are willing to master the rudiments of the sport — for one must strive for good form, deep breathing, strength of back and chest, and wear no tight or stiff clothing about the waist. Correct rowing induces an erect carriage and finely poised head, a full chest and well-

170

placed shoulders. Incorrect rowing disturbs all harmony of the figure. One can row one's self round-shouldered as easily as erect!'

C'mon, Clare, pull your finger out! Settle down, Lady Margaret, and get stuck in!

It must be said, however, that Henley's male preserve has, over the century, helped foster the image of the dotty little woman. The girls with their pastel parasols this week will look as dishy as ever, but, for most of them, the actual rowing will get in the way of a jolly good day out. They will not have a clue — nor will they be expected to have — about the real object of the exercise.

My favourite line from an uncomprehending woman, on being told a certain race had finished in a dead heat, remains 'A dead heat? How awfully dull.'

The Oxbridge colleges and the public schools still make up the bulk of entries at Henley. The clans gather — Eton, Radley, Bedford, Belmont, Shrewsbury . . . At times, the whole shindig is no more than an extended Old Boys' reunion. Particular school rivalries are carried on, summer after summer, as though they were founded in pre-history. Some schools consider their rowing VIII far higher than their cricket XI. Some years ago, in *The Field*, the writer Jeremy Alexander recalled his schooldays at Shrewsbury: 'As for the school eight, they were gods or thought they were, except when they lost in the Princess Elizabeth Cup to Tiffin. At that stage, Tiffin, subsequently recognized as a rowing force to be reckoned with, were almost unheard of. When the school went to first lesson next morning not a chair was in the classrooms. Under cover of darkness 500 of them had been removed to the 1st XI cricket field where they were set out to spell in monster capitals, TIFFIN. It was a remarkable operation which, incidentally, the sternest inquest never solved. It was man's revenge, to bring the gods down a peg or eight. If they wanted to swagger in their special treatment they had better not lose like that.'

The weather's bound to be balmy. The girls will be as gorgeously refreshing as the Pimm's and the Plymouth pink gins. The skullers skull, the skiffers skiff, and all the time the eightsomes reel on with symmetrical, rhythmic grace, past Temple and Fawley, Phyllis and Remenham Rectory.

Last year, an American arrived in a brand new, $1,000 denim

suit from Brooks Bros. 'Sorry, sir,' sneered my snotty Fogey, barring his way, 'no jeans!' He was probably imprisoned in the place they kept the confiscated perambulators — as well as my trannie. By tea-time, I was wondering how the cricket was going, and muttered such a thought in the Members' marquee. 'The Test?' replied a Robert Morley next to me, 'the Test's a river for fishin' in, not for rowin' on.'

If you can't beat 'em, and all that. *C'mon Jesus, f'Chrissakes!*

Words of Wisden

Words of Wisden

Some scholars have pronounced the year of our Lord's, 1864, to be the very crucial founding one for that love-'n'-marriage, horse-'n'-carriage, salt-'n'-pepper pairing known as Cricket-'n'-Englishness. Well, that year saw the first, generally-accepted County Champions (Surrey); overarm bowling was allowed for the first time and, in spite of it, a 15-year-old Bristolian with no more than baby's-bottom fluff on his chin, scored a clinkingly precocious century at Brighton. His name was Willie Grace. It was also the year that Wisden was first published.

The almanack which was to become, at one and the same time, the game's veriest old and new Testament, was brought out that year by a tiny, former spin-bowler from Sussex, John Wisden, who had set up stall as a corner-shop tobacconist in London's Leicester Square. Down the road, the much more important Lillywhite's store was boasting the capital's 'most superior foreign cigars' as well as 'unrivalled shag' — and also publishing a successful annual called *The Young Cricketers' Guide*. As we all know, it did not, for long, remain the best of such sellers.

Including 'Little John', the bible has had only, appropriately, eleven editors. The twelfth man can be introduced with the 124th edition. He is Graeme Wright, a placid, thoughtful, comradely and (obviously) meticulous New Zealander in his early forties. He 'learned' the almanack's tabulations and texts by being proof-reader on the 1978 and '79 editions and thereafter was assistant editor to John Woodcock who, in a comparatively short stewardship, unravelled a few straggly, flapping strings and tied them neatly into the second half of the century, and gingered up the traditional *Notes* to re-assume their place as the quirky and trenchant annual manifesto for the innate goodness and charms of the game.

Since Wisden himself, Wright may be the first editor of the now twelve apostles who would not describe himself as 'a Fleet Street man'. Sixteen years after the little spin-bowling tobacconist's first slim volume — opening sentence, '*Jan 1st, British Museum Closed,*' and, last, '*Tom Brett is the fastest and straightest underhand bowler ever known*' — three brothers, called Pardon, founded the Fleet Street Cricket Reporting Agency; and seven years later, exactly a century ago this spring, one of them, Charles, became editor of *Wisden*, when the firm added the book to its 'list' of sporting handbooks. Then brother Sydney remained in charge from 1891 till he died in harness, checking the averages of the 1926 edition. By then, it was an institution round the whole Empire.

Four other partners continued the line, and when Hubert Preston (who had first double-checked an errant leg-bye for the book in 1895) hung up his ear-trumpet for good in 1951, and pushed the chair over to his son, Norman, *Wisden's* style, accuracy and solemnity — and occasional, almost scary, well-aimed two-barrel damn-and-blast — was indelibly positioned in the English sub-culture. In 1977, three years before he died (in the saddle), the Pickwickian Norman Preston was awarded the MBE by Her Majesty. What did he do for a living? she asked him. 'I am, Ma'am, a General and Sporting Reporter,' replied the old man, proudly. Any relation of Victoria's must have approved.

Graeme Wright's cv makes him a very different kettle of collator. If his famous primrose dust-jacket stooped to an author's blurb, then his would read more like that of a typical blood-and-thunder crime-writer from the colonies — for he has come to *Wisden* by way of being a university drop-out, beachcomber, tobacco picker, wine harvester, coalman, lorry driver, ad-agency hack and ghost-writer. All such odd-jobbing fore-and-aft his arrival from new Zealand in the early 1970s. Then, after researching the Marshall Cavendish partwork, *The Game*, he spent three years at Queen Anne Press with responsibility for Rothmans Football Yearbook and the *Playfair* series, thus setting him up for cricket's harbinger of summer.

Wright's exalted predecessor, Woodcock, was already lording it up in the pressbox as correspondent of *The Times* when the 11-year-old Wright skipped school at St Patrick's, Wellington, to see the England touring team's Test match at the Basin

Reserve in 1955. The nipper far preferred rugby and athletics at the time, but now the wide little eyes saucered with delight — for that very first morning's introduction to real cricket was as witness to Tome Graveney's voluptuous century. Says Wright: 'I know it sounds ridiculously romantic and corny, but Graveney that morning showed me how cricket was more than just an athletic exercise. I was only 11, but I saw the beauty and grace of the game. And then, after Graveney, Johnny Wardle came out to field and he entertained the whole bank where I was sitting... and then Godfrey Evans took off to hold a legside catch, and suddenly I knew there was far more to cricket than just something on the school's games-playing syllabus.'

Four years later, in the Wellington bookshop, the boy came across his first copy of *Wisden*. That 1959 edition had the New Zealand captain, John Reid, as one of the Cricketers of the Year. That was the trigger. Reid had once coached young Wright at school. The rest was a book of revelations on cricket's big wide world out there. And now, less than three decades later, that same Kiwi sprog himself is guardian of the faith.

Like cricket itself, Wright is a small 'c' conservative. But liberal, refreshing and reforming with it. His introductory *Notes* are chummy and confident, crisp and concerned and unstuffy. His monograph on Botham — 'the guerrilla fighter impatient of discipline' — itself goes a long way towards recouping the hefty cover price of £15.95 (paperback, two quid cheaper), and Wright sets out his stall with chivvying counsel, sense and sensibility, on many of the legal and general headlines in the game. For instance, he signs off his impressive announcement of himself: 'It does concern me when, for example, I perceive a drift towards more limited-overs cricket . . . because if cricket does indeed reflect stages of social history, our lives too must become more and more restricted to a set number of permutations. When the American short story and baseball writer, Ring Lardner, died, Scott Fitzgerald wrote that "Ring moved in the company of a few dozen illiterates playing a boys' game. A boys' game with no more possibilities than a boy could muster. A game bounded by walls which kept out danger, change and adventure." Cricket must always be more than that. So much life.'

For the rest, the 1987 weightlifter's 1,296 pages include not only every wide or no-ball bowled in first-class cricket last year, every double-century or *not out . . . 0*, but also a cracking good catch of diverse essays — Marlar, hitting the spot triumphantly, on dear, lamented Laker; Bannister applauding friend Amiss; Warr's warmth for Sir Gubby; Swanton on the bicentenary; and Vic Marks with a current player's delightful reflection on times past and present, and how there might not be much that's really new under the suns of summer.

Plus, of course, reams and reams (and reams) of Frindall's facts and figs; and, as ever, a splendid Errata ('In 1973 Wisden stated on page 577 that Worcestershire were 202 all out v Somerset, not 202 for nine dec.' C'mon, Wright, we need a grip on that sort of thing). And, always, the most poignant *Obits* of the year, this time such sons of summer as Aird, Budd and Edrich, Fishlock, Laker and McCool — plus a mourned massed cortege of others, right down to the touching *'ROSE, ALFRED, who died in hospital at Worksop on June 21, aged 91, made one appearance for Derbyshire as a bat in 1924 and failed to score. He was asked to play again later that summer but replied he was too old for that class of cricket.'*

Nothing else; nor nothing needed. Aahh! *Wisden*; all of human life — and more.

One-Hit Wonders

There has been some monumentally daft pin-sticking over the century, to be sure, but it is hard to believe that any batch of England cricket selectors can have been so contrary, illogical, or downright eccentric than those serving recently under the chairmanship of Peter May. If he is on the look-out for a knighthood, this is an extremely dodgy way of going about it. If the cricket ultimately resulting from their deliberations has not been overbright, I suppose the selectorial vagaries themselves have at least been less than boring, and have considerably added to the gaiety of the nation in a perverted sort of way.

Up to the start of the first Test match against New Zealand at Lord's in July 1986 — and having shown evidence on only one occasion that one-day games can be different to five-dayers: Richards for French in the gloves — they had already chosen an astonishing 25 players since the end of aptly-named May, and were showing, as Matthew Engel despairingly wailed in *The Guardian*, 'no pattern, no underlying theory, no sense of direction: the classic hallmarks of a divided committee with a weak chairman.'

Mr May does not watch much first-class cricket. He is a busy man in the City. He says he 'takes soundings' round the county grounds, though I have yet to meet even an umpire he has telephoned. Since he gave up playing cricket, May might be a bit bored by watching the game, rather like one of his not-too-distant predecessors as chairman, Robert Walter Vivian 'Robbie' Robins. He (as Alec Bedser once told me) would turn up to the opening overs of a Test match for which he had chosen the team, be totally bored by noon, cadge a squint at a local paper to see what was on, 'and spend the afternoon at the local cinema, seeing the programme round twice and popping back to the ground for close-of-play.'

Of Mr May's eccentric picks this summer, I dare say poor Mark Benson, the Kent leftie, will not be the only one-off-wonder — that is, being chosen to the accompaniment of fond expectations and promises, and then being promptly discarded. Guillotined without fair trial.

Mind you, over the century, you could write a very large, very downbeat, book on the one-cap wonders of English Test cricket, starting with probably the most famous of all, old Fred Tate in 1902, whose solitary game saw him bowl like a drain, drop the crucial catch off the Australian maestro, Darling, and then, as last man in, get clean bowled with only four runs needed for victory.

Offhand — or, okay, with only the most passing of peeks into *Wisden* — there have been a lot of Test match players since Fred whose first was their last: Ken Smailes, Jack Durston, 'Father' Marriott, Jack MacBryan, Dennis Brookes, J.C. Clay, E.R. Wilson, Fred Price, Alan Wharton, Johnny Arnold, Harry Lee, and another father-of-his-son, Jim Parks Snr. Of the moderns, still intently determined to get out of the 'club' and catch Mr May's steely eye once more, are there any others than Andy Lloyd (whose wretchedly rotten luck was to zig into a Malcolm Marshall zagger), Paul Parker, Tony Pigott, Alan Butcher, and brave old Arnie Sidebottom, who bowled his boots off for Mr May last year (till blood seeped through them), and then was asked no more?

A comparatively horrendous run of results by England, in 1921, resulted in just as much panic by the selectors as now. In that summer, Durston was given the debutant's bum's-rush with the same speed as Dipper, Evans, Hardinge and Ducat. The latter, who also played soccer for England, forced his way back into the headlines when he died at the wicket at Lord's, in a wartime match, while shaping up to essay a leg-glance. *Wisden* records him as *not out 29*, but Benny Green, in his masterly anthology, reckons him, 'one of the few figures in history for whom the next ball was literally his dying thought.'

I once hit a four off a guy who had one cap for England. He was three years older than me too. When I was at Belmont Abbey junior school, we played Worcester Cathedral School. Peter Richardson, later to open for England, was captain of their 1st XI; his brother, Dick, was captain of the Colts. I was a la-di-da tyro with clean white pads: Dick was devilish fast. I almost broke-second-slip's kneecap with my first snick, which ricocheted for a one-bounce four. Next ball hit off, before spearing out both leg and middle. When he was picked for England a few years later, as a batsman in 1957, Dick went in No. 6 at 510 for 4. He laid about him spectacularly for 33 — but the Cambridge theological student, David Sheppard, was preferred for the next match and Dick never nudged a selector again.

My own county of Gloucester have had most of all single debs, and the further west you go, the worse it becomes: when Alan Jones won his one cap against the Rest of the World, Lord's later took it away from his as 'unofficial'. As well as Dipper in 1921, there's been Harry Smith, Charlie Parker, Reg Sinfield, Sam Cook and George Emmett — not to mention the Doctor's two brothers, E.M. and G.F., who were probably only chosen in the first place so they could carry W.G.'s clobber and buy the pork-pies at the Swindon buffet.

Emmett — dapper, dancing feet, whipcord-wristed on-drive, and sarn't-major-y Silvicrined hairstyle — dauntingly took Hutton's place in the Old Trafford murk against Lindwall and Miller in 1948. He made 0 and 1 and never had another postcard from Lord's. The year before had been a match better summer — for batsmen, that is. It was just Sam Cook's luck to be picked as a bowler — slow, very slow, left arm — on the Trent

179

Bridge Dunlopillo. When he packed his bag and left Bristol Temple Meads the night before, his aged spinning 'boss', Tom Goddard, advised him, 'There's still a last chance, Sam, to ring 'em up and say you're sick.' Such was the batsman's paradise at Nottingham, that when Sam was preferred to the established leg-spinner, Doug Wright, of Kent, he put his arm round the tyro and said, 'M'dear ol'Sam; rather you than me.' Cook was hit for 127 and never looked like taking a wicket. In the next seventeen seasons for Gloucester, he dismissed 1,618 batsmen, never got near the England side again — but continued to wear his England cap and blazer at every single opportunity.

And why not? Jack Martin, fast bowler for just one time of asking in the same match, probably did the same at Kent games, as, next year, did Alec Coxon, of Yorkshire, till he gave up the county grind. Years ago, I did a TV interview with Bill Grundy on the footballer, Pelé. The Brazilian mentioned he had met the Pope. Enquired the well-lunched Bill, in that puckish, questing style of his, 'You refer, of course, Mr Pelé, to Mr George Pope, the former Derbyshire all-rounder who had one game for England in 1947?' Pelé thought we were both mad.

Two Palmers made but the one pilgrimage each for England. Charles, donkey-droppist and later scholary President of MCC, played one match against the West Indies in 1953, made 22 and 0 and was entrusted with only five overs. Much the better player was Ken, the current Test match umpire. He was a sound bat and very capable seam and swing bowler for Somerset, who was coaching in Johannesburg in 1965 when he was called to the colours overnight and told to take the new ball with Ian Thomson, of Sussex, against South Africa in Port Elizabeth.

It was all too much for Fred Trueman, who had been dropped yet again by England from the tour and was picking up the odd copper on a charity trip to the Carribbean, organized by Rothmans cigarettes. When the English papers finally arrived in the West Indies, Fred went totally potty. He came out of his holiday hut brandishing *The Times*: 'Ah joost don't know what's goin' on out there. It must be t' end of t' world. There's Ian effin' Thomson and Kenny bleedin' Palmer openin' bowlin' f' England — and me out 'ere bowlin' f' ruddy cigarette coupons!'

If he goes on much longer, Mr May looks very capable of reviving the long established membership list. Fair enough on second thoughts — for it is a most respectable club.

Parting Shots

I had been nursing, uncharitably as it turns out, a mean-spirited little nag all summer that MCC were churlishly going to 'drop' Ian Botham and David Gower from their Gala XI to play the Rest of the World in the bicentenary Test: Gower, because he has cavalierly decided on a winter sabbatical from international cricket; and Botham, well, because he is Botham and authority would have passionately loved to summon the nerve to get in the last V-sign for themselves ere he departs to bomb out Brisbane.

But, glory be, they have both survived for this one final curtain call and last rousing encore. The power and the glory. They have been my two most favourite cricketers through the last ten years of turmoil — and I still find it ridiculous, as well as astonishing, when I count the times I have been the only drunk defending their style, record and sheer sporting *hooraymanship*, in dingy, low-lit, late-night bars around the world. Thin-lipped Puritans, especially when tipsy, do not like real men who are so generously profligate with their talents.

So it will be good to be at Lord's when the People have their say and, first Gower, and then Botham make their entrances and their last exit. Whatever they score, nothing less than a raucously prolonged standing ovation will do. As history will undoubtedly show, they have, between them, given us a truly privileged decade. Botham first played for England in 1977, Gower in 1978. They will both continue to play county cricket in English summers — but I have this irresistible hunch that their Test match record books will be firmly closed and locked this week. They are, to all intents, putting themselves out to grass.

Botham undoubtedly will take to Australia, and vice versa: they like guys who stroll off the beach to hit sixers in their sneakers. Gower's holiday will take in another few helter-skelters on the Cresta Run, a trip to the Winter Olympics at Calgary, and a cameraman's safari in East Africa. They will both report, refreshed, to their counties next spring — but by which time, surely, Gatting's England XI will have had a clearout and a brand-new look.

Where do they go, these sons of summer, when their nights draw in? It must be a devilishly difficult job for a superduper sports star to adjust to 'real' life when he's already crammed everything into just the third decade of his allotted seven-age span. Gower is 31 next April, Botham 32 in November. What follows now for these men who, as Spender had it, have 'travelled a short while toward the sun, and left the vivid air signed with honour'?

Once upon a time, old sporting heroes opened corner tobacconist shops and felt really grateful for it. Really ace operators chuntered on about their glory days — and how no modern could match up — on the radio: till the producer was changed and he'd bring in a new crop of more recent 'greats'. Likewise those with a newspaper 'column'. I remember John Snow, demon paceman and poet, saying as retirement approached that he had nightmares about being an umpire. (He's now a travel agent.) And Tony Greig saying the same about being an end-of-over summarizer on *Test Match Special*. (He's now a millionaire insurance broker for Kerry Packer, and a part-time TV meteorologist.)

It is impossible to imagine Gower or Botham as wireless wofflers; their game was innate, instinctive, off-the-cuff carefree, and never droningly analytical. (Talking of which, however, credit where due, and what a revelation this summer to have had such knowing, incisive, and enlightening contributions on both BBC television and radio from those two old seamin' swingers, pros who have really seen it all recently, Jack Bannister and Robin Jackman — no garbage, everything pared down and succinctly presented: thus enjoyment increased tenfold).

Some years ago, an insurance combine ran an advertising campaign, angled not so much on *Where are they now?* but *Where will they be?* in twenty years when such-and-such a policy matures. It was accompanied by touched-up pictures showing the likes of Gower and Botham at fifty — balding, bloated and bleary.

I hope they made a lot of money from it, but it was a good campaign, I suppose, because I remember it. Now, a beer-gut can happen to any of us, but that apart (and without any evidence from either horse's mouth) I reckon both our two great cricketers will increase and multiply their status and their savings most handsomely once they finally hang up their bats in the belfry, or wherever it is they discard them. By his fiftieth birthday, I fancy David will be executive director of Europe's most upmarket travel agency, specializing in champagne trips to, well, the Cresta Run, the Winter Olympics, and East Africa safaris; plus a very select, say, Royally Appointed little wine business on the side. While Ian will be sporting director of the largest estate in Scotland, relieving Germans and Japs (and Pakistani princes) of extremely large wads of money in return for showing them how to shoot, fish, stalk, and drink better than they've ever done in their lives. He will only very occasionally be seen down south — when his superstar son, Liam, is rallying England at Twickenham or Lord's.

Different from the old days, though, when our leading professional sportsmen were treated by their game's amateur administrators to minimum wages as horny-handed toilers, disposable once they'd run their crowded hour about the stage. My all-time hall-of-famers from boyhood were Bruce Woodcock (now a Yorkshire pub keeper); Tom Graveney (former publican, now TV summarizer); Tommy Lawton (another lovely man, who's just had his first phone installed in his Nottingham council house); and Arthur Milton (last-ever of the 'double' internationals, and now a postman at Clifton in Bristol).

Not one of them moans for one moment that they were born a generation too early really to cash in on their talent. Graveney, remember, was dropped by England for ever, just because he played in a charity benefit match for £1,000 without permission. And what would Milton — England colours at both cricket and soccer — have earned today? A fortune. Or the maestro Lawton, if he'd been allowed to go to Barcelona? Or Woodcock, had he had the TV money and accountancy team that the touchingly inept, almost defenceless, Bruno has?

Most players these days who reach the very top in Britain's major sports — and stay free of injuries and in the selectors' good books for a longish span — should salt enough away to keep them out of the tobacconist's corner site. Since soccer's abolition of the maximum wage (£12 a week in the winter, £8 in the summer) over a quarter of a century ago, a number of footballers have even become millionaires. Most notably, there is Francis Lee, hunky barrel of an inside-forward in England's best-ever team of 1970, who fastened on to the soft tissue-paper boom of a decade ago and whose firm has now expanded into a multi-million empire; and his international colleague from Leeds, Paul Madeley, whose Superstores have grown from one outlet in Otley to a national, high street network.

But, steady on, kid, this ramble is too much, surmising on the millions that Gower and Botham are going to earn once they've left the big-time platform. For they are both still very much on it — downstage too, and as ever in the starring roles. And you've only got my (as you know) notably wayward hunch for it that this week's rousing ovation might mark THE END of their Test careers. If it were to be the sunset clip-clop over the credits, though, 'tis good it's at Lord's, where Gower's languid elegance has so often riddled even the crusty spirits of the Long Room members, and Botham's astonishing oomph and unbridled competitiveness has had the free seats on a roar at the Nursery End more times than you can remember.

They both made their Lord's Test debut on the same day — against Pakistan on June 15, 1978. Gower made a serene half-century, and Botham a blitzkrieg whole one in double-quick time (and then finished off the match with a peppery eight for 34 in 20 overs).

The so-different, but dynamic duo had stormed into our consciousness and were off and away — for ten short summers and ten long winters. Now, voluntarily, they are both cantering out to grass — neither quite realizing how very much they are going to be missed.

Following On

In over a century, there have not been as many Test cricketing chips off the old block as you might imagine in a pastime traditionally so family orientated. England can boast only six before the Cowdreys: the Townsends and Tates, Parkses,

Manns, Huttons and Hardstaffs. I'm bound to have forgotten somebody (don't all write in at once) but offhand, apart from Damien D'Oliveira of course, I can think only of those two delightful current Hampshire players, Tim Tremlett and Bobby Parks, who are in line to add to the list. The former, whose father was longtime and loved as Somerset's straight-driving captain, has already made the England 'B' team; and if Bobby was called upon to wear the gloves for England it would be a *Frindallus uniquus*, for both his father, Jim, and his grandfather, old J.H., were capped for King and country. What a player young Jim was when you think about it — chirpy, bristling, always grinning, as he held his free-flowing follow-through; though he was a bit of a long-stop at the end, in his youth he was a quite electrically good cover-point.

There is an intriguing parental anniversary with us this summer. Exactly 50 years ago, one of India's legendary all-rounders, Lala Amarnath, was sent home from the 1936 tour of England 'for disciplinary reasons'. This season his son, Mohinder, is touring as one of the senior members of Kapil Dev's side. At England's final Test match in 1982 at Kanpur, up in the northern plains, I sat next to Lala in the Press box. He was a flea-fit, sharp-eyed, laughing man in his seventies. When I asked him what he had done in England all those years ago, he just laughed all the more, but would divulge nothing.

The true story, I now learn, is still enmeshed in India's colonial princely politics of the time. When there were at least two outstanding and proven cricketers, capable of captaining that 1936 touring team, in Col C.K. Nayudu and the Nawab of Pataudi — or even the brilliant young Lala himself — it was contrived by the British administration to give the job to a myopic, bearded, plump little minor prince, Maharaj Kumar of Vizianagram. The Viceroy himself, Lord Willingdon, and a Major Brittain-Jones, representative of Rajputana on the Indian Board, felt princes should be encouraged as a bulwark against the rising tide of nationalism.

The tale is told by Mihir Bose in *The Maidan View* (Allen & Unwin), a genuinely original cricket book, for it can take only an Indian writer to re-align the perceptions, presumptions, and, sometimes, patronizing myths that have always clouded Indian cricket round the great wide world. The team was duly led by the Viceroy's Vizzy — well, as Bose says, 'not so much a team as a prince's retinue; Vizzy travelling with 36 items of personal luggage and two servants.' Major Brittain-Jones was Tour Manager.

It was soon evident that Vizzy — who had never played a single game of first-class cricket before — could not captain a coracle, let alone the All-India CC. Amarnath, the no-nonsense Punjabi, let his views be known about bowling changes, as well as the positions he was being put in the batting order. The Captain told the Manager and the Manager told the Viceroy. Amarnath (who had nevertheless managed 600 runs and 32 wickets thus far) was sent home in disgrace. Highly satisfactory Empire-wise for, as Bose surmises, 'the Government of India Act 1935 had just been enacted and Indians were being given greater powers, but such public displays of disunity in an Indian cricket team playing in England could be a handy weapon to use to answer Indian nationalists' cry for more freedom. If Indians couldn't manage a cricket team, how could they manage a whole country?'

I hope Mohinder gets a sackful of runs in England this summer. If only for Dad's sake. Vizzy, by the way, dropped all but one of the many catches that came his way at first slip in the three Test matches, and totalled 33 runs off the edge — but he was awarded a knighthood and elected an honorary life member of MCC.

Not that the Brits didn't know all about their own caste system. Only the year before, another son of a famous father had been unaccountably spirited into the England team because of his connections. D.C.H. Townsend (Winchester and Oxford) remains the last man to have played for England without ever playing for a first-class county. He got in on the strength of a century in the 'Varsity match, but he was out of his depth for England, totalling just 77 runs in six innings. He never did play county cricket, unlike his father, C.L., who had been a brilliant amateur prodigy for Gloucestershire and, briefly, England, at the turn of the century.

The oldest 'father of a son' was Fred Tate, one of the saddest figures of the legend — for he played in only one Test match which, they say, he lost single-handedly by getting out for nowt when he should have stayed in, and then dropping a sitter off the Aussie, Joe Darling, at the crucial end. That was at Old Trafford and at deep square-leg — 'both difficult places', as the kindly Robertson-Glasgow observed many years later. Fred came off the field that evening in 1902 knowing he would never play another Test. But, in tears, he told reporters, 'I've a little lad at home who'll make it all up for me.' And so it came to pass that Fred Tate lived to see young Maurice take 155 wickets for England, as well as one grand century — and 11 catches.

Old Joe and Young Joe came next. When he retired from cricket in 1927, Hardstaff Snr became a first-class umpire, but he had no prouder day when, a few years later, he was sent a wire demanding he stand down from the Test panel — for his son had been chosen to follow him in the England colours. Both, by all accounts, were laid-back, almost lyrical, summertime right-handers.

The two Manns, of the brewery family, were both amateur captains of England and both very decent attacking mid-order bats. They both captained MCC to series victories in South Africa with very strong sides but both were worth their places. When the bespectacled Springbok left-armer, 'Tufty' Mann, dismissed the England captain, John Arlott growlingly summed up on the wireless: 'Ah, a case of Mann's inhumanity to Mann.'

Nor did Richard Hutton let the illustrious name down when he was England's all-rounder — sandwiched between Dolly and Greig in the early Seventies. One time, Richard was playing at Lord's and, on his own admission, bowling most ineptly. At the end of the over, the stentorian PA announcer was heard to be clearing his throat at the microphone to introduce, as often happens, a famous player to appeal on behalf of somebody's benefit or whatever. After being savaged for several boundaries, poor Richard was trudging back to his fielding position when, suddenly, the stadium was enveloped by sound, as if from heaven itself: '*This is Sir Leonard Hutton speaking . . .*' Recalled Richard, 'I was suddenly panic-stricken with the appalling thought that I was about to receive a public admonishment from him for improper bowling . . . I stood breathless and prepared for the worst. What followed was an appeal by my father on behalf of John Murray's benefit fund.'

I'll tell you two things that Christopher Cowdrey can do better than his father — bowl and write. The young captain of Kent has recently brought out a refreshing and fizzy collection of reflections and essays called *Good Enough?* (Pelham), a title based on the text, 'I don't mind if I'm not as good as my father, as long as I'm good enough.' Why the book needed the Head of English at Tonbridge, Jonathan Smith, to keep butting in with asides, only the funk-ridden publishers know. Cowdrey's stuff, as you would expect, is full of vim and vigour, good cheer and opinioned insights. His good father's ghosted autobiography some years ago was, alas, the best bedside reading any insomniac could have prayed for, if you get my meaning.

When Chris took a wicket with his fourth ball in his first Test match, *père* Colin was listening on his car radio — and promptly drove up a one-way street. At home, after his police warning, Colin answered the phone. It was his son, gloatingly asking, 'Dad, how many Test wickets did you get?' And answer came there, 'None.' What a nice phonecall to make after twenty-eight years of waiting.

Away from the Manger

Christmas Day on a Friday means a full League soccer programme on Boxing Day, so at least a hint will be stirred, in the memories of those of a certain age, of the ghosts of the sub-culture past when Christmas morning itself afforded the opportunity to stomp up an appetite on the terraces while at home mother slaved at the hob. Vast crowds would turn up in the Forties and Fifties — even a total of 361,000 attended the wartime Christmas Day matches of 1943. It went without saying that the programmes were spattered with as many printer's blocks of holly as were available and the usual drawing of a football — that separated the list of the two sides on the middle pages — for this issue, only, took the form of a Christmas pud.

On a Christmas Day morning in the early 1950s, 49,000 watched Manchester United beat Sheffield United by 5-2, and in the *Guardian* next day, Donn Davies began his report: '"Ah'll noan grumble if hoo's nowt but bread and jam for tea,' boasted one elated United supporter on his way home for his meal, 'them were five o'nicest ah've seen 'i youn sin' Johnnie Morris took 'is 'ook."'

They were the best of times as well as, in a way I suppose, the worst. Now we never venture forth with the twirl of a striped muffler, but just sit like slobs, centrally heated and wined and dined by Tesco, and watch Julie Andrews warbling on he television. Even the Boxing Day fixtures are organized by computer, these days. In olden times, the Christmas day match was invariably a local derby. This year for heaven's sakes, poor old Liverpool have to go to Oxford, for instance, and glum Brum City all the way down to Plymouth. A handful have come out of the lucky dip with some neighbourly festive fixtures — Chelsea v QPR, Burnley v Rochdale, Hereford v Newport, Bury v Wigan, but not many.

One of the best Christmases I've had away from England was with the England cricket team to India half a dozen years ago. I went to Midnight Mass in the Cathedral at Delhi with the two wicket-keepers, Bob Taylor and Jack Richards. It was packed. The hymn singing was tremendous. All the carols; every one a winner. When the lilting air, 'Amazing Grace', came on I let rip in full throat the Portman Road anthem *Ipsw-ii-ch! Ipsw-ii-ch!* and nobody was any the wiser, but I felt warmly in touch with home and knew the Blues would be playing the Canaries about that time in their East Anglian derby. I could almost see the snowflakes feathering down into the cattle market against the raging beam of the arclights. Good, evocative local derbies, those. Alas, temporarily suspended, with Ipswich in the Second and Norwich (just) in the First. This year, Crystal Palace go to Ipswich and Norwich slog to Derby. Not the same sort of thing at all.

Christmas on a cricket tour is reasonably good fun. That tour to India will be remembered notably for the century by Geoffrey Boycott in the Delhi Test on Christmas Eve, during which he broke the all-time Test batting aggregate of 8,032 runs set by Sir Gary Sobers. The Yorkshireman was, understandably, reet chuffed, and though later that night he would sip only his ginseng tea in celebration, it did not stop us getting early into our Christmas present bottles — so much so that, well past midnight with Geoffrey long tucked up in bed with his bat and box, I found myself tipsily pushing under his door this drunken Christmas carol I had just amended in homage:

Hark! E'en Hindu Herald *sings*
Glory to the Yorkie King.

189

Peace on earth, 'cept Kapil's wild,
Geoff and History's reconciled.
Joyful all the nations rise
(E'en the Doctor in the skies).
With your morning toast proclaim,
'Boyc's the Best in All the Game.'

An hour or so later, even worse for wear, I corkscrewed along the corridor again to deliver the next carol:

We three tweaks of Orient are
Bedi, Venkat, Chandrasekhar.
We rejoice in, can we join in
Applause for y'Ayatollah?
Oh, Star of Wonder in bad light,
Star that wears White Rose so bright,
Hairpiece preening, sweatbands gleaming,
Surely He will soon be Knight?

Geoffrey took the drivel totally in his stride and after Christmas lunch with all the liquid trimmings, he was beating me hollow at golf on the course near the hotel when I had to retire — to curl up and sleep somewhere near the bunker on the fifth. In India, drunks can get out of practice. Even at Christmas.

It was a different matter on Mike Brearley's England tour to Australia a Christmas or two before. The eminent, head-boy captain had instituted, at the beginning of the trip, a revue committee to organize the Christmas party, and also decreed a fancy-dress parade. The novelty of that first one made it fun. Now, the players tediously hire their rags from theatrical costumiers simply for the photo call on Christmas morning. This year, mercifully for us but unluckily for the Fleet Street picture editors, the lads are being allowed home for a brief three-week holiday between Pakistan and New Zealand, so we are spared the posing.

Different in the old days. Ninety years ago, on Christmas Eve 1897, the England touring party to Australia had two days off from the cricket and — fancy dress, bah! — went up-country to shoot. The all-rounder, J.T. Hearne, kept a diary: 'Finished up by getting about 40 brace of snipe, one hare (very large), one blue crane and two very fine specimens of black snake and all of

190

us soaking wet through up to the knees. Poor Tom Richardson got a rare fright . . . I may say we were all walking in a most careless and reckless manner when Tom came across this brute within a foot of him and then he only saw it just as it shot up its head ready to strike. He says he cannot describe his feelings at that moment. However, he got back a few yards and gave him both barrels.'

What would one of Mr Murdoch's ghost-writers today have made of that sort of stuff? Or same day, two tours later, 1903, the diary kept this time by the Sussex bits-and-pieces bowler, Albert Relf: 'Very hot. Good morning in bed. Got up and went out about 11 am. Had good look round Melbourne. Crowds of people doing Xmas shopping. Received a few cards etc conveying compliments of the season. Spent a happy musical evening, and drank a bumper to those at home.'

A deservedly relaxing Christmas, for the day before Relf had 'had a good bowl, got four wickets, they could not play well enough to touch me.'

Thirty years later, the journalists were keeping the journals. On Christmas Eve, 1936, Gubby Allen's recorded England 2-0 up in the Tests, but Neville Cardus still feared the worst (rightly, they were to lose 2-3): 'The happy Christmas was a Mephistophelian preparation for the disillusionment of the New Year. I stood on the rocky edge called the "Gap", looking towards the sea. I saw the *Awatea* sail through the heads, glowing with rosy lights. The moon was a feather, and the Southern Cross a symbol of the night and the season of the year . . . The streets of Sydney twinkled welcome. In the crowded lounge of Ushers, a man came up to me and asked if I would have a drink. I thought it was very nice of him to be so quick with his congratulations. But apparently he was celebrating for another cause. "You are Neville Cardus?" he said, and when I said I was, he went on: "Well, here's to you. I've been looking for years for an uglier man than me, and you win easily!" '

Aussie put-downs, I suppose, don't change. At last year's fancy dress do for the England team, the doughty podge, Mike Gatting, led the parade dressed as a musketeer. He had to wear that, muttered one Australian journo to another, because it's the only three-syllable word he knows. 'No,' replied his mate, 'the fat man knows one other: *ham-bur-ger*!'

Lord's and Ladies

On July 26 1745, the *Reading Mercury* reported: 'The greatest cricket match that ever was played in the South part of England was on Friday, the 26th of last month, on Gosden Common, near Guildford, in Surrey, between eleven maids of Bramley and eleven maids of Hambleton, dressed all in white. The Bramley maids had blue ribbons and the Hambleton maids red ribbons on their heads. The Bramley girls got 119 notches and the Hambleton girls 127. There was of both sexes the greatest number that ever was seen on such an occasion. The girls bowled, batted, ran, and catched as well as most men could do in the game.'

On the very same patch of olde Englishe, sheep-cropped turf last Sunday — and in its usual, appealingly scatty, inexact way — the Women's Cricket Association celebrated the 241st anniversary of that first match with a re-enactment game between sides captained by two of the most stalwart current players, Jackie Court and Carole Hodges. 'Throughout the day,' said the advertisements, 'commemorative programmes will be available from suitably attired sellers.' They were expecting a goodly crowd, and let's hope the weather held.

The beribboned gala, however, hit spot on the diamond jubilee of the WCA itself. Sixty years ago a group of hockey playing 'gels' gathered for hols at the Park Hotel, near Malvern. There was Vera and Mildred, Rebecca and Audrey, Marjorie, Biddy and Beatrice. They did a bit of walking, a lot of laughing and larking — and played two days of cricket, one at Cheltenham Ladies' College, the other at Malvern boys' school. No scores were kept, but one of their diaries did pass into posterity that Rebecca Blaxland collided with a fence on the boundary edge and cut her lip something rotten.

The upshot was an autumn get-together a few months later in London when, on October 4, a quorum of 19 founded the Women's Cricket Association. Only a Miss Brown, of Cobham, was reported to have disagreed with the idea;

192

her reasons were not minuted.

Coincidentally, October 4 is an auspicious date for women's cricket. On the very same day, 93 years before that inaugural WCA meeting, the *Nottingham Review* had reported: 'Last week, at Sileby Feast, the women so far forgot themselves as to enter upon a game of cricket, and by their deportment as well as frequent applications to the tankard, they rendered themselves objects such as no husband, brother, parent, or lover could contemplate with any degree of satisfaction.'

There is more gentility about these days — though the fun remains. So does the Malvern Week, centred on Colwall, the village snug in the shadows of the humpy, plump, sea-monster roll of hills. I went there once a few midsummers past, and watched the gentle, gym-slipped cricket from a deckchair. And in the evenings, there was a very decent amount of beer drinking (but only in halves), and a great deal of the aforesaid larking. One night, the Test team even put on a concert, in which the in-jokes were as deviously mysterious as a Chandrasekhar googly. All the sketches in the Village Hall brought the house down, as if it was midnight in the dorm on Angela Brazil's last day of term. One of the show-stoppers, I remember, was when the game's senior all-rounder, Glynis Hullah, played Eamonn in an hilarious send-up of *Rachael Heyhoe-Flint - This Is Your Life*. Rachael responded in the necessary way with tears of surprise at every turn ('F'gawd's sakes, someone throw her a tissue!') and the script went something like:

Eamonn: At nine-and-a-half you saw your first high-class cricket match when you were taken to Edgbaston. And thus were your lifelong ambitions firmly implanted . . .
Rachael: Ooh, you dirty beast!

Later that year I accompanied Rachael's team on a tour to Malta where they played a number of games at the old colonial Marsa Club. They called themselves 'Flint's Bints'. After one match, I snogged the night away in the hotel disco with the side's round-the-wicket slow left-armer. It was better than having the last waltz with Derek Underwood, I'm telling you.

I am extremely partial to women's cricket. So was Robertson-Glasgow, best of all cricket essayists. He once reported a women's county match for the *Observer* and he was enchanted by the athletic trimness and the delicate shots and placement in the batting. But the fielding was deplorable: 'Perhaps it was the heat; yet this alone does not explain the garrulity of the slips, out-doing any post-prandial discussions among men. Nor am I convinced that the conversation turned solely on the artistry or eccentricities of the opposing batsmen, but rather, I fear, on hats and cookery, or other matters of personal adornment and reflection.'

Such magisterial male chauvinism was echoed by Sir Leonard Hutton when he was prevailed upon to play in a charity match against the England women's side at Chislehurst. The gallant old Yorkie Bart stood at first slip. The wicket-keeper was that endearing chatterbox, Brian Johnston. When Rachael came in to bat, the deadpan old deadbat knight gave a despairing stare to Johnston and muttered, 'Well, suppose it's like a man tryin' t'knit, ain't it?'

It is a notable jubilee they drank to at Guildford on Sunday. It is the same game as the men's — but a different one: women's cricket is much more subtle, sensual some might say; certainly graceful and often very skilful.

Once Miss Brown's unknown objections were V-signed back to Cobham those sixty years ago, the WCA got to grips at once. Within a few years an England women's team set sail for a tour to Australia. *The Times* saw them off with a warning: 'Do not forget that these women are, after all, women, and it does not seem quite nice to think that they are future mothers charged with a responsibility of setting an example of gentleness, refinement and restraint to the coming generation.' Two years later in 1937, before the Australians in turn left Sydney to tour England, their players were each presented with the set of rules: 'No member shall drink, smoke, or gamble. No girl may be accompanied by a man. On board ship no girl shall visit the Top Deck after dinner. The team shall retire to bed before 10 pm. The team will participate in all deck games.'

Matches were also played in New Zealand, who had formed a women's association only the year before in 1932. On receipt of a letter from England enquiring about the possibility of a tour, the cable winged back by return: 'Delighted . . . Can guarantee billets, entertainments, matches, but regret no travelling expenses.'

The men, it must be said, have continued to be pretty stuffy at

194

the thought of their very good game being played by girls, dammit. The male bastion at Lord's relented once to let the women play there, though next year they are allowing a jubilee match in their fixture list only if Middlesex get knocked out in the early Benson & Hedges Cup rounds. Snotty and ungenerous. Not much has really changed since Belloc's chauvinist run-te-tiddly –

I wish you'd speak to Mary, Nurse,
She's really getting worse and worse.
Just now when Tommy gave her out
She cried and then began to pout;
And then she tried to take the ball
Although she cannot bowl at all,
And now she's standing on the pitch,
The miserable little bitch!

Long since, they have learned to ignore the men. I hope they had a good day at Gosden. And, later, raised the other half to Vera and Mildred, Marjorie, Biddy and Beatrice et al.

Gale Force Windies

In the tiny Caribbean island of Antigua the other week, taxi-drivers were diverting their journeys — but not to show visitors the stately magnificence of the deep-water dockyard that Nelson built, nor even the sumptuous Clarence House, which was made by British masons for Prince William Henry two centuries ago. Top tourist attraction for taximen, these days, is Andy Roberts's spectacular deep-sea fishing boat. It is the very pride of the coracled fleet.

Caribbean Dick Whittingtons, in the last quarter of the twentieth century, characterize the handful of devilishly fast bowlers who have maintained the West Indies' pre-eminence in world cricket since the turn of the 1970s. Not even the most devoted of Marxists on the islands begrudge them their fortune, and certainly not their fame. In Barbados, they insist on every visitor making a pilgrimage to the beautiful home — appropriately, and comparatively, as tall as a Dallas skyscraper — that Joel Garner has built for himself, on the very same plot of scrubland where once stood the plyboard shack in which his mother brought him up. It is no new phenomenon. Why, didn't one of the West Indies' most electrically-charged fast bowlers, the grandson of a slave, Learie Constantine, become a QC at London's Middle Temple; a Governor of the BBC; Rector of St Andrews University; a Cabinet Minister in Trindad; and first Baron Constantine of Nelson and Maraval?

The difference now is that there are more of them about. They used to hunt in pairs — Constantine and Martindale, Hall and Griffith. Now, it is a relentlessly encircling quartet that savages the poor batsman. Turn and turnabout. Four apocalyptic headhunters. And why not? England would readily play four fast bowlers, if they had four decent ones. There is no legal stipulation about playing 11, if you so cared.

Bowling furious fast has suited the West Indian nature for almost a century — just as Indians have always enjoyed the arts of mystic spin bowling, and Celtic poets have always supped pints. When Lord Hawke's first English touring side island-hopped in 1897, they declined to play sides which included black men, at both Barbados and Demerara (now Guyana), but were obliged to in the then more multiracially advanced Trinidad. They played two matches there and lost them both. Pelham Warner, scion of a wealthy plantation family, cabled to *Wisden* — both prophetically and with a dashed fine, and surprising, lack of patronizing paternalism: 'The chief credit for victory rested with the two black bowlers, Woods and Cumberbatch, who between them took 39 wickets in the two matches. Woods bowls very fast with a somewhat low and slinging action. He is very straight and every now and then breaks back considerably. Cumberbatch, who is perhaps the better bowler of the two, is a medium-pace right hander. He breaks both ways and varies his pace with much judgment.'

By the by, he also added: 'The fielding of the Trinidad team was splendid. The black men are especially fine fielders: they throw very well and seldom miss a catch.'

Three years later, Pelham's elder brother, Aucher, included Woods (nicknamed 'Float'; his surname was chosen after hearing of the dashing exploits of the then Somerset captain,

196

Sammy Woods) in his team for a short tour to England. On June 28, 1900, they played Gloucestershire at Bristol. Woods had been kitted out with cricket boots for the first time in his life. They made him feel like he was tramping in concrete. Gloucester's crouching hitter, Jessop, sprang at him mercilessly, hitting an astonishing 157 in an hour, during which humiliation he approached his white-man captain at mid-on. 'Please, Mr Warner, sir, I can only bowl if I feel the pitch with my toe. Can I take my boots off?' Certainly not, my good man; this is England! 'Just for one over, sir; then I will get him out.' Out of the question, my good man, this is a first-class county!

Woods passed the new ball on to another Trinidadian, George John, who was built like a pocket battleship 'At the end of the day,' wrote C.L.R. James, 'he strode back like a man just beginning. Before almost every ball he was rolling up his sleeves like a man about to commit some long-premeditated act of violence . . . Many a poor batsman hit on the inside of the knee collapsed like a felled ox.' Malcolm Marshall's forerunner Constantine's buddy was Manny Martindale, another smallish man with a whippy ferocity. When Douglas Jardine's England team came back from Australia after the notorious Bodyline tour of Larwood & Co, Constantine and Martindale gave the English a dose of their own medicine — and the colonial masters did not like it one bit. In the first Test at Lord's, Martindale swept away the cream of England's top order, and at Old Trafford, he peppered Hammond with bouncers, before producing the sharpest of risers which split open the chin of the English champion. As he was being attended to, Hammond is said to have muttered, 'If this is what Test cricket has come to, I have had enough of it.'

Since when, successive England batsmen must have smiled wryly at that, as they have ducked and danced and dodged to miss the continued bombardment of screamers from the likes of Gilchrist, Hall, Griffith, Croft, Holding, Garner and Roberts. Plus many more from whence they came. Roberts, of course, has now retired to comparative luxury — as is testified by the clutch of tourists who are taken to see his fishing boat, whenever she lays moored off Antigua. Andy had also bowled in bare feet till he was seventeen. He was born in Urlins, a tiny fishing village, one of a family of fourteen. Fishing, of necessity, had to come before an apprenticeship in cricket. His father could teach him only about currents and eddies, potting lobster, netting snapper, and spiking marlin. It does one's heart good now to see him the most spectacular leader of the fleet.

When the England team left Barbados for Antigua, at the beginning of their tour a few weeks ago, I stayed behind for a couple of days to watch the reverberating inter-island match between Barbados and Jamaica. It was awesome in its warning for the English batsmen. Every other ball cruelly reared at the batsman's helmet. Three or four of them were badly dented. In four full days' cricket only four overs of spin bowling was seen. The crowd bayed as if at an execution. Tyburn stuff. In the end, the fires of even Holding, Patterson, and Walsh for Jamaica, burned not half as hot as those of Garner and Marshall of Barbados.

Marshall is the physical successor of John and Martindale — a slight, spring-heeled assassin with a gymnast's suppleness and a hurry to hurt. He slithers in off a short, dramatic run: everything is coiled to strike. He reintroduced himself to the English last week — and within ten minutes of the first International beginning in Jamaica, the horrific pictures of Mike Gatting's smashed nose were winging round the world (and another of the ball with the piece of bone in it). Marshall is building himself a lovely seaside villa in Barbados, and off the field, he is a popular cricketer in every dressing-room, with a particularly engaging and comradely giggle. Though don't tell that to Mrs Elaine Gatting.

Patterson is the tyro, long-legged and a mean gleam in his eye — like Croft, a predecessor at Lancashire who was also considered pretty ordinary when he played a few games for Lancashire a decade ago. But there's something about these home-fires burning

Holding and Garner showed they had at least one, last, lethal Test series in them. Holding, the athlete, retains that liquid grace in his approach and 'glad animal instinct' in his action that Frank Tyson once wrote about. On bouncing, his deliveries take on, still, a wicked, fizzing venom. Holding is the son of a Kingston builder, a middle-class charmer off the field. Garner is the A1 working-class hero of Barbados. He is 6ft 8ins tall and proportionately savage, with a chilling bouncer, a rotten rib-tickler, and an often unplayable yorker. At the Foundation School, Bridgetown, he was taught by

198

Manny Martindale, who once chinned Hammond.

And so the line goes on . . . the English quake, the crowd bays, the sleek, smart fishing boats are built, and the new masters design their mansions.

Quite right too.

Vital Statistics

Harbinger of spring these days is neither bird, bee, blossom, nor daffodil. You know that April has turned to May by the thud of cricket books on the morning doormat. There is another glut — large, small and medium. It is no accident that *Wisden*'s cover is primrose.

While *Wisden*'s 1,200-plus pages weigh in as the heavyweight champ, it is good to see again the appearance of the sprightly little flyweight *Playfair* annual. It has put in a lot of years now. As kids, we could not afford *Wisden*. In our satchels, in the filthy clutter alongside apple-cores, half-eaten sandwiches and an autograph book, was always a dog-eared *Playfair*. I fancy it is still the same — unless the comparatively recent, livelier, and more perky ('I adore classical ballet' — G. Boycott) *Cricketers' Who's Who* has superseded it for all but the true schoolboy swots.

Like *Wisden*, *Playfair* has also had a change of editor. Bill Frindall, BBC radio's 'bearded wonder' and the most ink-stained swot of them all, has taken over from Gordon Ross, who died suddenly at the beginning of the 1985 season after editing *Playfair* for thirty-two years. Ross was a spick and dapper ex-RAF type, always sprucely turned out and with a carnation in his buttonhole. An admin-man sort of journalist, more of a careers' master chap than the obsessed and obsessive maths teacher, Frindall. But Ross had a romantic edge. One of the last paragraphs he ever wrote was published posthumously in the *Journal* of the Cricket Society. It showed he had died content, for he had spent his last hours watching Middlesex v Worcestershire at his beloved Lord's (April 27, Kapil Dev 100): 'Of course I enjoy Test cricket, but perhaps in a strange and unrelated way I enjoy Lord's more when Middlesex are enjoying a three-day county game . . . where there is the peace we used to know, when you can drift round the old place, chatting to players, umpires, scorers, groundsmen, administrators, friends, acquaintances, even to perfect strangers. As the shadows lengthen, stumps are drawn, and the sun sets, you are in the mood of thankfulness that it has been your great piece of luck to enjoy a lifetime of cricket as a profession . . . when at the moment hordes would be walking over London Bridge and spilling on to trains at Victoria to earn a living in a much less appealing way. I am forever grateful to the gods for their kindness.'

Ross's successor, Frindall, is far less rheumy-eyed. Just give me the facts, man. No warm, adjectival simperings for him — though, as David Benedictus once gloriously pointed out, 'If cricket scoring is an art, then Bill Frindall is an epic exponent, a Canaletto of the game.' And as the cartoonist, Kenneth Mahood, had his Test Match commentator saying some fifteen years ago: 'Would you believe it, Wilkins is the first red-haired left-handed slow bowler to be no-balled in the third over of a second day and incidentally Bill tells me that is the fiftieth piece of useless information he has given me today and his five thousandth of the season . . .'

Mind you, editing *Playfair* is only one more task for Bill. His cottage industry — his amateur filing systems used to bulge from every wardrobe of his north London flat — is now a big business. He churns out books like the Irish do butter. Reams of facts and figs. This summer he celebrates hi 21st birthday in the game. It is a touching story of haphazard fluke, accident and dedicated design.

In 1965, at 26, Frindall was an enthusiastic club cricketer, not long out of the RAF, and training as an insurance inspector with the Legal & General at Fenchurch Street in the City. One evening, he commuted home to Surrey, made himself a cup of tea — and heard on the radio that Arthur Wrigley, the BBC Test Match scorer, had died.

Totally unaware that calamity had struck the whole trade, and that the game's other two leading statisticians, genial Roy Webber and gracious Jack Price, had also not long gone, Bill sat down that night and, bold as you like in his careful copperplate, wrote to the BBC applying for the job. Lo and behold, he got an interview — and quakingly sat in front of Max Muller, head of radio outside broadcasts; Michael Hastings, the cricket producer; and the commentator, Brian Johnston.

He had been asked to bring along examples of his 'work'. Desperate, he could only think of taking along the scorecharts and analyses of his own small-time club cricket 'career'. Unbelievably, they did the trick — homing straight to the lovable Johnston's prep school spirit 'Jolly good, Frinders, eight for 29 for Banstead against Ashtead. And five clean bowled! Jolly good show! And what's this red inked column marked DFI?' They were our hero's few 'Double Figure Innings', topped by an underlined 59 against the Oval Nondescripts). He got the job, even though his two rivals for it were pretty top candidates — Michael Fordham, who was unsure about taking time off from his job with Kent County Council, and Wrigley's protégé, Arnold Whipp, who was the ace compiler of timetables at the Manchester transport depot.

Frindall had a winter to swot before his first trial match at Worcester the following April. He began growing a beard and bought as many *Wisden* back numbers as he could lay his hands on. He stayed up at night learning *Playfair* by heart. When spring sprung in 1966, he was racked with nerves. The West Indies were kicking off at Worcester. He drove down, his little Hillman Imp crammed with every reference book imaginable. He loaded them into two huge cardboard cartons, and staggered up to the commentary box with them before waiting, petrified, for his new colleagues to arrive. He shivered with dread at being stumped, yards from his ground, by every question the commentator posed. If someone had asked him his name that morning, no chance. Let alone how many Hutton had scored at The Oval in 1938. Come to think of it, where was the commentator? He seriously considered driving straight back to Fenchurch Street.

With just three minutes to transmission, John Arlott ambled in, carrying a plump, tightly full, leather briefcase — 'full', thought the bearded tyro, 'of questions I won't be able to answer.' Arlott squeezed past him in the little box, briefly held his great bear's arm on the young man's shoulder and burred a greeting, 'Welcome, friend.' Then, while the seconds were being counted down to 'on air', the commentator unpacked his briefcase — a large hunk of Cheddar, a packet of Ryvita, a corkscrew, and two bottles of claret.

Then it started raining. Not a question was asked. A dream

201

debut. Since when the nation's bearded cricketing Canaletto has never looked back. Except, that is, to treble-check a bowling analysis.

Crowe's Feat

SINCE Somerset's pitchfork rebellion, 1986-style, was ruthlessly put down earlier this month by its cricket club's vote and resulting banishment of its three mighty emperors — Vivian Richards, Joel Garner and, in sympathy, Ian Botham — the world and his wife have been asking for details of the young pretender who, single-handedly, must take their place in the lists next summer. Martin Crowe was 24 in September and was born in Auckland, New Zealand. He bristles with potential — but will need to put it into immediate effect to stop the rebels regrouping and mounting another angry march on Taunton.

Crowe is a tall, powerful, thoughtful batsman, combining elegance, instinct and muscle. He has scored four centuries in his 30 Test matches. Botham scored his 13th in his 70th Test, and Richards his 20th in his 80th, so the young man has some way yet to catch up. His wicket-taking as an occasional change bowler is so far behind Botham's and Garner's in Test matches as to be invisible. As a performing crowd-puller, he has a daunting job on his hands. Not only Watchet, Wedmore and Westonzoyland are watching: the whole cricket world will be keen to see how he copes.

I have a fancy he will rout the doubters. In his one season for Somerset, in 1984, when he stood in for Richards, who was touring with the West Indians, the 21-year-old displayed considerable mettle and courage — as well as an upright, clean-shaven, Boy-Scout manner that endeared him to the county establishment. He began with a candy-from-kids century against Oxford University; but thereafter a pretty embarrassing nudge and nurdle of 77 against Leicestershire was the only relief from a humiliating run of scores (the sequence of which ran 1, 10, 1, 0, 3, 5, 3), all the way through an unmerry May. All Somerset, devoted almost in idolatry to Richards, thought they had bought a pup. Well, they had. But a gritty one.

Suddenly, on June 11, and against Cowans, Daniel, Emburey and Edmonds of the crack side, Middlesex, he creamed a blissful century — and then laid the whole month to waste with four more centuries in successive matches, scoring 719 runs at an astonishing average of 143.8. He finished the season with 1,870 at 55.97 in first-class matches, plus no end of thrillingly chunky all-round performances in the one-day competitions, and *Wisden* said (we should have noted the hint for two years hence): 'He virtually filled the huge gap left by Richards, and his mature influence and general deportment rounded off his wonderful introduction to the county.' Did we but know it — the battle-lines had been drawn.

I wonder if the potentially heroic young Crowe might just be the fellow who caused John Arlott to rejig the proofs of his sumptuous new claret-table book *Arlott's 100 Great Batsmen* (Queen Anne press), which should solve many an auntie's Christmas present problem. 'Only as the Preface was being written,' he growls, relieved, 'was the final alteration made. One man *had* to go in,' and it was a heart-searching business to decide who to leave out of his final-final list. Could it have been the old sage's sudden realization that, while the book was still on the shelves *next* Christmas, Martin Crowe would already have proved himself a world beater?

On his record so far, Crowe could not remotely qualify in a litany of the hundred greatest batsmen. Not that Arlott seeks to be definitive. Whatever any critic might 'prove', he says, it remains a *personal* list. 'It's only my opinion — I'm not the voice of history.' Like the old tyke who was interrupted by Cardus one day at Bramall Lane, when he pointed out that his 'perfect' English XI was packed full of Yorkshiremen, but had left out the Master, Jack Hobbs. 'I know,' said the old bloke, 'but I just don't see 'ow I can fit 'im in.' We are all schoolboys at heart, doodling over our ideal World XI to play a Select XI from the Gents and Players of Mars and Venus.

Arlott twigs: 'In the back of the mind there lurk names that sentiment would have put in; the cricketer's urge is to include rather than exclude. Real-life selectors, of course, are realists; even ruthless. The ordinary enthusiast is more weakly human. Especially he has qualms about including so-and-so — whom he knows to be a such-and-such — at the expense of a nice man.'

(Though I must say, on another occasion, when I asked John if he liked all professional circketers, he had to ponder long before having to say, 'No, in my time there have been just two *absolute shits.*')

His choice falls on not only the canon's obviously relished player, but the *relishable*. There are some, at first glance, unlikely names who make the list — Archie Jackson, who died at 23, a year younger even than Crowe, and after only eight Tests (av. 47); and another Kiwi, Martin Donnelly, who played only seven (av. 52) and 'Tuppy' Owen-Smith, av. 42 in only five tests. But as is usual in these matters, the omissions, however much regretted, are those that will fuel the debate round the home this winter. No Bill Edrich; nor Colin McDonald; nor India's record-breaking stylist, Dilip Vengsarkar. The tragically stricken, one-eyed Colin Milburn and the Nawab of Pataudi Jnr get in, but 'the Noob' Snr misses the cut.

Eddie Paynter makes it, but Old Trafford stalwarts, who enjoy a moan, will munch sadly on their sandwiches over the omission of the jaunty-capped happy hooker, Cyril Washbrook. Charlie Hallows, and the immortal 'Shake' Makepeace. I rejoice to see my first-ever batting hero of boyhood, Charlie Barnett, make Arlott's team: 'High-shouldered and deep-chested, he batted with infinite gusto . . . with immense power, immense strength of arm and innate timing.' His was the first autograph I coveted. He was very fierce with schoolboys. He is still on the go, only four birthdays away from eighty, and only gave up riding to hounds a winter ago. The other day I had occasion to stop off at Cirencester — and popped into his shop on the corner of Market Place and asked for a souvenir brown bag marked 'Charles Barnett — Fish, Game and Poultry'. Just for old time's sake.

barnett hit 'only' 48 first-class centuries. But Dennis Amiss, pipe puffing accumulator who this season became probably the last Englishman ever to score a century of centuries, does not make Arlott's 100. Nor does Keith Fletcher, the canny chuckling eminence of Essex, who is next on the table of most prolific present-day English centurions with 62. Graham Gooch catches the boat, but another thunderous opener, Harold Gimblett — Somerset's best before Richards and Botham — misses the SS Arlott.

Jeff Stollmeyer gets the trip — 'relaxed in air, easy timing, strong on the legside, undisturbed by pace . . . and never lost his sense of humour' — awarded Alderney's nod over such as Lawrence Rowe, Roy Fredericks, Seymour Nurse, Larry Gomes or the older Clifford Roach. But Sir Garfield's cricket, of course, 'simply transcended all records'.

There is no place, either, for Cyril Walters, the master stylist; the oddly underestimated Douglas Jardine; quiet, firm and polished Ernest Tyldesley (the only other member of the '100' club to fail to make this list); the gamely determined Ian Redpath; the poised and polished Alan Kippax; the under-valued and neglected Jack Russell; or the man 'doomed to be remembered as Herbert Sutcliffe's partner', Percy Holmes, of the two-man '555' club.

Three New Zealanders with higher Test averages than Martin Crowe — and in many more games — Graham Dowling, Mark Burgess, and Geoff Howarth — have never-theless failed to clamber aboard this singular vessel. Arlott can 'sniff' class like an old dowager. Of Crowe, Arlott says with unknowing prophecy (this being written many months before the Wessex revolt blew up), 'He would be welcomed back in Somerset or, if not, in any worthwhile corner of the cricket world.'

It will be intriguing to see how long it takes the bonny young prince totally to quell the rebellion.

Hit Parade

And the Egg Ran Away
with the Spoon

I WENT to a school summer sports day last week, and a trampoline exhibition broke out. There wasn't even an egg-and-spoon for the Under-fives. Too competitive, you see. If they had put on a three-legged race, even the two Davids might have won a prize. But no competition, no first, second, third, and definitely no Booby.

And after Trampolinex, came the Mixed Maypole Dancing. Not a winner in sight. Before tea — all uniform rock buns, so no aggressive sporty type could be first in the queue to polish off the best jam sponge — we had Throwing the Cricket Ball. But nobody measured the distances; no marks even for artistic impression. They are dreary days on Britain's school sports-fields. Lots of Pansy Potters, and no little Victor Ludorums.

No more for the sake of a ribboned coat, or the selfish hope of a season's fame . . .

> *There's a breathless hush in the Close tonight,*
> *Ten to make and the match to win . . .*

Not any more there ain't.

Radical educationalists see sporting competition as a social evil. The modern view is that Muggins shouldn't excel at the crease, if Diddums is having to spend all day fetching the ball for him from deep square-leg. As Stuart Biddle, the secretary of the British Society of Sports Psychologists, put it last year: 'For many children, established school sports are sheer purgatory. Remember, only about five percent ever make the school team. Now team games and competitive events might serve a valuable purpose for those who excel, but the modern view is that sport is most beneficial when everyone can participate at their own level — and today tens of thousands of British children are partici-

pating in activities that once would have been considered
"'exotica.'"

Like sailing and mountaineering — and trampolining and
mixed maypole dancing, I suppose.

Many of these 'activities' are not even on the school
curriculum. They are voluntary and 'coached' outside school
hours — the more so since the teachers' dispute ran (ironically)
and ran. Though the good, earnest, misguided folk who plan
policy for the Inner London Education Authority have their
reasons — always passionately and cogently argued — fact is
that the world as we know it in these matters may never be the
same again. Apart from the odd bit of trampolining, probably
the only organized team games the majority of this year's state
school-leavers will play will be Monopoly, or those inside pin-
table frames. A comprehensive, you might say, disaster. Oh, my
Gatting and my Botham long ago . . .

Soccer, because it really is the people's game and for the ease
with which just a handful of guys can throw down a couple of
goalpost-coats, should manage to survive among the Yumpies
— that is, the Young Unfit Municipal Park players. But both
codes of rugby (though the League clubs are fashioning a
healthy enough Saturday morning out-of-school yahoo) and
cricket, especially, could be deprived totally of their whole and
wholesome plebeian intake within a generation — and the
heritage of these two great national games would revert to the
public schoolboys of last century. That would be a tragedy.

To be sure, it is a good bet that Mike Gatting will not only be
the first, but also the last comprehensive schoolboy to be
England's cricket captain. He was at John Kelly's Boys, whence
he graduated to Brondesbury CC, after answering an ad for
coaching sessions in the *Willesden & Brent Chronicle*. Meanwhile,
of course, Ian Botham had been the first sec.mod. skipper of
England (having gone to Bucklers' Mead in Yeovil after
deliberately failing his 11-plus, he says, because they didn't play
soccer at the local grammar school); and Keith Fletcher was the
first village school former pupil to toss for England (Comberton,
in Cambridgeshire, which was too small even to have a cricket
team).

These three, hitherto class barriered, social advances in
English cricket happened only in the last half dozen years. A
breakthrough no sooner achieved than thrown away, it seems.

It is odd, don't you think, how the competitive ethic in sport has become so unfashionable in Mrs Thatcher's macho reign. But it was easy: the PE teachers of ILEA simply dispensed with any judges or 'tribunals' — for any pastime, even trampolining and mixed maypole dancing, can become a ruthless competitive sport if played and judged on a strict set of codified rules. Why, even the waterlogged and breathless synchronized swimming of Tracey and Debra left off being a recreation and became a narrow-eyed Olympic sport, once some ruddy twit decorated it with a set of regulations. Plus, of course, a team of po-faced judges, wearing gold-buttoned blazers, and marching about, poolside, with clipboards.

The Victorian values of Dr Arnold's missionary Muscular Christians in Dickens's inner city had it that if you saw a group of street urchins throwing rocks at random, you did not call the Peelers and have them locked up — but went out and organized the rules for a rock-throwing contest. And everyone was happy. And thus the Modern Olympiad.

There are new rules now. Or, rather, none. *Decline and Fall* is the sum of it — as even the most unathletic Mr Waugh so gloriously chronicled in his first great novel. Hear ye this, for olde tyme's sake:

' "The course," said Paul, "starts at the pavilion, goes round that clump of elms . . ."

' "Beeches," corrected Lady Circumference, loudly.

' ". . . and ends in front of the bandstand. Starter, Mr Prendergast; timekeeper, Captain Grimes."

' "I shall say, 'Are you ready? one, two, three!' and then fire," said Mr Prendergast. "Are you ready? One" — there was a terrific report. "Oh dear! I'm sorry" — but the race had begun.

'Clearly Tangent was not going to win; he was sitting on the grass crying because he had been wounded in the foot by Mr Prendergast's bullet. Philbrick carried him, wailing dismally, into the refreshment tent, where Dingy helped him off with his sole. His heel was slightly grazed. Dingy gave him a large slice of cake, and he hobbled out surrounded by a sympathetic crowd.

' "That won't hurt," said Lady Circumference, "but I think someone ought to remove the pistol from that old man before he does anything serious!" '

Happy days at the school sports. When childhood summers were bathed in sunlight; when winners swanked, and losers blubbed. Now all together please, folks, let's hear it for the final formation of the mixed maypole dance . . .

Amateur Dramatics

We should have twigged. It was all gruesomely inevitable. Ten days ago I went to Paris to welcome back to Europe that brooding, dangerous, little tugboat that had last steamed away, bells ringing and sirens bleating, after the Wimbledon tennis tournament of 1985. I went to Paris to check on his fitness, form and frown, after his six-month sabbatical to take in fatherhood and marriage, and gauge if he was in the trim for London's prestigious and lucrative Benson & Hedges indoor championships at Wembley this week. But it may be that little Johnnie McEnroe ain't coming any more.

Paris was blissful. Sunlit days as crispy as spring. Leaves on the trees and some colours still in bloom. The new tennis centre at Bercy was wintery in the evenings. In his first round doubles, McEnroe bawled out a lineswoman. In his singles quarter-final, he went totally ape, threatened a British umpire, Jeremy Shales (our old friend of whom Ilie Nastase once demanded, "*Ey, punk, you call me Meestaire Nastase Sir, all right?*", and in so doing ran up enough fines to ring the jackpot on the swearbox to over $7,500, which these days means an automatic ban of three weeks. McEnroe's comeback, to all intents, was over for the year.

This sublime player really has got a slate loose. You feel he is allowing himself to fade away, to vanish up his own tantrum, without even seriously logging a claim to being one of the all-time greats. It is tragic — though I admit it has been compulsive viewing. It is hard to believe, but he is 28 in February 1987 — already ten years older than Becker and a veteran, too, to the sudden, new, swirling mass of grasping youngsters in the pack with stony faces, deadpan personalities and unpronounceable names. It really does seem unlikely now that Mac's manners will mature, that — as, somehow, one had always presumed he would — he would coat the court with sweetness and light and chivalry (adjectives, in fact, that have always gone with his actual tennis-playing game). But The Brat we loved to hate has suddenly become The Prat we hate to berate. In Paris, I found myself up in the gods *willing* him to get his act together, and just play. Not a hope.

Many will say good riddance, but there will be far fewer beating a path up Neasden Way to the Wembley box-office this week, with a spring in their step and a palpitating sense of anticipation. In a game which seems to me to be dominated overwhelmingly, all of a sudden, by massively shouldered serve-and-volley merchants, the comparatively weedy, light-welter-weight feel and touch and fast hands of McEnroe were among the truly rewarding saving graces.

The warning signs had been there when I first came across him in Paris. His mind wasn't totally on the job. Well, how could it be, surrounded by new bride, new son, Mom, Pop and other family, friends and minders that bigtime sportsmen seem to need to cart around with them these days. He seemed edgy about admitting that domestic bliss had cured the tantrums on court, or 'caged the rage' as the press handouts assured us. Indeed, an American reporter friend told me that in John's very first 'come-back' tournament in Vermont he had got into such a lather over one line call 'that he was almost physically sick on court'. He didn't stain his gym shoes — but the first of the fines was ticking away. Said McEnroe, who can use understatement as effectively as that feathery backhand approach volley, 'I guess it's a bad habit that I tend to revert back to when I'm nervous out there.'

What he can do, also, is give the lie to the still often held belief — by those of us in the bleachers — that top professional sport nowadays resembles anything remotely to do with fun. 'Every tournament is a worry. How can I pretend I'm happy down there? You have a job to do and you do it to the best of your ability. You are in a state of worry to the very last point, whatever the tournament is. A lot of you people just don't realize that. I suppose, one day, I might look up my record and say, "Hey, did I win there in Antwerp? Or Houston? Or wherever? Or, was I really No. 1 player in all the world between 1982 and whenever? Gee." Now that sort of thing stays with me. In the end it's a far better pay-off in terms of satisfaction than pretending to you that I'm kinda having fun out there on the court.'

212

It has taken sixty years to get that sort of admission out of a tennis player. To the very month. This week, in London, represents a jubilee for pro tennis. To all intents, it began in November 1926, when a zingy US razzmatazz merchant called C.C. ('Cash-and-Carry') Pyle booked Madison Square Garden, laid out a tennis-court and looked round for a killing. He had already introduced the six-day cycle race, the roller derby, and dance marathons to the frenzied 1920s, but now he was to put a real whizzer up the starched shirts of the US and English tennis authorities by signing up the incomparable Wimbledon ladies' champion, Suzanne Lenglen (for $23,000), and the American favourite, Mary K. Browne. Four male club players provided an overture, and the packed house were apparently delirious when the two ladies did their stuff. Pyle pocketed his profits of $30,000, and then moved on, smiling, to other Barnum or Bailey projects.

But, thereafter, the amateur authorities were always looking over their shoulders. Others, in turn, made their pile for a bit — and then struggled, for too often the one-night stands reeked of uncompetitive exhibitionism. Tilden, Vines, Cochet, and later Budge and Riggs, each took a turn at driving the caravan through good times which were often bad. Half a century ago this autumn, Fred Perry turned pro after his hat-trick of Wimbledon wins. Every amateur club in the country, including the All-England, demanded a return even of the club tie they might have presented him with. Perry wanted to play a pro match against the American champion Ellsworth Vines — but it looked as though they wouldn't be able to get a court to play on *in all Europe*!

In the end, the British industrialist, Bernard Sunley, built them a portable wooden court. The two finest players in the world trundled it around the English football grounds for a month or two here and there — but then played, by all accounts, a sensationally vibrant five-setter to a clamorous audience at the Empire Pool, Wembley (where this week's lucrative little lot is being staged), that had the genuine tennis fans still buzzing by the time Jack Kramer attempted to revitalize the professional game after the war.

From Kramer's amateur win at Wimbledon in 1947, it still took another two decades for Wimbledon to give up their sham payments — but, increasingly, they lost their champions as soon as they had been presented with the famous gilt biscuit by the

213

Duchess of Kent. Sedgman, Hoad, Laver and most of the other Wimbledon champions all went over. Once the latter (another leftie and McEnroe's boyhood hero), had signed up, the writing was really on the old ivy-coloured wall of SW19.

The millionaire kids of today don't realize what sacrifices those early pros put in to get this generation's gravy train out of the sidings. I had tea at the Westbury a couple of years ago with Jack Kramer. 'We scrimped and saved and laughed and played,' he said, 'just to get the show on the road. Now these young guys today don't seem to give a damn for the collective, for the *idea* or the dream — they are just looking for the top dollar for *themselves*.'

Jack's friend, and one-time fellow traveller, the ever engaging Butch Buchholz, piped up to recall their days, 'as wandering vagabonds wallowing in obscurity, filling whole years with one-night stands'. He said one vital thing drove them on, as well as earning an honest buck for themselves. It was being able to say to the coming generation, 'One day, friend, all this will be yours.' But he, too, was now disillusioned: 'A hammer and nail were as much our standard equipment as rackets and balls. Otherwise there was no place to hang your clothes when you went out into the rain to take a shower. We once played 30 matches in 31 days and slept in 29 different beds. The kids today are millionaires many times over — yet they do far more bitching and moaning. If they could only understand what it was like for us, I think they might appreciate their life a little more.'

This week at Wembley we might miss the skills of McEnroe, sure. Shame. But the really warm thoughts should be for the likes of Buchholz and Kramer, Vines and Perry and good ol' Cash-and-Carry himself. It is a notable sixty years they celebrate, whichever way you look at it. Not that the deadpan kids out there on court will give them much of a thought.

Champ Gets Into Ring

Marriage might yet be the weapon which wins the world heavy-weight title for Frank Bruno, Britain's amiable pugilist with the chandelier chin. Not his nuptials, but those of the fearsome milky-bar kid, Mike Tyson. The muscular multi-millionaire of 21 was married in Chicago the other day to a TV soap-opera actress, Robin Givens, and while his co-managers, Jim Jacobs and Bill Cayton, pronounced themselves well pleased — 'She's an exquisite girl who will end any contemplation of a carefree, bachelor life' — wizened old sages, fingering their scar-tissues and chewing their dentures, were mumbling knowingly round the ringside how history showed that, more often than not, a wife would soften up a fighter.

Whether Robin will soften up hubby in enough time for our Frank is another matter. In March 1988 Tyson reaches up to put the landing lights out for terrified Tony Tubbs in Tokyo. Then, in June, Mike Spinks is next on the hit list; with Bruno logged, apparently, for August (logged being the operative word, unless Mrs T. works particularly well).

There is quite a history of Mr and Mrs in boxing. In fact, the only world heavyweight champion with a British connection, Bob Fitzsimmons — who left Helston as a boy for New Zealand — won the title, it is said, on the direct advice of his missus, Rosie. It was ninety years ago, at Carson City, Nevada, on St Patrick's Day, that spindly Bob met Gentleman Jim Corbett, an adroit and upright champion. For thirteen rounds, Bob had failed to land a decent punch. No women were allowed in the body of the arena, and Rosie had been watching from a box above the bleachers.

At the beginning of the fourteenth, she could stand it no longer and made her way through the throng to ringside. 'Don't waste strength trying to punch his head off,' she bellowed. 'Go for the bread-basket, alug him in the slats!'

Henpecked Bob, as always, obeyed, and at once let fly a terrific left into the poor Gent's solar plexus. There was a

215

pained, almost pitiful shriek — and Jim first made a move as if to tie up his shoelaces, then went the whole hog in a heap and signed on for full membership of the Flat Earth Society. Rosie slunk back to her box, satisfied, and Bob was champion of the world. Slugger of the slats.

Nearest thing to Rosie Fitzsimmons in my experience was Cheryl Finnegan, wife of Chris, the middleweight, and one of Britain's best post-war boxers. Cheryl was an absolute smasher. Chris was the last Brit to win an Olympic gold medal, in Mexico City twenty years ago. Before he left, Cheryl spent months on a diet of Golden Wonder potato crisps. Their little flat near Slough was littered — positively carpeted — with used and unused packets of the stuff. You see, Golden Wonder were having a competition in which you had to send in as many empty packets as possible — and give your reasons for wanting to win the first prize of a free holiday at the Games in Mexico. Cheryl sent in the most whopping parcel you ever saw, and enclosed the entry form with *Reasons for wanting to visit Mexico in exactly ten words*. Nobody could possibly have had a better reason than Cheryl — she wrote: 'Because my husband is going to win the gold medal.' Exactly ten words. Golden Wonder didn't even send her a reply.

When he won his medal and turned pro, Chris was responsible for many a rousing show as he worked his way towards his world title fight. But it was all hard work, all a long slog, for he did not have one single, dramatic knockout punch, not one explosively concussive 'Sunday' special. Nevertheless, Cheryl was always in the front row, just behind the press seats, and throughout the fight her plaintive West London squeal would rise above the general hullabaloo at least twenty times each round: 'C'mon, Chris, darlin', *kill'im!*'

But of course, her hubby up there was capable only of accumulating the points, which he did more often than not with bruising ease. When he retained his European title at Nottingham, in 1972, against Conny Velensek, of Holland, Cheryl was in particularly sharp voice. 'C'mon, Chris, *kill'im!*' At the end of one of the middle rounds even her hubby had had enough. He came back to his corner, took his gum-shield out, spat in a bucket, and leaned round his second to shout down, ''Ere, Cheryl, doll, turn it in, can't even 'ear meself fight up 'ere! An' anyway,' he added, truthfully, 'you know I'm not supposed to bleedin' well 'ave a punch!'

Quick as a flash, Cheryl retorted, 'Well, what's that right 'ook you got when you put the cat out every night, then?' It brought the house down.

Prize-fighting lore has usually demanded that the game and the gels don't mix. The greybeards watching this month for evidence of Mike Tyson's strength being sapped by his sexy spouse will quote you one of the tenets handed down by one of the greatest of all fighters, Sam Langford, at the turn of the century: 'Boy, you can sweat out beer, you can sweat out whisky, but, son, you can't sweat out women.'

Yet it is all a myth. I suppose the two great heavyweights of my lifetime have been Muhammad Ali and Joe Louis — with Master T. on course to take the bronze from Rocky M. (And don't all write in if you disagree with my placings — it gets so tedious opening those envelopes of yours, let alone reading the contents. Sorry and all that.)

As a bright-eyed youth I was brought up to believe that Louis ('a credit to his race, the human race') got where he did by clean living, not even his wife, the cute little stenographer, Marva, being allowed near training camp at Pompton Lakes for at least six weeks before a fight. But as soon as the title had been retained, he would be off home at once for some of her favourite boiled chicken 'n' rice.

Not a bit of it. Once poor old Joe had died, they queued up to tell the real tales. So, from Gerald Astor's illuminating biography of the Brown Bomber, *Gloves Off* (Pelham): 'Shortly after Louis had established himself as a figure of note through the Carnera fight, he began a lifelong career of consorting with women. "He would come into town, go up to a club in Harlem," said an acquaintance from that period. "The manager would bring out all the girls in the show. Joe would pick one out, and spend a day or so in the Hotel Theresa with her before returning to camp." '

Even my onliest hero, the nonpareil Ali was, it turns out, laughing not only all the way to the bank, but also the bunk. In his biography, *Fight Doctor* (Stanley Paul), Dr Ferdie Pacheco, Ali's physician during most of his fights, tells how the great man strayed: 'Before his first fights, in the St John in Harlem, Cassius would sit quietly of an evening sipping his orange juice, while beautiful long-legged ladies strutted by with their pimps, and if

217

they hesitated their man would say, "Naw, babe, he is fighting this week in LA. What you trying to do, girl, hurt our man?" . . . Never again in his boxing life would Cassius have such will power. Later in his career, where ladies were always available to Ali wherever he would go, he would always accommodate them.'

Ah me, dreams shattered. Anyroad, it's something to think about, isn't it, that the chances of Britain having a second world heavyweight champion, ninety years after the first, rest solely with the former Miss Robin Givens, of Chicago. Take him, Frank, he's all yours!

Only Four Can Play

The caravan has moved on. The dust has settled. Every year, it strikes me as poignantly right that the grunting sounds and furies of the Wimbledon fortnight is ended with the final of the Mixed Doubles late on the last evening. With it, in a way, the big-time hurly-burly is giving back a pleasant pastime to its soft, suburban heartland. The singles' wars have raged the full 15 rounds, and the toffs and their tantrums have long been chauffeured back to their international hotels, their agents holding their hands and their cheques . . . and now the net is elongated, the sun dips more mellow, and endearing matchstick shadows criss-cross the court to the sounds once again of the age-old lawn tennis garden party.

Bees buzz around the buddleia. Mums get out their thermos flasks. *Plick, plock!* Comradely screeches, and other olde tyme sounds of competitive fun and, would you believe, laughter. On the Centre Court, too! We can relate to this. This is the tennis you and I once attempted long ago on provincial parks in the golden evenings of youth. Not to mention the corpulent tea-times of middle age. *Oh, good shot! Yours! Mine! Well left! Drat it! Sorry, partner!* Hooray for Mixed Doubles!

Such piffle might make for a pretty and pastoral piece, to be sure. But we all know such guff represents a damnable lie. Down the years, mixed doubles' tea-parties at tennis have wrecked

218

more marriages than any amount of wife-swapping orgies round midnight. The war of the sexes, you see, is engaged to ferocious intent *on both sides of the net.* Mixed doubles allows you to hate your opponent's partner — but, most times, you end up hating your own partner. The deadpan manuals might tell you that the prime strategies of the game consist of no more than getting your service in court — or your return — playing your hardest at either 15-30 or 30-15, and 'no poaching' at the net, but the subtler coaches, like the splendid American sporting guru, Art Hoppe, know different: 'The proper method for playing mixed doubles is to hit the ball accidently at the woman opponent as hard and as accurately as possible. Male players must not only seem to retain equanimity on their side of the net, but create dissension on the other.'

Another learned Yank, Doctor Theodor Saretsky, chimed in with his spoofingly unsubtle Oedipal paper for Pagoda Books last year, *Sex as a Sublimation for Tennis (from the Secret Writings of Freud)*: 'The psychopathology of Mixed Doubles persists in a preconscious state during the latency period only to be reunited with the tennis urge in early adulthood: the subtle melding of sex and tennis through wedlock is one of the foundations of real love. The gradual erosive effect of playing mixed doubles with one's spouse is not felt until the thirties and forties. The flagrant disregard for reality and the generally poor judgment displayed by those who choose to risk their marriage on the Scylla and Charybdis of this infernal invention of mixed tennis reflect masochism at its worst.'

Which, I guess, is a Woody Allen-ish way of saying Don't Mix With Mixed.

As a well-adjusted and long resigned loser through the years at any mixed double from tennis to kitchen plate-throwing, I am qualified enough to be serious about tactics on the court. Absolute No. 1 rule, to my mind, for success at Mixed is to hit the ball back down the middle, (a) because there is no doubles' net, even in a Wimbledon final, that does not sag like a hammock, and, (b) the midcourt ball gives far fewer angles for the opponent to open up. My rule No. 2 states that, when smashing, aim (a) for your male opponent's groin, or, preferably, (b) straight between your female opponent's eyes.

The one and only Jack Kramer, among many other things, was the US mixed doubles champion in 1942. A couple of Julys ago, I had tea with him at the Westbury in Mayfair and, bless him, he was gallant and most delicate when I raised with him the tactics he employed: 'Lob to the lady always — and in a spot where the man cannot cheat and take it.' He winced when I expounded my theories, as witnessed on the public parks of England. Perhaps, in his day, the gentlemanly old cove from California played only with poetic, petite and pretty, pencil-slim partners. Nowadays, there is a size and strength and sinew about top tennis girls — as the great Davis Cupper, Abe Segal, observed the other year: 'Some of these new young women players shouldn't be allowed out alone — they could fell me with one hand.'

Most of the 1987 Wimbledon programmes and magazines carried a glossy full-page ad for 'The Most Important Piece of Sports Equipment a Girl Can Wear', namely 'The Minimal Bounce Bra', which claims, 'Unique Cupless Design in special blend of cotton/Lycra, comfortably and effectively to minimize painful breast bounce and the accompanying irreversible stretching of Cooper's ligaments and equally painful nipple soreness — only £11.99p.' But are they useful armour for a ruthless set-to at mixed doubles?

One of the most amply endowed of comparatively recent champions was our very own Ann Jones, the Brummie left-hander with the lovable lilt to her larynx and the 40D bra-cup. Ann was a very good mixed doubler, usually with Fred Stolle (they won Wimbledon in 1969). Down those years, they had a series of epic matches with Billie Jean King and Owen Davidson. And it took a gel to spot the other's weakness — as the wise old bird, Billie Jean, glintingly remembers: 'With Ann's big boobs, the tactic was to bring her to the net and make her hit backhand volleys — the hardest shot of all for a girl with a well-endowed chest. "Oh, no," Ann used to moan at me, "I've got to hit over them or under them: I just can't hit through them."'

No man, surely, would stoop to such a cruel and canny ruse. And indeed, at its most piquant form, the battle of the sexes in the mixed doubles of life is waged only in the mind. As Stephen Potter, that maestro of up-manship defined in his treatise on mixed doubles:

'Play to the rules, which are:

    1. When changing ends, know exactly when to stand

elaborately aside in order to allow your female opponent to come by first; and equally when to allow her the minimum room for getting by;

2. Know when to make a great show of encouraging your partner and exclaim "Good Shot!" whenever she gets the ball back;

3. Know how to apologise profusely for lobbing into the sun;

4. Know exactly the moment to get the scoring wrong — always, of course, in your opponents' favour.'

By the same token, mind you, men have the most to lose. Did you notice last week on the strawberry fields of SW19, for instance, that the losing man of every mixed double tottered off court, face blanched, spirit diminished. Beaten by a girl! And *in front of* another girl! Like Wodehouse's dear Mr Garnet, humiliated by the Royal Navy lieutenant called Chase and his battery of Wimbledon-like shots. It was a bearable beating — but not in front of his beloved partner Phyllis: 'I felt a worm and no man. Phyllis, I thought, would probably judge my entire character from this exhibition. A man, she would reflect, who could be so feeble and miserable a failure at tennis could not be good for much in any department of life. She would compare me instinctively with my opponent, and contrast his dash and brilliance with my own inefficiency.

'. . . my ball flew in a slow semi-circle, and pitched inside the correct court. At least, I told myself, I had not served a fault. What happened then I cannot exactly say. I saw the opponent springing forward like a panther and whirl his racket. The next moment the back net was shaking violently, and the ball was rolling swiftly along the ground on a return journey to the other court. "Love-forty," said Mr Chase. "Phyllis!" "Yes." "That was the 'Tilden Slosh'." "I thought it must be," said Phyllis.'

It was, of course, the inventor of that 'slosh', the legendary (and homosexual) Big Bill Tilden (Wimbledon champ 1920, '21 and '30), who first warned his fellow man of the inherent dangers of playing mixed doubles. Tennis with, or against, a woman was emasculating, said Bill: 'Women partners are a lot of bitches. When someone is a genius, when they have a great task in life like me on court, they cannot afford to be depleted by a woman. Women on the same side of the net as you, wear down a man — they have no right to make a man of genius share their petty demands and ploys.'

To Tilden, the battle of the sexes was writ 6-0, 6-0, 6-0. And never, ever, said Big Bill, congratulate your woman partner for her intercepting volleys at the net: 'Anticipation is just a woman's fancy word for guessing right.'

As in mixed doubles, so in the hectic three-setter of life and love itself. *Quiet please! Play!*

Eights, Nines, Thames

RIP. The soggiest of winters is officially confined to a watery grave in the deep of the Thames this next couple of weeks. The oarsmen are messing about in boats at their rowlocking spring festival down on that mucky, murky, flotsamy flood between Putney and Mortlake. It's Tideway time, folks, for the next three Saturdays. First up is this week's gorgeously crazy Head of the River, as congested a jam of skiffs as to make Hong Kong harbour seem as serene as a drowsy, dawn dewpond in Dorset.

You've heard of the Severn Bore; well, next week rolls in the Thames ditto — namely the 134th Oxford v Cambridge Boat Race. The following weekend has the heaving, seething solo merchants bending their backs for the singularly obsessive Sculls' Head. As March turns to April, there's always more obsession littering this stretch of the old towpath than even discarded gumboots. Rowing chaps: great fellows, great fanatics, great frenzies.

The old ones are always best at this time of year: 'Eight men with but a single thought — *if that.' Proud but bewildered auntie to stroke of the winning crew*: 'Well done, my dear, you all rowed fast, but none so fast as you!' Or, *football fan walking across Putney Bridge to Fulham's Craven Cottage, just as Boat Race is starting below him*: 'Yeah, dead borin' innit. Bound t'be, s'pose, when same ruddy teams always reach the final.' Actually the best joke is probably the oldest. It was Mr Punch's the week after that dramatic dead-heat of 1877. His headline read succinctly: OXFORD WON, CAMBRIDGE TOO.

'*Are you ready? Go!*' is the traditional rowing command from the starter on the stakeboat. Any damn fool can start on the order 'Go', but a chap's got what it takes when he starts on the word 'Are'. That was doubtless said by a coxswain. Mighty, megaphoned midgets, coxes; I've been hanging about with them down on the towpath. Far sharper, too, than the lofty, muscled brutes they boss about. It's called an Eight, but of course it's a Nine — very much so.

I've been muffled and duffled down by the riverside watching them work — all of us bent double against the wind that skims like a flat pebble off the chill and chop of the water; it threatens even to bring down the condemned meccano pylons of Craven Cottage yonder, and it rocks and shudders the buses as they crawl like friendly red slugs over Putney Bridge.

Coxing strikes me as by far the hardest thing about rowing. Okay, the hulking hearties have to heave, but that's all; they aren't even allowed to see where they're going. The cox has their fate in his tiny, frozen hand — and gets a mention in the papers next day only if he, as you might say, 'cox' it up, like steering into a stationary barge which that poor Cambridge tot did a couple of years ago, or hit amidships the middle balustrade at Hammersmith Bridge, or run aground on Chiswick Eyot.

I was honoured to be taken out on a launch with Andy Green, who coxed Oxford two or three years back. He talked me through the whole dramatic jag and geog: 'At "Are", aim straight for that white boathouse over there and get them to put their foot down . . . the Middlesex wall is actually a heck of a curve, but keep parallel to it, that's your line of stream . . . then straighten them up and go like the clappers for that clump of three poplars on the towpath, right opposite the football ground . . . stay gentle now with the wall, softly, softly, it's all smooth curve, no zig, no zag . . . and now you'll find we're pointing full ahead for that crane exactly over the Surrey prong of Hammersmith Bridge . . .'

Ships, towers, domes skim by, the Riverside Theatre, temples, wharves, Harrods depository, the bandstand at Duke's Meadows and the pubs to both left and right. Every landmark logged and lined up by the cox, the little fellow with the booming voice who is producer, director, choreographer, theodolyte expert, chivvier, bully, nanny and nursemaid. In front of him the great brutes heave and strain, creak and grunt in unison like a toiling operatic chorus in a biblical epic. The wee cox is emperor.

Green again: 'There's a critical point where the stern of one boat is on the bow of another; your oarsmen cannot see it but they can sense it. it's somehow as if the two boats are tied together for a moment. It's the absolute crux. "C'mon," I urge, "put your ruddy backs into it, let's get going, start motoring, give me another 'ten'" . . . and slowly, relentlessly, our spurt is roping them in alongside us, and I'll start counting off their men as we edge past them, I'll say "We're on their six seat," then "We're on five seat," then four, then three. It's a fantastic feeling, calling out like that when you knew the crew alongside were really travelling, and that we first held them, then started hauling them in, and now we're going away from them, and I can't see them any more, but I know they're dispirited. They're stuck for any retort, they are broken, they are dead and gone . . .'

Because they knew the waters and the currents, professional watermen were always hired as coxes when rowing started to get organized last century. Then the young gentlemen thought to have a go themselves. In 1839, ten years after the first Boat Race, C.J. Selwyn, of Leander, suggested that in future they 'allow no waterman to have anything more to do with the matches, but to leave it all to gentlemen: I do not mean to say a word against watermen, but watermen's ways are not our ways, or watermen's notions our notions.'

There was general acclamation, and later that year Selwyn set out his Boat Race Principles: 'First, Gentlemen shall steer; second, Fouling shall be abolished; and last, not least, Victory should be its own reward.'

In 1844, the pioneer amateur cox, the Rev A.T.W. Shadwell wrote *A Treatise on Steering*, in which he set out the coxswain's duties: '. . . To watch the peculiar motions of each man, to teach diligently and temperately, to trim the boat when lurching under uneven rowing, to calculate the advances made in speed as rowing improves, to time accurately . . . to keep up his heart and nerve in trying circumstances, to keep in good humour with all his crew, and to keep them in good humour.'

One of the outstanding coxes of recent times is Colin Moynihan, who plotted Oxford's sprayful stroll in 1977 and also medals for world and Olympic crews, always zestfully living up to Shadwell's definition of cox as 'maker of the crew and presiding spirit of its work'. He is now, of course, our own dear Minister of Sport, needing even more so the qualities ascribed to him in Christopher Dodd's classic, *The Oxford and Cambridge Boat*

Race: '. . . He knows all the tricks; always point the shell the way you wish it to point; never give an opponent the advantage of position or start if you can possibly avoid it; have the measure of your own men as well as the course, being aware who can take insults and who cannot; and do not be averse to speaking just loud enough for the other crew to hear if you want them to. And know how to wind your crew up and also wind them down, and sometimes wind some up and some down simultaneously.'

The lad should go far in politics. By the by, Moynihan's Boat Race win was just a year before Cambridge's famous sinking when the BBC man, Jim Railton, set the nation on a roar by describing the unfortunate (but to those warm at home, hilarious) waterlogging as 'leading to a dolphin effect which could yet cause a drowning situation'. I think it was Moynihan's year that, at the finish at Mortlake, he was generously and sportingly congratulated by the missus of one of the beaten Cambridge oarsmen, at which the BBC commentator, Harry Carpenter, announced, 'Ah, isn't that nice, the wife of the Cambridge President is kissing the cox of the Oxford crew!'

Yeah, we knew what you meant, 'Arry. The Tideway gets everyone like that as March turns into April.

No Success, Please, We're British

I HAVE a friend who must be coming up to fifty now. He is a six-footer and remains handsome enough — if you like that sort of thing, namely, a chubby face of blotches and a button nose, topped by a Gower-like, tight nest of dull blond curls. Well, there we were, the two of us, minding our own business in the loo queue behind the Tavern scoreboard, on the last of a Lord's Test some twenty or so June-Julys ago, when a fierce English fellow bowled up and started brandishing his brolly at my companion.

'Scared to show your face down there, are you? And I'm not surprised, you clammy, spineless, little drip!' And many more expletives deleted to that effect.

My pal, taken aback as well by the intrigued crowd that was gathering, muttered that, sorry, he did not yet follow the drift of such an explosion. But the bloke was only warming to his theme: 'You, sir, are a drivelling, disgusting disgrace to the flag; a pusillanimous, cowardly, yellow-bellied un-British oik, sir!'

Scared as he was, my friend continued to look genuinely perplexed — so the puce-faced accuser momentarily stopped ranting, to ask, 'Don't try and come over all innocent and deny it, *everyone knows you're ruddy Mark Cox!*' The crowd, twigging, rhubarbed their own menacing certainty that such a bounder deserved everything that was coming to him.

Bank cards and driving licences had to be produced before the flare-up subsided in grudging apologies for mistaken identity — but with mutual agreement all round that, had he in fact been the British tennis player (whom he did, come to think of it, more than slightly resemble), then the patriotic outburst would indeed have been quite in order. For a couple of days before, down the road at Wimbledon, poor put-upon Mark had led the tame annual retreat of the homesters by losing on Centre Court in an early round, grieving and gasping, against some unpronounceable foreigner who was far lower down the world rankings than even he had been placed. It was ever thus. And ever more shall be so.

At least Cox got into that first-round draw by right. This year, not one homegrown laddo made the 'Gentlemen's' singles on merit — all qualified as 'free' wildcard entries to make up the numbers. They may have found it consoling that there has been a shortage of the usual, pre-Wimbledon stories of 'Brit with Grit To Go Whole Way This Time' variety — but I'm afraid, the reason was that none of us occasional feature bods know even their *names* any more, so we can't even begin to look up last year's drivelling determined quotes and reshuffle them into a new piece. British tennis, quite simply, went into this year's All-England Championships at its lowest point to date.

Mark Cox was once, at least, a doubles semi-finalist. The lugubrious Yorkie, Roger Taylor, also a leftie, made two singles semi-finals — and we must not forget, either, that the former Mr John Evert-Lloyd twice won the mixed doubles. (Calm down, calm down, you know-alls, good ol' Drob, whom the Brits took to their hearts and claimed as their own when he *did* win Wimbers, in fact was born in Prague and Davis Cupped for Egypt!)

In awful, awesome truth, the Anglos have been sadly saxing,

waxing and wailing for over fifty years. For half a century, it's been sweet love-all. Of course, like every other, this year was going to be different. Winter turned almost to spring and the annual, daisy-fresh, bonny optimism once again lifted the spirits. The British men's team in the Davis Cup drew a nice little looser for the first round against Mexico. In the best-of-five tie, alas, they were 0-3 down in next to no time. With the match won, the Mexicans then compounded the humiliation by fielding two substitutes, to give them some experience in the final two rubbers. They won them, to complete the whitewash — but still the British team manager, Paul Hutchins, summoned up the gall to complain about it. He should have known — as we all did — that the Mexicans could have fielded Pancho Villa (or even Aston Villa) and the poor Brits would still have lost.

So the only thing to do was to indulge in the old standby: Blame the Press. Hutchins had a go; so did the president of the Lawn Tennis Association, Geoff Brown — and at the LTA annual dinner, no less. Even the British women's team manager, Sue Mappin, tossed her oar in about the 'knocking copy' that sports-writers had produced being the only thing stopping her players winning a cupboardful of trophies — though I must say I know a fair few even in Fleet Street far fleeter than her galumphing gels between the tramlines, but that's another sad story.

Even the British No. 1 men's player (hang on a tick, while I look up his name . . . oh, yes) Andrew Castle waded in. He had grace enough, mind you, to wait till he had recorded his first victory, in a grand prix tournament match, in the long twelvemonth stretch since he sprang to 'fame' by taking *two* sets off Mats Wilander at last year's Wimbledon. 'I've been meaning to get this off my chest for a long time,' he glowered. 'This last year has been an eye-opener. You Press go wild when I win; but when I lose, all you ask is, "How come you had such a disappointing match?"' Seems a fair enough question to me.

For all the threats and promises and practice, the loot and the love, the Five-year Plans and Ten-year Plans, it remains, nevertheless, 51 years since a Brit nursed and nuzzled the old gilt biscuit for the photographers down there on Centre Court, at the end of the Gentlemen's singles final. That, of course, was Fred Perry, working-class son of the Labour MP for Kettering, when he clinched his famous hat-trick in 1936.

227

Why, 1988's smasheroo celebrations at the snotty old straw-berry fields of SW19 will be to hoist the half-century anniversary of the last time a native male of these islands actually *appeared* in a final of the singles. That was Bunny Austin, who lost the finals of 1932 and 1938 — in the former, becoming the first finalist ever to come out in shorts — 'after getting my tailor to run up a prototype modelled on what was then being worn on the rugby union fields'.

One of my treats of this week in recent years has been to cadge or wangle a visitor's tea ticket from an All-England member on the afternoon that Fred Perry was taking Bunny Austin to tea. Both in their time were blackballed by the often ludicrous Club — Perry for turning pro after his hat-trick, and Austin for joining Moral Re-Armament during the war. Neither cares a fig now for such snubs, especially when their talk turns to old times and good times. Perry is still the ramrod-straight six-footer, handsome is as handsome does, with a vice-like handshake clawing out from his massive right wrist: speed, suppleness, stamina and strength were his hall-marks. Fred has never not been a superduperstar.

Bunny was obviously more the Rosewall type. The last time I saw him, pale and grey and bright-eyed, he looked still like an elderly little 'Muscles'. Including those two finals, in his eleven years at Wimbledon between 1929 and '39, he failed only once to reach the quarter finals. He is as chivalrous now as he obviously was then: 'Oh, good gracious me, no, I never had a big serve or volley. I was a ground-stroke player. I reckoned to return well, keep the ball in play, search for the angles and wait for the opportunities. In my first final in 1932, Ellsworth Vines won the match with an ace. I still don't honestly remember which side the ball passed me: all I can still hear is the clap of thunder as it hit the backstopping behind me. I didn't play well that day, Ellie didn't let me. But, by Jove, he was simply tremendous. Did you know, he served 30 aces in 12 games.

'Six years later, in my second final, I think I played much better, though if you look up the scores you wouldn't think so, for Donald Budge was so superlatively good. He was almost unplayable at times. It was tremendous to be out there with him in a way. He simply devoured all my best shots.

'Don and Ellie were so tremendously powerful, you know. So was Fred, of course. The three of them would have been among the really great of any age. They had all the equipment to match the leading players of today — though of course there are far many more ''good'' players in the top pack today.'

This weekend's men's singles winner will pocket an almost obscene £155,000 for his pains. The runner-up will dust himself down and, with a face of snarling gloom, just about bring himself to accept a cheque for £77,000. Even Britain's first-round losers sloped away to count £2,500 for their brief three-setter and their one further chance to lay all the blame on the Press.

Bunny Austin's reward as runner-up on both occasions was a voucher for £2.10s to be spent at Mappin & Webb, the jeweller. 'Though I must now confess it,' he twinkled the last time we met, 'I asked if, instead, I could have my voucher made out to Tooth's Picture Gallery. And both times, they let me. Awfully good of them, don't you think?'

Watch the Birdie

Doubtless the Ryder Cup golf tournament organizers at Muirfield Village, Ohio, this week, have spent years reading, referring back, and acting upon the minutes and memoranda produced by their various bodies and sub-committees. I bet the Greens Committee is hot stuff, and the Catering Corps, the Fairway Stewarding and the Crowd Control. The Divot Replacing Squad is all in hunky-dory order, checked and re-checked, and the Media Relations Commission. As you would expect from a club inspired, built and captioned by the supreme perfectionist, Jack Nicklaus.

But is there a sub-committee, answerable to the Locker Room Relations Group Management Executive, entitled *Marriage Guidance Sub-section*? The world's leading golfers can handle the birdies; but not many of them seem much cop in coping with birds. The divorce-rate has currently reached epidemic pro-portions. Wife-losing-wise, the Ryder Cup will finish on Sunday in a tie. With no play-off.

Offhand (although there are doubtless more), of the leading

golfers who contest the dramatic US v Europe Ryder Cup this week in Ohio (and I write, of course, before the exact teams are nominated), the divorced men on each side well outnumber the married. Within the last two years, to my certain knowledge, the marriages have broken up of: (Brits) Sandy Lyle, Nick Faldo, Sam Torrance, Howard Clark, John O'Leary, and Eamon Darcy; while Yanks who have remarried recently are Lee Trevino, Ray Floyd, Lanny Wadkins, Ben Crenshaw, and Hal Sutton (who, at the age of 29, is already with his third wife).

It surprised all but their closest friends when Christine Lyle called a press conference in the spring to announce she was seeking a divorce. She blamed the constant travelling. Since when, Sandy's game fell apart. Last month, he told the *Mail on Sunday*, as he sweated on his Ryder Cup place; 'My game is in a shambles, and so is my love life. Obviously I've got to refind my form. It's no good pretending my personal problems don't affect my golf. They flash into my mind at unexpected moments in the middle of a game.'

Marriages in golf obviously appear at risk regardless of success. It is a game for obsessives — and the obsession can take a grip on even the most uncoordinated weekend hacker. Through a year, every provincial divorce court grants hundreds of decrees: cruelty, adultery, desertion might be cited, but in a great deal of cases, I bet *golf* itself is the culprit. In fact, on the United States pro tour, it might be easier for a wife to cope with her obsessive golfer, for recently the organizers, recognizing the problem, have been endeavouring to make the circuit as hassle-proof as possible, with crèches for the kids and courtesy cars for wives. But there is more to it than that. As the fount of all such wisdom, P.G. Wodehouse, wrote over half a century ago: 'His handicap was down to 12. But these things are not all. A golfer needs a loving wife to whom he can describe every aspect of his day's play all through every long evening.'

About the same time, Henry Cotton, now well into his eighties and not long widowed after a long and happy marriage, told why he married comparatively late-ish: 'I would not advise any pro to marry till after the age of thirty. Marriage demands a division of interests and golf, particularly tournament golf, demands every minute of a man's time.' (I particularly like that *particularly*, Henry.)

Sandy, who was five years married to Christine (who was a

230

pro golfer herself), is not thirty till his next birthday. He was Open champion in 1985. This year's Open winner was Britain's other hunky six-footer, Nick Faldo, who was thirty on the penultimate day of his famous championship — and already three years divorced. In John Hopkins's harrowingly revealing biography, *In Perspective* (Allen & Unwin), Nick confesses: 'I'd come home, throw the clubs down and fiddle around. I just wasn't happy at home. Golf was my escape. I went to the course, enjoyed it and won. If I had to be at home then I would fiddle with my clubs or go and see Barry Willett, the clubmaker at St George's Hill.'

At which his former wife, Melanie, had to admit: 'Being a golf wife is a terribly secondary existence. You're always orbiting round a tremendous star. You're never shining on your own. You exist only as a satellite . . . I was screaming out for some kind of life, whereas Nick would play golf for twelve hours a day, come back to the room, have a shower, go out to dinner, and then go to bed.'

But there is one man who submerged any of his upset with humour. You would expect it of him. At the last Open, at Royal Birkdale, a few years ago, Lee Trevino introduced us to his new wife, Claudia, a sparky-eyed 26-year-old redhead. His previous wife, of twenty years, was also called Claudia. 'So I didn't have to change the name on the towels,' joked the Mexican. He said his divorce had come as a complete surprise to him — 'though I suppose I should have expected it; it's the sort of thing that happens, I guess, when you haven't been home for eighteen years.' He had, he said, to win this particular tournament for his new wife (who sat giggling next to him), because 'she went out and bought $50,000-worth of designer furniture last week — and she now needs a house to build around it!'

Rather like the line of the tennis player, Ilie Nastase, just before he divorced his lovely Belgian, Gabrielle: 'No way I'm reporting the loss of my American Express card. Whoever stole it can't possibly use it as fast as Gaby.' Though in tennis-and-matrimony, the best throwaway was uttered by a friend of Pancho Gonzales, who was married five time — 'and the nicest thing he said to any one of 'em was "*Shuddup!*"'

Test cricket, being longer to play, by a day, than a four-day golf championship should give golf a good run in the divorce stakes, though I can't think of all that many cricketing break-ups. Bill Edrich, the old Middlesex dasher, was married five times, however. Just before he died (on the very first day of the 1986 season), at his 70th birthday lunch, I asked the delightful old twinkler if his wives had ever interfered with his cricketing. 'Not really, old boy,' he said, 'but one or two of them did get in the way of my drinking.'

Best grounds for a cricketing divorce, I reckon, could have been obtained by the girl-friend of Ms Vicky Rantzen, who contributed to a correspondence on male chauvinism in the *Observer* in 1978, thus:

'Dear Sir,
When we were living in Sydney recently, a friend told me that one night, while she and her husband were making love, she suddenly noticed something sticking in his ear. When she pulled it away and asked him what it was he replied, ''Be quiet! I'm listening to the Test match from England.'''

There was also poor Mildred Rowley, who won her decree at the Stourbridge divorce court, in 1981, after telling the judge: 'I had cricket for breakfast, dinner and tea. It was like an obsession bordering on madness. He could tell you who scored what in any match played even years ago — and even what the weather was like. But he could never ever remember my birthday.'

After which the *Daily Express* traced Mildred's husband, Mike, for a comment. He was playing for the Worcestershire Marauders. 'There is nothing much I can add,' he said, then excused himself, 'Look, I'm sorry, I have to go now, I've got to get on with the game.'

Quite a few thousand golf widows, too, I fancy, know what Mildred went through. Though many do survive. In the half century between Cotton and Lyle, only one Brit won the Open — Tony Jacklin, who is, of course, the European's Ryder Cup captain this week in Ohio. Tony is still only 42, but he and Vivien celebrated their 21st anniversary in May. A couple of years ago, I had a warm, rewarding day with the Jacklins at their home in Jersey. We sat for hours drinking coffee in the kitchen, waffling on about this and that and golf. Hanging on the wall, proudly, is a poem Tony had written to Viv years ago when he was on the US tour:

I'm never happy when I'm not with you
When I'm away I'm always blue
Words cannot say how much I care
It's everything when I know you're there
Stay by me all of my life
My friend, my lover, my woman, my wife.

My love, Tony

Ahh. There's more captain Tony could be doing this week than working out the order of play. And, doubtless, he will be.

King Levinsky De Foist

I watched the televised boxing from America at the weekend with a dear, sensitive soul who winced and covered her eyes every time one of the fighters so much as cocked a fist. But she opened them, quite mesmerized, at each appearance on the screen of the American promoter, Don King. Of which there were many. His unashamed, *Hi, Mom!* camera-hogging makes Fatima Whitbread look like a Carmelite. The sound of his own voice is a black-tied orchestra to his ears. Like the late Mike Todd, Don King is an impresario singularly more impressive than any of his own productions. Certainly he has sewn up heavyweight prize-fighting in a far neater and more secure way than the mailbags he used to thread in the Ohio State Penitentiary.

King is both a manager and promoter. He can't lose — especially when, as often happens, he's manager of *both* fighters. Olde tyme cornermen were meant to say little more than, '*We'll* moider the bum,' and, '*He* got shellacked in the eighth,' before counting our their percentage. And promoters never, ever, made a profit of so much as sixpence, as successive generations of taxmen learned to jab and move and ride the blows to their professional esteem. King is different. His ego can't allow him to announce a loss.

I met Mr King in London's Park Lane hotel in 1987. He was over to listen to the entreaties from Master Frank Bruno's syndicate that their boy was ready to be hoisted on to the international gravy train. For just one gory, golden handshake anyway. It must be, I said to the affable-seeming Don, a heck of a job, this promotion lark? What did it take to be a promoter?

His spectacles steamed up. His henchmen cowered. So did I. A great voice rolled up like thunder. 'A promoter? A promoter? I am *The* Promoter. First, there was the Prophet Isaiah, yeah, then that ol' forecastin' dude Nostrah-deemuzz, then P.T. Barnum and Buffalo Bill — and then there was *Me!*'

He obviously meant every word. Sorry, sir, I said. He turned his back on me, but at least he didn't signal for a crony to throw me out. He began to comb his hair at the dressing-table and at once the frown vanished.

His hairstyle is one of eccentricity's great glories. It is an almost frightening Friesian frizz, a piebald mane that screeches up from his scalp, like a cartoon cat's whose tail is caught in an electric-light socket. I didn't dare ask him about it, but in *The Black Lights* (Robson), Thomas Hauser's dramatically successful book on boxing, King's stepson, Carl, explains how the cataclysmic crimp was first conceived: 'The style happened by accident. It was always short and combed straight up. Then, with the Ali-Foreman fight in the Congo, Pa was gone for a couple of months and didn't get it cut. It got longer and longer, and he kept combing it up. Finally people started to notice and comment. He liked that, and he decided it looked like a real king's crown.'

And hadn't the prophet said, 'And lo, the hair of my flesh stood up,' Job 4, v. 15, yeah?

That morning in his Park Lane suite, I think I got back into Mr King's good books by telling him the story of the previous American boxing 'King' who had visited these shores fifty years before, the Chicago fish porter with the telegraphed, right-hander haymaker, King Levinsky, who fought the hunky and often hilarious heavyweight from Ireland, Jack Doyle, just before the war at Wembley. At a publicity lunch to promote the fight, the toastmaster had boomingly proposed the toast to 'His Majesty the King'. Everyone solemnly stood, as is the custom. Levinsky remained seated at the top table, beaming proudly and clutching his hands above his head like the champ he wasn't. Doyle leaned down to whisper to his opponent, 'It's not for you, it's for King George the Sixth.'

234

'King Goige de Sixt?' queried Levinsky. ''What's dis Sixt? How can he be better than King Levinsky de Foist?'

Don King liked that. 'Good, yeah,' he said — then lit another cheroot and ordered an aide, 'Send some ringsides for my next lotta fights to the Queen of England, yeah, and that Princess Fergie, and that Mrs Thatcher; now there's a fighter for you, your Margaret, yeah.' One can only presume they got the comps for last weekend. What a shame they never turned up.

I resumed the conversation more carefully. How was he liking England? 'Your little country,' he said, 'has the grace and style and elegance which suits me fine, yeah, just as it suited Captain Nelson, Winnie Churchill, Maggie Thatcher, the Marquee [as in tent] dee Queensberee, and that cool cat of yours, Willie Shakespeare, yeah.'

He had, said Don, read all of Shakespeare's works in prison. His four-year stretch had been his Harvard and Yale, his Oxford and Cambridge. In 1967, he had been found guilty of second-degree murder after a street brawl; the verdict was later reduced to manslaughter. Between mailbags, he says, he devoured books by the crate. He started at the beginning — 'dat Genisis thing's real mind blowing, yeah' — reading, he tells you, 'from the chinks of light under the door in solitary. For ''They that dwell in the land of the shadow of death, upon them doth the light shine,'' Isaiah 9, v. 2, yeah.' Then the New Testament. Then Aristotle and Homer. 'Then that Sigmund guy, yeah, Freud. Then Marx, Karl Marx, a cold sunuvabitch, Marx, but I learned a lot outa him. But most from your Willie Shakespeare, yeah, a cool, fun-living dude that Willie, eh?'

King is 56, born into an impoverished family of seven in the mean suburbs of Cleveland. His first job was delivering crates of battery chickens from Hymie's Chicken Shack to the city abattoir. Escape lay in the underworld's murky numbers game. His backstreet fist-fight happened when he was almost *numero uno*, and had just taken delivery of his first pink Cadillac. But, as he tells you with pride, four years in the slammer was the making of him, and matched his intellect to his energy: 'Yeah, for as Willie-boy, your Bard, says, ''Adversity is ugly and venomous like a toad, yet she wears a precious jewel in her head,'' yeah.'

King and a mischievous Norman Mailer once apparently compared reading lists. 'Yeah, philosophy — Masters and Johnson, Kinsey, that cat, Freud, and, what's the guy . . .?' He

235

hesitated momentarily, 'Knees Itch, I read a lotta him. Who? 'Knees Itch. You know Nig Zitch.' Oh, Nietzsche. 'Yeah, that's the dude, I learned me a lot from him.'

And all the time the fingers saw the air like dazzling disco strobe-lights. For on each is appended the front window of Tiffany's. Gold and diamonds, rings as square as matchboxes, or as round as glinting new half-crowns: and a watch which is a bejewelled Big Ben. They could start *News at Ten* with a close-up of Don King's wrist.

Once the tap is turned on it continues to spout with scarcely a pause for breath. A quip a minute, a quote a minute. I just managed to get in my last crucial question. What chance, in Mr King's scheme of things, had Frank Bruno of becoming world heavyweight champ? The very same potty poser (well, who in his right mind doesn't know that the answer lies between slim an none?) was being asked after last weekend's little lot.

Young Frank will get his opportunity, said The Promoter — even though 'your noble British boy can't fight and is too dumb to sell many tickets in the States, yet "oppressed and afflicted, He will be brought as a lamb to the slaughter, and as a sheep before her shearers," yeah, Isaiah 53, v. 7. Yeah, that's Job talkin' to the Lord, yeah, Job talkin' to the Lord through me, Don King. A neat ol' cat, that Job, yeah?'

George Plimpton wincingly once turned away when King boasted he was the man who turned 'colossal' into 'super-colossal'. Said Plimpton, 'He can't really turn lemon into lemonade.' Another American journalist, Mark Cram, said King's ambitions in fact remain small time: 'He only wants to swallow mountains, walk on oceans, sleep on clouds.'

King, for sure, is one of the anti-heroes of our dotty sporting times, in which the gamesman and the gamecock are far bigger than the game. Yeah, and yeah again.

Fields and Tracks

Not Just a Pretty Race

In her relentlessly droning effort to get the message across and damn, for the campaign, all quirky British diversions (even down to those potty daily letters they read out on Radio 4's *PM* programme) I'm surprised Mrs Thatcher hasn't even considered asking Tebbit, N., to ban the Derby this year.

Perhaps, as the nation has continued to weigh up the pros and cons of every runner and rider this week, she's simply presumed this Derby business was something to do with Rolls-Royce shares. Well, Legal Bid, Reference Point, Shady Heights, and even Ascot Knight have all got a City ring to them, haven't they? (By the way, Dr David Owen, I am reliably informed by my man in the hedge at the dawn gallops, has put his mortgage on Don't Forget Me, fast fading from the favourites' lists as the 'Off!' approaches.)

Mrs T., alas, is not a sporty type. When Her Majesty talks of The Lincoln, her Prime Minister thinks of The Marginal. The weekend she launched her election campaign, Central Office wheeled their boss off to the Cup Final. She wore not the powdery-blue of Coventry, the winners, but the dark blue of the Hotspurs, who were so surprisingly walloped. Omens, omens, everywhere.

Every time I caught a glimpse of her at Wembley — at the most thrilling game in years — Margaret Hilda looked totally bemused by the whole plebeian fandango. She spent not only all of half-time, but most of the climactic extra-time, studiously and frowningly engrossed in her match programme, as if some explanation of the whole mysterious hoo-ha might be secreted in its small-print.

Mind you, this tactic could look very good indeed if they persuade her to the Derby in the interests of grabbing an extra vote or two. Spending an afternoon at the races, with your nose deep in the race-card or form-book, is quite in order and suggests you really know what you're on about. So do watch out this Wednesday for Grantham's petite chestnut mare in the blue polka-dot silks — the experience at Wembley might have encouraged her to think that the in-thing at Epsom was likewise to dance about on tiptoe, waving scarves and chanting *Erewego! Erewego! Erewego*! all around the Royal Enclosure.

But, on the whole, I fancy it would be safer for the Tories to ban the Derby till after the votes have been counted next Thursday. Unless Saatchi Bros can contrive to get the hot favourite to walk it, that is, and so put the populace in relieved good humour about Them and Us for the next eight days.

If Mrs Thatcher did manage to ban the race in her effort to persuade the country to concentrate on 'the issues', however, she would verily crown her wilful, constitutional career. For two World Wars and quite a few other Second Division colonial skirmishes have not once stopped the top-hatted Derby starter mounting his rostrum at the tapes, for the big one in this first week of June.

By the spring of 1915, for instance, the Epsom Grandstand had been commandeered by the War Office and Red Cross to serve as a hospital for the poor wounded soldiers who had been ferried back from the trenches. Fair enough, said Mr Dorling, the owner of the course, as long as they were out by Derby Day. All hell broke loose in glorious, insane Britishness. The Jockey Club was split on the matter and so, it was rumoured, was the War Cabinet itself. The Duke of Portland, a leading owner, withdrew his entries for the race, announcing: 'It is beyond the comprehension of the French Government that people should turn wounded men out of a Grand Stand or even go to the Races when their sons are in the trenches. The Epsom Grand Stand authorities have, indeed, aimed a heavy blow at the prestige of our grand old English sport.'

The Editor of *The Times* waded in: 'The frame of mind which can contemplate turning wounded soldiers out to make room for luncheon parties is beyond conception . . . (and) the whole atmosphere of the racecourse crowd is utterly abhorrent to those who realize the character of this tremendous war. We are convinced that any attempt to hold the great popular racing festivals, such as Epsom, will make a deplorably bad impression on our neighbours, the French . . . (As) the Ascot meeting falls on

239

a date when the war may be at its climax, can it be seemly to hold it when millions of men, including great numbers of our own people, will be at death-grips?'

Raucous debate bounced around the chamber of the House of Commons. *The Times* had to clear its letters column of opinions on the War itself. Lord Rosebery, for one, was horrified at the very thought of cancelling the Derby. He wrote: 'This, the greatest of all Races, had been held only ten days before the Battle of Waterloo, to not the slightest detriment for the British troops' morale.'

Another appalled correspondent recalled how the result of the Derby had been given out in General Orders to all troops in the Crimean War; and yet another fired off an incensed signal to the newspaper in heroic remembrance of his finishing his first day's march with Lord Roberts, from Johannesburg to Pretoria, in June 1900 — and seeing Britain's Boer War army, 'just settling down in their bivouacs, when suddenly we saw heliographs flashing and mounted messengers galloping to their various units, their arrival being greeted by loud and prolonged cheering.' The message, signed 'The Field Marshal Commanding in Chief', read: 'Epsom Derby. Winner by $\frac{1}{2}$ length, Diamond Jubilee (by St Simon out of Perdita 11), 6-4 fav., ridden by Herbie Jones, trained by R. Marsh, and owned by HM Prince of Wales.'

In the event, in 1915, the 'wets' won the day — sort-of, for though the Epsom Grandstand was kept as a hospital, the Derby itself was transferred for the four-year duration of the War to Newmarket, Steve Donaghue and Joe Childs each winning twice. Tradition was established and in the Second World War, the Derby encamped again to Newmarket, this time calmly and without any parliamentary debate, Bill Nevett riding three of the five winners. (The first at Newmarket, by the way, was won in June 1940, only a couple of days after the evacuation of Dunkirk! Not only that — the 1940 winner was called Pont L'Eveque, Sam Wragg 'up', and it came in on the very day that Hitler's tank divisions were rolling over the same bridge to take the little town across the Channel.

In the age of our Iron Lady, to be sure, it is difficult to credit that Parliamentary Victorian Values invariably demanded that the House of Commons would officially recess every Derby Day. The first proposal for an adjournment on the famous day was

240

made by Lord George Bentinck in 1848 — and granted to a chorus of 'Ayes!' The custom continued more or less annually till, towards the end of the century, the House got bogged down with Irish Home Rule and conscientiousness got the better part of sportin' fervours.

Hansard records it all, deadpan. There was a wild adjournment debate, for instance, on Derby Eve, 1894, when, on the morrow, the Liberal Party leader, the same Lord Rosebery, was running his hot favourite, Ladas. Even the Tory MP, Henry Chaplin, put in an impassioned plea for an adjournment: 'Political enemy I may be, but I hope the Liberal Party will return from Epsom tomorrow conscious of the enormous advantage they have gained by winning the Blue Ribbon of the Turf . . .'

To no avail. The 'dries' were beginning to be outnumbered and they were well routed that day — though one Tory, Mr Maclure, rose to say the division vote to him was of complete indifference: 'For to the Derby I will go; I have not missed that event in all my thirty years in this House, and I am not going to miss it again in my present advanced period of my life.' Thus, next day, the old boy saw the Leader of the Liberal Party lead his 9-2 on favourite into the winner's enclosure, Johnnie Watts up.

By the turn of the century, the Derby adjournment was not even debated. A new breed had taken over. On Derby Eve, 1907, Horatio Bottomley mischievously rose in the House at Question Time to ask of the Prime Minister, Campbell-Bannerman, if he would grant the House the following day off, 'on account of the nation's great National Festival'. The Premier had not the forggiest idea what the Hon Member was talking about. Racing-buff Bottomley persisted, much to the merriment of those hearty members in the know, as the pinched-lipped Campbell-Bannerman looked even more vacantly bemused. Finally, Bottomley put him out of his misery. 'Has the Prime Minister forgotten,' he enquired with rascally double-bluff, 'that tomorrow is the Poet Laureate's birthday?' Laughter, as they say, from the hearties of both benches.

The unsporty Campbell-Bannerman continued, apparently, to be totally perplexed by it all. He must have looked rather like Mrs Thatcher at Wembley.

First Class

They are heading for the last rev-up this weekend in, of all places, dozy Adelaide, Adelaide, ever dozin' Adelaide. This one will sure unhibernate the Aussies, for the din will be quite ridiculous — and so will the attendant ratpack of conceited, obsessive, greenback-and-girl-greedy glitzy folk who feel obliged to follow motor racing's Grand prix circuit to the ends of the earth. I've gatecrashed it a few times over the years and, always, the best thing about a Grand Prix is the day after a Grand Prix.

Come to think of it, 1987 has been one heck of a year for *speed*, both ancient and modern. Man's most primitive propulsion, shanks's pony, was ridden faster than ever before, i.e. Ben Johnson's electric dash to the (surely unbreakable?) 100 metre running record. Then the four-legged variety, and the horse-racing fraternity have just finished doffing their trilbies, en-thralled at the months-long round Britain whizz of the two midget millionaires — Cauthen, the Yank with the 'hands' from the heart of Marlboro country, and Eddery, po-faced, prow-nosed pixie from green Galway. There had been nothing like it for at least a quarter of a century, when the gnarled little Breasley, of Her Majesty's colonies, would annually charge, head-to-head to the final wire, alongside the parchment-faced Piggott, now of Her Majesty's pleasure.

The motor racing year has been dominated by just as riveting a rivalry. What made the challenge between Nigel Mansell and the new champion Nelson Piquet so singularly intriguing right through the spring, summer and autumn till Mansell's prang in Japan, was that they went on snarling at each other even though they were in the *same team* and, more often than not (and sometimes literally), miles ahead of any other car on the circuit. If the turbo-charged partnership of Williams-Honda was working smoothly, then the highly-charged human partnership of Mansell-Piquet certainly was not.

But it's all over now, for Sunday's final race in Adelaide represents the end of the era in motor racing. It is all-change

242

both in the cockpit and the pits. New rules begin turning back the all-conquering turbo-charged entines into obsolescence by 1989 — and with Honda's fire-power dramatically divorcing itself from the Williams chassis, and taking up with Lotus and McLaren, 1988's interim season promises, politically, to be a very different bore game.

That is the sketchy gist of it, I gather, but the rude mechanical exactitudes are quite beyond me, so I won't attempt to elaborate. But I hope the 'new', normally-aspirated Williams car next year will not be humiliatingly left chugging along at the rear of the field. Not so much for Nigel Mansell's sake — he'll still get his wages — but for Frank Williams's. A hell of a guy is Mr Williams.

Funnily enough, in this season of form-filling for the various awards for the Sportsman of the Year, it would be far more appropriate to get one for the *Backroom Boss*. His talent depends on how you tot up the scores in sports these days. For instance, in horse racing, while the world and his wife were hollering home either Cauthen or Eddery, the one genuine and indisputable man of the racing year was quietly, even shyly, going about his business without so much as an *hooray* from the fancy that lean so intently over the low white rails of the paddock.

The Newmarket trainer, Henry Cecil, outrageously smith-ereened the 120-year-old record of winners saddled from a single stable — overtaking John Day's 1867 tally of 146 with over two months of the season still to run. Silver spoon and all that — but you cannot deny the 44-year-old's spectacular knack with nags. He may be the stepson of Sir Cecil Boyd-Rochfort, and the son-in-law of Sir Noel Murless — but if anyone deserves a knighthood for sporting excellence this new Year, then I reckon young Cecil does.

Unless it's Frank Williams. A year older than Cecil, the head of the racing car company had got 1987's Grand Prix Constructor's Championship trophy in the bag even, propor-tionately, earlier in the summer than the racing trainer had his bit of silver for the mantelpiece. Home and dry, even though he had one or two other things on his mind through the previous twelve months or so.

In the spring of 1986, WIlliams was driving himself back to Nice airport after supervising a practice session at the Paul Ricard circuit, east of Marseilles. He was in a rush as usual to catch the aeroplane. He took a B-road short cut, and in the village of Moulinon he careered off, wrote off his car and, it was presumed by the ambulanceman, himself. 'Totally my fault,' he says now, 'I was always a pathetic driver, I'm afraid.'

He has (there is no better word for it) masterminded this season's series of astonishing one-two Williams coups from a wheelchair. He is paralysed from the shoulders down. He has to be fed at meal-times, as he says, 'like a month-old baby by a nurse', and carried in and out of cars or aeroplanes 'like a legless octogenarian by two strong men'. But the Williams has kept on winning — both for, and thanks to, the shattered Mr Williams himself.

Whenever I pass those fume-belching, doom-laden concrete hourglasses clustered alongside the railway line just outside Didcot station, I always crane my neck just to catch a reassuring glance of the span-spick, low-slung Williams Engine Works. I'd often said to myself that one day I should get off the train and pay them a visit. And one day, a few weeks ago, I did.

Frank Williams's welcome is so affable, so cheery, the face so animated, the brain (as you are to discover) so sharp and keen, that you totally forget yourself and stick out a mitt for a matey handshake across his desk. Without any rancour, he grimaces and wincingly endeavours to hoist an elbow, or even bend a wrist, which might crank up at least the tiny flicker of a hand in greeting. But he cannot even shake hands.

He can talk though — marvellously — and, as I say, *mastermind*, and later that week he was going to be wheeled into the pits for another Grand Prix, and, as he sat there seemingly broken-bodied and useless, they would clamp the earphones to his head, and a radio mike to his lips, and in direct, dramatic contact with his two drivers, he would tell them the score as they vroomed and fumed around their daredevil fortnightly dice.

Reception is usually perfect. The drivers have their earphones built into their helmets, though the boss will only speak if he's spoken to: 'No, there's no way I call up just for a chat, like "Hi, Nigel, you've left your rear onside winker on!"'

Mansell, said Williams, was more talkative than Piquet during a race; perhaps a bit more insecure, or even simply more interested in lap times and opponents' performances behind him. But when I asked which of his two fliers — it still looked likely that they were heading for a last showdown to the final flag at Adelaide — the boss, understandably, would not separate the different talents of his workers. 'Nigel's Nigel and Nelson's Nelson. Chalk and cheese, and both immensely quick. In the two-and-a-bit years he's been with us it's honestly been quite thrilling to see Nigel getting quicker and quicker and quicker. Then add his determination, his grit, his solid application — and, I suppose, the fact that he's an Englishman! Oh, yes, a strange fire and venom burns in Nigel now. Just as it has always ignited Nelson. With Nelson, brooding venom helps light up his astonishing driver-skills. Well, name me a more genuine contender for any championship in any year he has ever entered? He has the speed all right, the raw, untarnished stuff, but he also has the innate ability to steer through, well, let's say that 190mph right-hander at Ricard, and not lose a single millimetre of control on his racing line — and do the very same for every one of 80 times through the full 80 laps. That's car control at speed, right?'

Right, 1987 — last of the fast years.

Biddlecombe in the Springtime

Spring has sprung — official. Because it's Cheltenham next week, the veriest fall-game festival in the history of the world. To any hunkydory, genuine horse-racing man from the British Isles — as opposed to the pinch-lipped, narrow-eyed, international balance-sheet syndicates of The Flat — Cheltenham is a sporting celebration of the nation's enthusiasms that knocks your Wembley, Ascot, Lord's and Wimbledon into one tatty cocked hat.

That's not me tub-thumping with such certainty and relish, mind. It's a fellow who really knows about these matters; and its a delight to let him have his final say. After next week, Cheltenham will not be quite the same for men of my generation: Terry Biddlecombe, ever-cheery champ, the bombing, blue-eyed blond from up the Tewkesbury Road, is emigrating to Australia. He is, it goes without saying, mustard keen for new challenges — but, by golly, the late-night cheerios will be heartfelt and bleary next week.

It is just on forty years ago that the chubby little urchin of eight was allowed to play truant from his Gloucester school for the day — and father Biddlecombe stood his son, entranced and palpitating, by the water-jump at Cheltenham on Gold Cup day. 'We didn't pay, just shoved through a hedge. Cottage Rake won it. I can still hear the roll of thunder as the hooves approached us. The sound, the speed, the cursing jocks. Sensational. I must have thought then, 'This is for me".'

It is all very well for you and me and the world and his wife to get softly sentimental about how the Cheltenham meeting heralds the spring and all that: the early train down from Paddington; the glistening sun popping out of hibernation; the comradeship, the crowds and the colours; the winning scrum, the losers' luck, and, oh, the liquor that's lapped up — and in Lent, too.

It must be mighty different for the jockeys. They see Cheltenham from inside the rails. I bought Biddlecombe breakfast, a whopping great racing man's fry-up, plus a snorting couple of chasers of the five-star Napoleon variety. It was still pre-Cheltenham, so spring hadn't quite sprung, and it was yet very nippy up on the dawn gallops. You stir the spirit into his coffee, then mix in the still piping-hot memories. Twenty-one years ago Biddlecombe, local laddo and now champion of all England, lined up at the start of the 1967 Gold Cup: 'Just eight of us. Fort Leney, What a Myth, a copule of others. Stan (Mellor) was on the grey, Stalbridge Colonist, and Dave (Nicholson) on the great Mill House. But I had some horse, too: Woodland Venture was a bit temperamental, but lovely really, just needed settling — and at once, cripes, needed to be 'cos we hit the first so hard that we were still charging on the rebound through the second, scattering everything everywhere.

'Then we settled, comfy. Down the hill, first time round, Dave, alongside, shouts, "If we continue like this, Biddles, we'll be on the Queen Mum's Christmas cards this year!" We both got over — just — in a great explosion of birch twigs and swear words, and I looks across at Dave and says, "Well, that's cocked up her Easter cards for certain, boy!'

'Nice and easy now . . . round the great big curve to the lea of the hill. Easy does it, boy. It's like a musician picking up the tempo, gently, gently, not too much, not too little. Now it's really picking up, and so are your nerves. Only five or six left now. Still upsides, Dave coming to the ditch: I simply slew it, but suddenly there was Dave hanging on for dear life before finally dropping off. Hard luck — and, great, I'm in front, always the best place to have your little breather at Chelt, just there at the top of the hill.

'Then suddenly it's steep, very. And it's a hell of a downhill gallop, and those two ruddy fences that if you hit them with the foreleg at full pelt it is definite curtains, or worse. As we move in, his ears prick up, that first-aid hut is too close, he's distracted; we're going to go! The fence is charging at us. Crikey, that's it, finish! We leg it over somehow — give away two lengths, must have — but we're still in front.

'Two to go. The little bend, and the sanded road. Two to go, and now the hill's in front of you — uphill, and you can see the great crowds banked on either side. A great uphill tunnel. Still no sound, mind. Just eerie silence. Is it possible I'm going to win? No, just keep calm, keep control. You can win it here, but you can also lose it.

'We pop over easy. Don't look round. Keep control, boy. Are they cheers in the faraway distance or what? Yes. I'm their local lad, aren't I? They want me to do it. I will. It's going to be okay! Just one more, just one more, then home.

'Suddenly, what's this? Hooves upsides. It's the grey! Sod me, it's Mellor. The bastard! I'm a goner. No one can beat Mellor on the run-in if your horse is weakening. He's such a puncher and kicker, squeezing out the last ounce. He sort-of bounces them home; don't let him do it to me, please, not in the ruddy Gold Cup.

'Mellor's got that grin on him. And now the fear of God's really in me. He's going away; no, he isn't, we're holding him. Control, balance, here comes the last. Settle yourself, boy.

'Here we go! Stride for stride. *Hup*! What the hell! To this day no one knows what happened, but just as we land, my left rein goes. Just like that. I'm left with only a right hand. And that at once gets all tangled up. Just what I need for a motoring finish with ruddy Mellor. At once he's a length or two up. Grinning, I bet. At least we've landed. I grab and fumble at the rein in panic. Then we're re-balanced. Well done, boy! Let's go at him! Me and Mellor up that hill like bats out of hell. To beat Mellor is always mind over matter. Dig in! Go for it. Close the space. It's closing! Mellor's shagged out, too! Go on! We're upsides! The intensity. I shout and scream, "Please, post! Please, post!" I can't hear another sound now, just me shouting, and Stan pleading with his grey, "Go on! Damn you, go on!" "*Please post! Please, post!*" '

Woodland Venture (T. Biddlecombe up) won by half a length. They were on the Queen Mum's Christmas cards.

Now the old hero has one last Cheltenham left. After the final, final farewells, it's a new life to be lived (naturally) to the very brimming full Down Under. Cheltenham will be held during Terry's first Australian autumn. Not quite the same thing at all.

"Ey, look here, stop making me cry already. Australia doesn't wipe out memories, does it? Cheltenham was my youth. The big event; the colours, the buzz of it; the wind in your face as you turn and canter down to the start; that jellied-eel tent at the top of the parade where not once did I ever not say to myself I'm going to dismount and buy a plateful; and the Irish over, and the Fathers — "Bejasus, I never have a bet myself, sor," but the wads of money folded flat inside the rim of their dog-collars — and all around the local farmers, your family, your family friends and their cousins and aunties, and the whole wide world shouting up at you, "You trying today, Biddles?" and "Win this one for us, eh Terry!" and "C'mon, Terry boy, you can do it!" '

The English spring is officially reborn again next Tuesday. In Gloucestershire.

The Truly Incredible, A-Maze-ing Mr Walker

If, like I was, you were inclined to think that the sport of Grand Prix motor racing was one of noisy monotony, then you should have wincingly cocked an ear into the BBC television commentator's box at Silverstone on Sunday. Raucous, sure, but dull it ain't when Murray Walker's your man at the mike.

Murray does it standing up. Dancing, cavorting, swaying and braying at one and the same time, microphone in hand, he jigs about his hut as charged up with revs as the cars which, by the second, crescendo past his window. Distant voices, terse and passionate, are screeching into his earphones. His spectacles glint back at the monitor set. His bark has the bite of the passionate enthusiast. But even he cannot see the half of it, for the 200mph action is entwined round a hillocky three or four square miles. There is no other sports commentary that can be quite so difficult. But if Walker's voice wasn't being heard above the din on Sunday, well, to two or three generations it wouldn't *really* have been the British Grand Prix, would it?

In 1988 at Silverstone he celebrates the fortieth anniversary of his first Grand Prix commentary there — when John Bolster, in an ERA, came barrelling down Hangar Straight towards Stowe Corner, launched into a fearful roll, end over end, to finish up in a mangled heap right in front of the commentary box. The nation held its breath, and then, in his first introductory slice of understatement, Murray remarked calmly enough, 'I think John Bolster has gone off.' The Murray Walker Fan Club was up and running.

There will be another anniversary in 1988 — for it will be sixty years since his father, Murray Snr, became the world's first motorcycle racer to average 80mph, in winning the 1928 Ulster Grand Prix. Thus has young Murray been steeped in the fumes of motor sport for just about every one of his 64 years. His first bike was a 1928 Aerial Colt. I am not an *aficionado* by any means, but I have been riveted by conversations with Murray on the men and machines, the great and (often, alas) late of those pioneering days. He continued to see it all, travelling through Europe with his father who, after he popped out of the saddle, was the BBC's first wireless commentator.

After Highgate, Murray was apprenticed at Dunlop, then commissioned at Sandhurst during the war, ending up as a captain after the push from Normandy to the Baltic. Then he embarked on a highly successful career as an advertising executive — and he lists the national accounts he got off the ground like it was a sung litany: Pal, Lassie, Chappie, Kit-E-Kat; Trill and Treets; Mars Bar, Milky Way, Galaxy, and Bounty Bar.

All the while, almost as a weekend hobby, he was making every Grand Prix that little bit grander with his distinctive decibels and zanily glorious *non sequiturs*. Murray Walker is unique — or, as he might put it (and has), '*This leading car is absolutely unique, except for the one behind it, which is identical.*'

249

There is no broadcaster quite like Mr Walker. '*And now he's totally in front of everyone in this race – except for the two in front of him.*' No one leads Murray. I doubt if anyone alive has witnessed more of the screaming pageant that has whizzed past his window in the last half century. His father was a legend. And legends introduce sons to legends. Nuvaroli, he reckons, was the greatest of all. Murray first saw Nuvaroli fifty years ago: 'His manager was a family friend. I can remember it like it was yesterday, all of us going up to Donington that Saturday in 1938. He drove an Auto Union. He was in a short-sleeved cricket sweater, and wore a pre-Rockfist Rogan cloth helmet. Sliding around all over the place, but never not smiling. In a way he was a right scruffy 'erbert, but always a lovable, arm waving, laughing, archetypal Latin; all arms and elbows and thrills, and four-wheeled drifts round corners, all opposite lock, and brakes and slides and dust — and always that carefree smile. Nuvaroli was the one we queued up all night to watch, the guy who was always 50mph faster than he had any right to be. Unquestionably the greatest.'

Nuvaroli's bitter rival was Varzi, another Italian: 'Crikey, what a contrast. Varzi was all clinical coldness at the wheel. Aloof, detached, immaculately but sinisterly dressed in black always. He treated a car like he did his many women — with brooding disdain: he would just use them, do what he wanted with them . . . but he had none of the dash of his compatriot, which the whole world loved.'

Varzi settled in Argentina when he retired — and was one of the first to encourage a young man from the mountains to go and try his luck on the circuits of Europe. At last he came over, in 1948, and at once Juan Fangio 'proceeded to blow everyone off the track: we had never seen anything like him: a gracious gentleman who could drive like the wind: the furious European drivers just couldn't keep up with him.'

Okay, Murray had seen them all, so name me the top five of all time? He starts confidently: 'In spite of Fangio's genius, I must name him second to my beloved Nuvarolo as the all-time great.'

Then a long pause (a very rare thing for a Murray watcher), followed by a great room-splitting laugh (a most regular thing) as he conceded defeat: 'Yep, I totally funk it: third place has to be a dead heat between the two Germans, Rosemeyer (killed,

Frankfurt, 1938), and Caracciola (died in his bed, 1959), and in fourth place I just can't split the difference between Moss (alive and well and still gossiping for London), the truly incredible Clark (killed, Hockenheim, 1968), and the amazing Stewart (still geeing up the world).'

Truly Incredible and *A-Maze-ing*. These are the enthusiast's words Murray has given his narrow-eyed, loot-laden, corporate 'sport'. The fans on Sunday were wearing T-shirts bearing those two simple legends — and everyone knew to whom they affectionately referred. The one I liked best was more sophisticated, and recalls one of the commentator's decibel-drenched all-time classics. On the front is printed *Unless I Am Very Much Mistaken*... and, on the back, *YES I Am Very Much Mistaken*...

Of the present crop, I fancy the little French Aznavour, Alain Prost, looks the only one likely to make Walker's Top Ten: 'Alain's not only a truly great thinking driver, but a gritty little devil as well. He's so incredibly smooth, neat and unobtrusive, that he never actually seems to be going very fast. Like you're waiting for him to take a corner — then all of a sudden, crikey, he's been past and you never even saw him come or go. Then full pelt in a cloud of dust, might come, say. Keke Rosberg, rocketing round that same corner almost like a Nuvaroli — all flamboyant whizz and wonder and four-wheel skid. And then you check the times and find that Prost had been quicker through the corner by a full half second.'

Truly A-Maze-ing!

Twentieth-Century Fox

My neighbours have bought a big horse and put him in the old stable/shed in the yard behind my kitchen window. Ah, the clatter of hoof and the pong of pony. I discover I had never forgotten how to make that friendly clicking noise of tooth and tongue with which Roy Rogers used to converse with Trigger. Actually, this gentle-eyed, four-footed, new friend of mine is more than a horse: he's a hunter. For the past fortnight the whole holiday has been in hock, as my neighbours prepare their whinnying offspring for the New Year's Day Hunt. I have been mugging up — just for conversational purposes, you understand.

It is no easy matter trying to make sense of a world that calls scarlet 'pink', 30 hounds '15 couple', and says 'Good mornin'' at tea-time because huntsmen, traditionally, never stop for lunch. Also, did ye ken John Peel with his coat so *gay*, i a dead giveaway? It's *grey*, because he used to ride out with the Border, whose coats are the colour of steel-grey flannel.

Yet, in a way, anything goes. If, that is, you know *exactly* how far to go. One of the most touching obituaries for Charles Douglas-Home, the Editor of *The Times* who died, much mourned, at the very beginning of the present hunting season, appeared in that wonderfully unchanging, weekly record of a seemingly unchanging world, *Horse and Hound*: 'The distinguished Editor was noted for his occasional disregard for convention in matters of dress, and the hunting field was no exception. He caused Captain Ronnie Wallace and some other Heythrop stalwarts more than a few twinges of disquiet by choosing to appear in the hunting field in a brown velvet cap with a brown coat; then graduating to a black cap with a red coat, and when this was pointed out to be the prerogative of Masters he cheerfully treated the red coat with blue dye, producing a remarkable plum colour which he sported out hunting regularly, alternating it with a red cutaway, worn with a black cap.'

Nevertheless, it is said he remained the best of friends with Capt Wallace through a hunting career, 'punctuated by horrendous falls which he bore with extraordinary fortitude'.

By a tragic fluke, the week Douglas-Home died *The Times* carried a cracking good feature on the myths and manners of the hunting field, by Victoria Mather. It might even have been the last piece he ever commissioned. It has been an essay crucial to my research. Myths, manners . . . and menus. Thus have I started training with the huntsman's diet, that goes something like this: 'Breakfast: Porridge and cold pheasant or, for the less robust, kedgeree, and very strong tea with a tot of brandy. Lunch: A flask of Amontillado sherry is attached to the saddle (Asprey's) with a silver top that doubles as a cup. Supper: If you can make it through dinner, without falling asleep, then it is time to enjoy brown-bread pudding soaked in naval rum, blended with three eggs, clotted cream and strawberry preserve.'

Ms Mather's educational 'in' and intriguing piece also insisted you cleaned your hunting topper by 'devoting the evening before to stroking the edifice with Guinness to achieve a suitably distinguished shine'. Boots, she said, should be hand-made by Charles Smith, of Northampton, and cleaned with a caressing elbow-grease, plus 'champagne and apricot jam'.

See, I didn't say *caressin'*. Poor form that. Another help to my diligent swotting has been Wilson Stephens, the celebrated arbiter in all these matters, who was for over a quarter of a century the Editor of *The Field* in its heyday. Long ago, he decreed: 'The dropping of a final g, as in huntin', is often done. There is no law against it. Yet it causes anger among persons who are themselves not free of idiosyncrasies in diction. To drop the final g is no worse, and certainly no better than speaking with a regional accent, the shock effect of which went out with the suffragette movement. Many hunting traditionalists refrain, for undisclosed reasons, from saying "Good morning" on non-hunting days, the approved salutation being "Good day". When hounds are out "Good morning" comes into its own because there is no such thing as afternoon to hunting people . . . Such small details in speech loom large in hunting circles, since they mark a man as being one of the old school. To be of the old school is high praise indeed, even when fidelity to the past proves disastrous in its effect, as it does from time to time, and indeed ranks high as one of hunting's unadmitted problems.'

Pronunciation is proving more difficult than even vocab. In the local library, I found these two H's in a dictionary: 'HOLLOA (or "View Holloa", pronounced Holler). The shout or screech given by someone who has seen a fox; the noise informs the huntsman or hounds of the fact, HUIC HOLLOA (pronounced *Hike Holler*. Huic means "Hark"). A shout or screech to draw hounds or huntsman's attention to a Holloa further away. Thus a whipper-in (never "whip") might hear a good Holloa some two or three fields from a covert where hounds are drawing. The whipper-in might canter up a ride inside the covert shouting "Huic Holloa! Huic Holloa! Huic Holloa!"'

Quite so. I suppose it will soon be second nature to me. Meanwhile, I can stand at my kitchen window making amiable clicking noises to my new friend, Trigger, across the way as he strains to get out of his newly sawn-off, half door. I get on with cooking a brown-bread pudding soaked in navy rum.

Hunting folk, I learn, are as keen on correct colours in cuisine as they are in coats. Of an evenin', before the rum pud, a huntin' chap expects some sort of meat dish sandwiched between mousses 'of indeterminate flavour but different colours -beige to start with and pink to follow'.

In the bumper Christmas 1985 Number of *Horse and Hound*, there was a classic piece by Chris Collins, giving tyros like me instructions on entertaining the hunt Master to Lunch. Roast beef, schoolroom cabbage and lashings of claret are the only things. '*Nouvelle Cuisine* should be regarded in the same light as interval training — i.e. as a dangerous form of mumbo-jumbo to be avoided at all costs,' instructs Mr Collins with a marvellously magisterial certainty. Master does not want his roast immersed in a lake of puréed apricots. Nor will he appreciate conversation being drowned by the munching and chomping of raw vegetables. 'Pudding should be of the nursery variety, e.g. apple pie or spotted dick.'

More than one MFN is known to judge members of his field by the quality of his proffered port. As for cheeses, Collins says the order of the day should be Stilton, proper Cheddar, or a Blue Shropshire — 'All attitudes towards cheese should start with the certainty that things start going seriously downhill as one steams into Calais.'

I've asked the neighbours and a few of their friends to pop round after the New Year's Day hunt. Good morning! G'day! *Huic Holloa*! First I must clean my boots and topper. Will someone please pass the champagne, Guinness, and apricot jam!

If only Trigger twigged. Let alone our poor little defenceless friend, Reynard.

Point of Order

C'mon my son! I say, jolly good show. The point-to-point season began at Aldershot last Saturday. Soon the equally breathless whoops and curses of the eventers will be reaching a crescendo. It all means spring is springing fast. You don't need a calendar in England. You can tick off the seasons by what the nags are doing.

A point-to-point used to provide a remarkably good day out. As a mite, I used to go to the meeting at Belmont, near Hereford. One of the water-jumps was, honestly, an open sewer. But you soon got used to the pong, farmers all brought their own home-brewed, lethal cider, and the bookie cheerfully accepted bets of sixpence each way. You always backed the second favourite and, if my memory's right, it always seemed to win. It was a lovely gathering of the clan and everyone went home happy — and totally sloshed.

You used to meet fellows next to you in the Hillman Huskied car-park, alongside the 'rails', who would waddle off, pie-eyed, to ride the 3.10 (point-to-points, as a matter of principle, never start on the hour or half-hour; or certainly never did in my day). You'd never catch sight of him when they came round, even for the first circuit, but he'd be back (often, courtesy of St John's boys in blue) around 3.25, spattered in mud and blood. He'd take a large swig of apple-juice and insist, 'She went beautifully, bar that bit of trouble at the second . . . he's a great ride, even if he is taking his time to mature,' which, roughly translated, means, 'I was only on the thing for about 20 seconds when he tipped me into the sewer . . . I've wasted six years and a ruddy fortune on the beast, and now can't even afford to trade him in for a pit pony.'

I have a hunch, alas, that the point-to-point has been dragged up-market. Somebody told me the other day that they were charging a tenner for a place in the car-park, and that you can not only hear the PA announcements these days, but they've hired special experts from London to make them with BBC voices. Shame. And, oh dearie me, the fastbuck bookies . . .

A week or two ago there was a letter in that weekly treasure-trove of all matters neighing, *Horse & Hound*, that warned of a troubled point-to-point season, in East Anglia, at least: 'Sir — The number of blatant non-triers and the amount of obvious schooling reached new heights last year. In not one case did the Stewards announce an inquiry. One reason for this may be the eminence of those who perpetrate such practices, but the Rules should be enforced without fear or favour. If one also takes into account the appalling bookmakers in the area who make a book of 170-plus, it is no wonder that so many serious point-to-point fans are now going to South-Eastern and Midlands meetings . . .'

In the same issue, there was a brisk agreement in an article by Granville Taylor, who wrote that our friends with the bulging satchels 'are guilty of betting seriously over-round on most races (i.e. the 'book' is framed considerably to the layers advantage). The other ''popular'' measure often adopted at Bank Holiday meetings is a top limit of something like 10-1. Unfortunately, the majority of point-to-point organizers seem to take little or no interest in the betting proceedings, so there is scant prospect of improvement in this sphere.'

Traditionally, point-to-points were laid on by local huntsmen as a sort of open-day carnival to thank farmers for letting them tally-ho over their fields and kill their furry little foxes. Nowadays, the very same Barbour-jacketed, green-wellied brigade, who point-to-point on Saturdays, are those who turn up to horse trials midweek. Oddly enough, 'eventing' (typically British, the three-day event takes four) has not developed from hunting but from the military academies of France. You will still hear it referred to in the Olympic Games as *le militaire*.

Originally, the three-day event consisted of some ridiculously difficult, long-distance rides, which would be followed by some strict dressage tests to see if horse and rider still had their marbles about them. In 1892, the gruelling Vienna-Berlin ride was first instituted. Not many were standing for the dressage. Ten years later, in the Brussels-Ostend gallop, 16 of the 29 horses that started dropped dead on the way.

The dressage tests are now held before the long slog. The original French military orders still apply: 'Dressage is the harmonious development of both the physique and ability of a horse. It makes the horse calm, supple, and keen, to achieve perfect understanding with rider. Freedom and regularity of paces; harmony, lightness, ease of movements; lightening of forehand and engagement of hindquarters; the horse remaining absolutely straight in any movement along straight lines, but bending on curved lines. The horse thus gives the impression of doing his own accord what is required of him.'

It's even more high-flown in French, I'm telling you. Generally, the Europeans remain best at dressage. Some years ago, Lucinda Green, the Wantage convent schoolgirl who became possibly the best horse-woman this country has ever known, went to Germany to study dressage. She was staggered, realizing she had to 'unlearn' everything she had been taught in England — 'to stop using my heels and elbows and instead persuade my back, bottom and thighs that it was their responsibility to balance me and provide the necessary impulsion.'

In a way, the trouble with dressage as a sport — it is only one discipline of an 'event' but it applies to this one more than the other skills — is the same problem that afflicts other so-called 'competitive sports', like synchronized swimming, diving, or Torvillandeaning. The fancy of the judges holds sway. If you want proof that those well-bred, straight-backed women, with complexions of porcelain and accents of haughty disdain, can, in fact, outswear a Scottish fishwife, then hang around the stables after the judging of the dressage at Badminton.

Britain's best current Thelwell gel, Virginia Holgate, told the magazine, *Eventing*, in 1985 'It can be very depressing at the end of the day . . . when you get as much as 40 marks difference from one judge to another, whom do you believe? I have come home in despair, looked at my judging-sheet and thought, what do I do? I have nothing to go on.'

There are moves to get the dressage judges to agree on some uniformity. I reckon there is as much chance of that happening as there is of those East Anglian bookies giving all their money away.

The Hunters and the Hurdlers, the Hoorays and the Sloanes

It's not so much that Cauthen and Eddery are head-to-head to the wire in the flat-race jockeys' championship, the way to tell that autumn is *really* here each year is when Dick Francis asks you to the lunch that launches his new book at Plumpton. Alas, I couldn't make it this year, but the very invitation always signals the change of the seasons better than anything else. It braces you up for the clocks to go back in a fortnight or so. Drat the first frosts and darn those mittens. Cricket is hardly over, Dick's having his latest launch and, like the greatest ever clerk of the course at Stratford had it, 'Seasons alter so hoary headed frosts fall in the fresh lap of the crimson rose.' I always feel the *Jumps* are more British than the *Flat*.

Francis is in the silver ring this autumn at Plumpton: his twenty-fifth book, in the twenty-five years since he slipped out of the saddle, is called *Hot Money* (Michael Joseph). His party couldn't be at a more evocative place than the chirpy, almost scruffy, Sussexy little course in the lea of the Downs, with the commuter trains trundling by, and near enough to the sea to have the ploughman's sentry-straight lines on the curving ridges up yonder followed by excited squadrons of diving, squawking, white seagulls. And, higher up, the russet leaves are turning into litter as fast as the betting-slips down below on the racecourse forecourt. It is going to be a long, hard ride for the jump jockeys in their crash-hats and the legion in trilbies who follow them. They ride till early June.

Up country, at the likes of swish and stately Newmarket, or wide and windswept Doncaster, the fierce-eyed thoroughbreds of the Flat, mounted by their midget millionaires with wasted, waxwork faces, still have some weeks of business to settle. Theirs has been a long gallop, too, through the summer for the sport of kings. But no narrow eyes at Plumpton, just the warming buzz of anticipation for the eight-month cavalry charge ahead of the friendly free-masonry of better adjusted men and horses. The hunters and the hurdlers, the Hoorays and the Sloanes in headscarves; the snow and the sleet and the steambaths; the broken bones and the over-hearty ambulancemen. All orchestrated to the relentless tattoo of coconut-hooves on the frost-hard turf. Unless it's the skiddy splosh of mud when the thaw sets in.

The last time I launched (or rather, lunched) the winter off to a good start with Dick Francis was for his twenty-third bestseller, *Proof*. A couple of jocks came a cropper at the water-jump, down by the railway line, and it all came flooding back for Dick: 'I think I fell at the Plumpton water more times than at any fence in all of England. On one day, three times in four races! It was a very damp walk back each time. Only at the very end of my career in the saddle did it suddenly dawn on me: I lay there yet again, inspecting the fence at the closest of quarters for the umpteenth time when I realized that the landing side was far less cut up away from the rails, and, indeed, was firm and sound and safe on the railway embankment side. But, by then, I sighed

258

as they stretchered me away, it was far too late in my racing life to cash in on the revelation!'

Dick is marvellous value on the whole winter's round Britain whizz: 'From Sandown, Cheltenham and Aintree, to Cartmel, Wye and Plumpton, every racecourse has its own personality; no two are alike. Each has its own flavour, oddities and customs and, almost, its own insignia — like ribbed woollen stockings at Cheltenham, rain at Haydock Park, and straw bale grandstands at Bangor-on-Dee.'

Others are less romantic than Dick. That still irrepressible tub of laughs, Terry Biddlecombe, will tell you how Cheltenham was always his favourite course, and Hereford his second best. They are the two tracks nearest his home! Though he does add that Hereford was 'particularly handy if you were on a lazy horse because the stables were right next door to the winning-post and once you turned for home they would step up the juice a bit, to be quicker to get to their oats and have a rub down.' The other day I put the same question to one of our leading current riders, Richard Rowe. His favourite place, he said, was Fontwell, his pet hates Ludlow and Market Rasen. I thought it might be something to do with the curves or the fences or even the view. Not a bit of it. Says Richard: ' Sure, I could tell you that Fontwell appeals because it is a nice sharp track, friendly atmosphere, more downhill than uphill, nice and quick and all that. No, the reason I love Fontwell is that it's only 12 minutes down the road from my house — and, on the southern circuit, Ludlow and Market Rasen are the furthest away from my house!'

It can also pay if you're race-riding near home. In his most revealing and good humoured memoir, *Tales from the Weighing-Room* (Pelham), the former jockey and now popular locker-room 'valet to the stars', John Buckingham, tells of his old buddy, the aptly named Johnny Gamble: 'It was strictly against the rules of racing for jockeys to bet. Anyway, Johnny ignored this at Newbury one day and went into the ring to have a punt. As he was walking away, he noticed one of the stewards nearby, and wondered if the fellow had seen him placing his bet. Sure enough, soon afterwards, the public address system asked for the jockey, Johnny Gamble, to report to the Stewards' Room after the second race.

'Johnny was wearing a dark suit and a trilby. He also, luckily, lived in Newbury. He ran to the main gate, grabbed a taxi, and directed it to his house. When he got there he told the driver to leave the meter running while he dashed inside and swopped his suit for flannels and sports jacket and his trilby for a flat cap. Then he rushed back to the racecourse, and reported to the Stewards' Room as instructed. The man who had spotted him in the ring looked at him with some surprise, muttered, "Sorry, there's been a mistake," and let him go!'

Buckingham's book gives you a rewarding peek into the gregarious, but enclosed confraternity that, in fact, spends much more time through their long winter in their cars than in their saddles ('I sometimes wonder what the people who arrange the racing calendar are thinking about when they have us going to Folkestone one day, then all the way to Newton Abbot or Devon and Exeter the following day, and then back to the south-east for Plumpton the day after that'). He tells, too, of the occasional days when the seasons overlap — like this month — and the jump jockeys and the flat-race stars have to share the same weighing-room benches.

At such times, the jump jocks look at each other and are extremely thankful, he says, 'The Flat boys are so serious. No larking about or telling jokes for them. Between races they sit on the bench with their arms folded, chins on their chests, brows furrowed. Perhaps they are worried about how to invest the half-million or two, but whatever it is, if that's what riches bring, they can keep it. Over the years I have seen some of the top flat-race jockeys undergo a tremendous change since the time they were apprentices, whereas someone like Steve Smith Eccles hasn't changed a bit since the day he first walked into a weighing-room.'

Meanwhile, for another few weeks, while the bonny brotherhood of jump jocks get ready for the clocks to go back and the first snows to give them the *real* bracing feel of their long winter's ride, the two eight-and-a-half-stone midget millionaires, Eddery from Galway, and Cauthen from Kentucky, remain locked in their epic dash to the Championship wire. Bet on the Yank, collect your winnings in the appropriate, narrow-eyed way — then put on your best smile and loudest check tweeds, and go out and enjoy the winter.

Rather Beside the Point-to-Point

The first organized sporting event I'm told I ever attended was as a shrieking babe in arms (or, rather, in the back seat of an Austin 7), some forty-nine cold and crispy springs ago when one of the outings of the year for that part of Hereford's farming community was the Saturday of the Belmont point-to-point. I suppose they've moved on from there, from that softly soggy, low-slung field down in the dip below the squat and friendly Abbey tower — for, so I've heard, that old track is part of a rolling, handsome new golf course now.

I'll soon know for sure. because this March I'm leaving the frenzied din and the dust of London and going back to live in Hereford, at Marden on the Leominster road, to which old village church, centuries ago, the local laddoes played football with the severed head of King Ethelbert. (Even then, English soccer was already on the decline, and would never be the same again since Woodbines cost a penny a pint and all that.)

I will be to and fro, of course, here and there — slanting a jaded eye at the latest deaths and marriages of London's football clubs (homeless Charlton Athletic could yet enjoy an interestingly sexy merger with haughty Sloane Rangers, perhaps?), and the snort and snot and spit of seedy boxing; I'll still be getting hipflask happy at Twickenham, broke and blotto at Sandown, jaundiced at Wimbledon; I aim to enjoy the Oval, as ever, and stop gritting my teeth for one summer at Lord's because, after all, this is MCC's 200th birthday. So I'm not going far — and anyway, Hereford will be really rather near the centre of things, for isn't Master Blaster Botham's batting going to be stirring the leaves (and the fishes) round Worcester's previously calm Severnside cricket ground?

Even more appropriately, mind you, I return to roots with the point-to-point season in full steamy gallop. When I was a lad on the old *Hereford Times* some thirty years ago, you could make an extra bob or two by covering sport on a Saturday afternoon. Nothing to do with the world's backpages, though — you had to

261

gather in, meticulously, reams and reams of results, plus just one paragraph of winner's interview and one (if you were lucky) of local colour . . . on the weekend's point-to-point; or the hedging competition; or the ploughing match. Never a ball game in sight — and certainly not when you were operating from the paper's branch-offices at Ledbury, Leominster or Ross.

I suppose I served my sports-hacking apprenticeship, though I didn't know it at the time, at an Eardisley ploughing match, or the Woolhope hedging set-to. With the same, expert skills on view, and just as much concentrated passion (if a little less noisy) as anything laid on in the Maracana stadium of Brazil, or the Kensington Oval of Bridgetown. And still, I bet you, the hedges of Hereford remain the most sturdily neat in the land; and the red-soiled furrows the most slicingly straight.

But the point-to-point was best. A classless gathering of the class-ridden clan. I wonder how the sport has changed? Traditionally, meetings represented a sort of end-of-season 'Thank-ee!' from the local hunt to the farmers who had tolerated them jorrocksing all over their land through the winter. It was a kind of four-legged village fête. Now, I hear, the point-to-point is big business. Folk flock in for the famous ones, not only from the next county but the next county but three. With claret warming in BMW's boot.

Every fence seems to be sponsored, every whip and crop, every mare and marquee. But not, I hope, the fun. And certainly not, alas, the flutter. With wealthy, national firms such as Christie's, Land Rover and Times Newspapers sponsoring special series through the $3\frac{1}{2}$-month season till May, the sport can never have been in a healthier financial state. Last winter, for instance, 12,430 steaming, snorting hunters ran, jumped and/or stood still at a total of 176 meetings at 113 different courses. This season's figures will be even higher — and, with it, the prize-money. The Christie's series, for instance, will end with a grand final at Cheltenham, with £12,000 up for grabs.

The presumption — no, *stipulation* — remains that rider and horse remain 'amateur'. This certainly raises a few arched eyebrows and jodhpur slapping around the inner circuit of the bitchy bridle birgade — rather like it used to among the show-jumpers when a horse, in Olympic year, would suddenly find its name changed back to Dobbin after three years as Nippy Double-Glazed Pop-up Toasters Tommy IV or whatever. Also,

262

the rules demand point-to-pointers must have been 'regularly and fairly hunted during the current season' and must not be handled by licensed trainers. Even archer eyebrows are raised these days, I'm told, though there's nothing really new under the pale suns of February — for even Surtees was noting in Mr *Sponge's Sporting Tour* that: 'The horses were hunters; and grooms and fellows used to come up to masters of hounds at checks and critical times, requesting them to note that they were "out" in order to ask for certificates of regularity than which nothing could be more irregular.'

On the other hand, perhaps Hereford has gone soccer mad since my day. When I left (initially just to pop over the river to the great County Championship county of Grace and Graveney in the summers, and Boughton, Booth and Burton in the winters), any round ball sport took second place to the hunters and the hounds — not forgetting the hedging. But then, Hereford United were in the Southern League; now they've gone up to League Division Two (just for a year), so they might well have a far grander opinion of themselves; though I doubt it. And I see their attendance record remains 18, 114 for the famous non-Leaguers Cup tie v Sheffield Wednesday on January 4, 1958. Well, it would have been 18, 113 but for little me. I remain a digit in history.

John Charles, alternately 'The King' and 'The Gentle Giant', must be United's best ever, but he was almost in sepia and long past the green freshness of youth when he was player-manager at Edgar Street. Raddy Radford once scored television's Golden Goal of the Decade (or was it Century?) for United, and good ol' Joe Wade, once captain of Arsenal, still keeps a sports shop in the city, they tell me. Those two certainly can reclaim their fame any day they feel like it.

But I suppose Hereford's most enduringly celebrated sport remains Tom Spring, unbeaten heavyweight champion of England (and thus the world) in 1823 and '24, mine host at the Naked Boy (now the Green Man) at Fownhope, Wyeside pull-up a few miles west of the city. He was 5ft 11ins and 13½ stone, and he soaked his knuckles in vinegar for two hours each day. When he beat the Irish champion, Langan, at Worcester racecourse on January 7, 1824 (the 78 rounds took 2hrs 29mins, and were watched by 30,000), he rode from Fownhope in Colonel Berkeley's carriage and four. As the reporter, Pierce

Egan, described: 'The roads in every direction beggared all description. The adventures at the Inns would furnish subjects for twenty farces . . . the company in general so masquerade a character that it defies the pen; even the celebrated pencil of a George Cruikshank would be at fault to give the richness of its effect . . . in a word, it was a *conglomeration* of the Fancy. Where were you, Mr Hazlitt? What food for the imagination did it exhibit? Peers, MPs, Yokels of every cast, Cockneys and Sheenies . . .'

Botham this summer will not cause such a commotion down by the riverside, and certainly Herefordshire's best known current cricketer won't, good as *she* is. For such must be Miss Sarah Potter, demon bowler from Ross-on-Wye, who the county and country look to this year to bring back the female of the Ashes species. If the gentlemen at Lord's can tighten their wobbly chins and bite the bullet this year, Sarah and her England side should be taking on the Aussies at St John's Wood in midsummer.

At men's cricket, it is a *very* minor county — indeed the last Herefordian to play at Lord's in a Test match was Peter Richardson, over a quarter of a century ago; and though he was born and schooled in Hereford, he played for Worcester (OK, OK, *and* Kent). A great cove, though, was the left-handed Peter Edward, and he never lost his Hereford sense of humour.

Once, at Canterbury, he refused to take strike till the umpires had investigated, and stopped, a mysterious booming noise emanating from the balcony alongside the pavilion. It was disturbing his concentration. The game was held up for minutes; fielders fretted, and Richardson insisted. Finally, and in trepidation, stewards and umpires approached the din and demanded it desist.

It was Mr E.W. Swanton telephoning his testament through to the *Telegraph*.

National Anthem

Each year since 1847, the Grand National has increasingly represented what its title claims. Name me a more potently compelling pagan festival in the whole of the British Isles. It is only a horse-race, held on a sooty circle of ground, around a tatty clutch of dilapidated buildings in a depressing no-man's-land near Liverpool — yet annually the *Grand* of its title gets grander, and the *National* bit more national, as it brings together for one riveting afternoon sons and mums, nobs and nobodies, debs, plebs, and proles in their shoals.

It might be cruel to horses. Its object is heroism — as well as excessive cruelty to book-makers. For 139 years, always just as March has turned to April, the epic, breathless, cavalry charge exults in being, at one and the same time, the British Isles' living festival of the present as well as its certain folklore of the future. As the old Victorian refrain rum-te-tiddled, so this Saturday:

Ye lads who love a Steeplechase and danger freely court, sirs,
Haste forward all to Liverpool to join the gallant sport, sirs.
The English and the Irish nags are ready for the fray, sirs,
And which may lose and which may win, 'tis very hard to say, sirs!

I am not a betting man, but this Saturday I will put a couple quid on the back of any nag with *Cottage* in its name. There usually is one, for some reason. I remember only a few years back that grand old front-runner. Tied Cottage, setting off at such a lick that he was a couple of fences ahead of the field in no time, dear old Tommy Carberry hanging on to his mane like he was a Red Indian extra. Then they went and jumped Becher's Brook *lengthways*, and were left there, high, dry and skewered across the hedge as everyone else sailed past. 'Sure,' said Tommy afterwards with a cheery shrug, 'he's always inclined to do that if he goes a bit too quick!' Thanks for telling me.

The first two National winners to gallop into my consciousness were both Cottages — Lovely Cottage in 1946, and Sheila's two years later. Suddenly I find — without even trying too hard and certainly without looking up any record books — I can rattle off quite a few National winners of my time. I bet everyone could, come to mention it. Where are they now? Where Freebooter? Or Nickel Coin — who survived such a pile-up in 1951 that the old *Reynolds News* cleared its front page next morning to demand END THIS SHAME NOW! — or Quare Times, or Royal Tan? Remember Early Mist? And Teal, and good ol' ESB, who panted past when Devon Loch sank? And is Sundew whinnying, nostrils wide, this special week in Trapalanda, the place the gauchos know as heaven for good and faithful horses?

What about Mr What? Or Scudamore's hot Oxo? In 1963, Ayala won at 66-1, ridden by 18-year-old Pat Buckley. The week before, Pat, between races, had popped into the gents' loo at Sandown Park. On the way out he bumped into the leathery-faced old twinkler, Keith Piggott, Lester's dad and trainer of Ayala. 'Have you a ride at Aintree?' No, said the boy. 'You have if you can make ten stone by Saturday.'

Buckley was, literally, inch-perfect in keeping Ayala's nose in front of Carrickbeg in a heroically thrilling National run-in. Carrickbeg was ridden by John Lawrence, now Lord Oaksey. M'Lord dismounted sadly, weighed in, and went to the telephone to dictate 1,500 words to his paper, the *Sunday Telegraph*. It remains just about the best bit of sports-writing I can remember. The drama of the piece was intense: it shone through with chivalry; but the commas were smudged with tears.

Two years later (Team Spirit in between), there was another unlikely tale. The legendary Fred Winter, then newly out of the saddle himself and setting up his stables at Lambourn, told me about it last year: 'One night in the early winter I took a trans-atlantic telephone call from Maryland. A young blade called Tommy Smith wanted to have a go at the National, of which he'd heard some stirring yarns. Would I train both him and his American horse, which was called Jay Trump? They shipped themselves over, stayed with me and, well, the rest you know . . .'

Smith — brash, open-faced, all-American kiddo in a stetson and with a Lucky Strike dangling from his lips at the gallops — had all the knowing old Berkshire Downs smirking at his bravado. But Winter worked and worked him, talking him round Aintree again and again. The boy slept in Jay Trump's

266

stable some nights. On the morning of the race, Winter and Smith walked the course as if with a magnifying-glass. The American was told exactly where to be, and when, at every fence. Jay Trump won sensationally at 100-30 and even David Coleman was momentarily lost for words.

In 1967, Foinavon won at 100-1. He had touchingly worked his way up from pulling a milk-float to being a National backmarker and makeweight. He was steady, but very slow. Suddenly, at the thorn fence after Becher's second time around, the 27 horses in front of him concertina'd, bumper-to-bumper, in a gruesome pile-up. Foinavon, late on the scene, carefully tortoise-tiptoed through the cursing carnage and ambled on to win an awful lot of oats.

Gay Trip was first in 1970, when the two words still combined to mean only a jolly good day out. Lovely old L'Escargot had its day, and so did Lucius — but the decade belonged to the phenomenal four-legged friend who lived behind McCain's Secondhand Car-mart, Upper Aughton Road, Southport. Red Rum was, as they say, simply something else. His sensational hat-trick proved that the National wasn't just a lucky lottery 'on the day', as many believed. The jockey, Jeff King, once put it: 'You need all your birthdays in one afternoon to win the National/'

Another horseman — who had been spreadeagled by Devon Loch all those years ago — explained at greater length. In his outstanding autobiography, which for my money remains the best thing he has done in a whole shelf-full of good stuff, Dick Francis recalled the 'birthday' build-up in that rickety old jockeys' room before a National: 'We do with deliberation, and unconsciously as if all were new, the things we do every racing day of the year. Smiles have a different quality: they become an acknowledgment of the hazards ahead, a sympathetic recognition that everyone is suffering the same gripping hope. No one has slept well, many have dreamed they have won the race: no one dares to believe that he will . . . you have no heart for the chatter and jokes of ordinary days. Rows of silent jockeys sit on benches, elbows on their knees, staring at their boots. Half an hour passes until at last, at long last, the time has come . . .'

As it has, once more this Saturday. When Britain's 'two nations' will be one again — for twenty minutes or so.